The Lorette Wilmot Library
Nazareth College of Rochester

The Modern Cinema of Poland

THE MODERN CINEMA OF POLAND

Bolesław Michałek
and
Frank Turaj

INDIANA UNIVERSITY PRESS
Bloomington and Indianapolis

Library of Congress Cataloging-in-Publication Data
Michałek, Bolesław.
The modern cinema of Poland.
Bibliography: p.
Includes index.
1. Motion pictures—Poland.   I. Turaj, Frank.
II. Title.
PN1993.5.P55M56   1988   791.43'09438   87-45372
ISBN 0-253-33813-1
ISBN 0-253-20481-X (pbk.)
1 2 3 4 5 92 91 90 89 88

Dedicated to Andrzej Wajda

CONTENTS

Illustrations follow page 79

INTRODUCTION

The film industry in Poland is state owned. To those who know little about Polish cinema, it would seem therefore, at first consideration, that film production would mainly serve the narrow interests of the government in the sense of rendering its interpretations of reality, its diagnoses, its understanding of life in this socialist republic. Actually, Polish film in its most interesting manifestations—which are the subject of this book—somehow succeeds in becoming a general reflection of Polish social and spiritual life, an artistic record of changes, crises, aspirations, hopes, and disillusionments. This industry has become an important part of the national culture and has helped forge an instrument by which Polish identity receives definition.

A number of historical, cultural, artistic, and political elements are involved, some of which it would be useful to name before going more deeply into the story of Polish cinema and its makers from the end of World War II until now.

The Literary Connection

It is clear that one of the things that decided the shape of this cinema was its connection to literature. In fact, all national cinemas are to some degree related to literature; all use it directly or indirectly in their own way and to their own ends. But the tie in Poland was deeper and, it is justifiable to say, special. What was this link? First of all, the filmmakers hearkened to the serious writing of the late nineteenth and early twentieth centuries, to the most revered classics, works by Henryk Sienkiewicz, Władysław Reymont (both Nobel laureates), Bolesław Prus, Stefan Żeromski, even the esoteric Stanisław Wyspiański. These are the cardinal names among those who were the caretakers of Polish lore and letters for the stateless nation before World War I. During that time it was these men who constituted a sort of government of the soul and fulfilled the offices of magistrates of ideas. In their literature they crystallized the themes that were a foundation for the nation's intellect and its social direction. It is important to note the status and extraordinary mission of literature because it comes to share its calling with cinema. The most noble of the classics, and the most profound, had great influence.

This is a principle that held as well with the effect of modern and contemporary writers upon film. Again it was the best rather than the most fashionable who had persuasive force among filmmakers. Jerzy Andrzejewski,

Jarosław Iwaszkiewicz, Maria Dąbrowska, Stanisław Dygat, Bruno Schulz, Kazimierz Brandys, Tadeusz Konwicki, and others who were the cutting edge of letters gave film its complex narrative forms and its careful esthetic structures. There were special intonations—Andrzejewski, moralistic; Dygat, nonchalant; Iwaszkiewicz, existentialist; Konwicki, sarcastic; Brandys, intellectual—intonations of rare sophistication in movies. Those writers who were especially associated with films included such rare talents as Aleksander Ścibor-Rylski, Jerzy Stawiński, Józef Hen, and, again, Tadeusz Konwicki.

For decades Polish filmmakers manifested the richness of their lettered foundations and their literary approaches. By comparison, it is as if the mainstream of French cinema had depended fundamentally upon Stendhal, Balzac, Zola, Flaubert, and Proust, or contemporarily upon Gide, Malraux, Camus, Giraudoux, Cocteau, and even Marguerite Duras and Claude Simon. Would that not have been extraordinary? In fact that is precisely what modern Polish cinema was doing, growing directly out of the heritage of the national literature.

Contrary to the literature of much of Europe, that of Poland took relatively little interest in psychological and subjective material, with some important exceptions. Rather, it was full of more social concerns, its two main themes being man versus society and man in the light of history. The problems of nationhood, the fate of the individual caught up in the historical process, choice in the face of social crisis—these were the subjects of Polish literature. History had imposed them; consequently, with some few exceptions, there was little space for lightness, caprice, psychological play. Cinema inherited this national commitment and the job of analyzing the complex and painful experiences of the nation.

What did this mean esthetically? The filmmakers most inspired by literature carried out their tasks with the greatest fidelity. They did not merely select what was most obviously filmable, as had happened in instances of adaptation from Faulkner to Dostoyevsky to Joyce. In fact, they remained exceedingly faithful to their originals, not only in theme, but in artistic exploration as well, reforming the language of film to accord with literature. The result was characterization that was more complex and different from the kind often found in movies, relationships among characters that were more diverse, and less conventional motivations, situations, and tones. Not all experiments were fruitful, but the trend brought richness and variation to the art, particularly during the fifties and sixties. The influence serious adaptation from literature exercised upon film techniques and therefore upon film esthetics was one of the chief determinants of Polish cinematic style, especially after the political crisis of the fifties. This was so on into the seventies when a new generation of filmmakers came along who wanted to create their own themes and scripts and a film language based on their own experiences. This change is addressed in the chapter devoted to the cinema of moral concern.

The History Connection

History is equally as important as literature in the evolution of Polish cinema. It must be noted, and it can scarcely be overemphasized, that from the end of the eighteenth century until the beginning of the twentieth century Poland existed only as history. There was no Polish state, and there were few mechanisms for normal national expression. It was in the consideration of history that basic social, political, and philosophical ideas were created and in the context of history that they were debated. Writers and artists often interpreted history in lieu of contemporaneity, in that way raising questions of social morality, honor, national identity, or the individual in a context of historical crisis. In short, to discuss or portray history was to deal in fundamental values. It was not unusual for the most heated controversies to break out regarding historical events rather than current affairs (with contemporary parallels always in mind, of course). The cinema industry inherited this way of thinking about and using history.

Such was the sway that history held in moviemaking until the latter part of the sixties, when its role was somewhat diminished by contemporary concerns among a newer generation including, among others, Jerzy Skolimowski and Krzysztof Zanussi. Skolimowski developed a theme regarding the bourgeoise softening of Polish society, especially the intellectuals. Zanussi analyzed the plight of individuals sickened by cynicism and careerism. The newcomers, Feliks Falk, Agnieszka Holland, Krzysztof Kieślowski, and others, studied the phenomenon of the manipulation of individuals and of masses. At this point, history was pushed aside to make room for a more direct view of today's society.

The Status of the Filmmaker

In such a cultural situation, the creative position of a filmmaker, especially a director, is considerably enhanced. In Polish cinematography a director is no mere manipulator of mise-en-scène, nor simply an executor of a producer's projects, nor yet a combination technician-businessman-organizer (a paradigm familiar to Americans). He is nothing less than an exponent of universal aspirations and concerns, a creator who has gained the status heretofore reserved for poets, writers, and artists.

There are other intellectually salutary factors to be reckoned—for example, the problem of profits. While in a state-owned industry there is always an immanent threat to creative independence, the other side of the coin is that the threat of unprofitability is of no concern. The director need not worry about financial success. His salary is little affected by his popularity. He is free, theoretically, to worry only about his vision and the artistic quality of his work. The prospect of profit does not heavily influence the choice of theme, form, or character delineation. Therefore, the main stimuli in film work can be originality, innovation, and message. The total system, which includes the function of semiautonomous film units, has worked so as to give directors of film extraordinary status in the Polish cultural community and cinema itself a revered place among the serious arts. Within the industry the director has the initiative in taking up new projects provided (the coin turns again) they do not interfere with the political interests of the state; but on occasion even this limitation has not been rigorously observed.

Given such a background, it is not surprising that the *auteur* phenomenon should have manifested itself. Indeed, it came into being immediately after the creation of the film unit system of production, even before the theory of *auteurism* was articulated in France and the United States in the fifties and sixties. Not all filmmakers deserve to be called *auteurs*, of course. Some simply desire to make lightweight impersonal films or do not have the talent to do otherwise. But there were those individualistic, artistic creators who placed their imprint heavily upon their work. Wajda, Munk, Kawalerowicz, and Zanussi are among those and have separate chapters devoted to them in this book. There were also such capital talents as Kutz, Konwicki, Has, Skolimowski, and many among the younger makers who represent their own clear style and character, the fruits of their sensibilities, and the themes that preoccupy them. Many acquired the right to be known as *auteurs* within this limited and new film industry.

It is important, for purposes of accuracy, not to paint too bright a picture of the organization of the film industry. It is worth knowing how this bureaucracy functions, what its institutional basis is, how film art depends on political authority.

Since right after World War II, the film industry has been owned by the state. It was not so much a nationalization—for all practical purposes the industry was ruined—as the establishment of a state monopoly. At first, this monopoly controlled cinema directly. There was a government office for scripts, which was the source of film ideas, and the production process was likewise controlled by administrators. Officials had considerable influence on subject matter and even the composition of film crews. This was during the period of strong ideological pressure, the late forties and early fifties. Few filmmakers, under the circumstances, could rise above mediocrity. It became evident to all over the years that the system as it was led only to artistic, financial, and even ideological failure. Happily, political evolution made it possible to change things.

Film Units

By 1955 circumstances were such that the film community was able to propose the creation of separate film units as semiautonomous creative entities. The idea stemmed from before the war, when the avant garde proposed such formations to free filmmaking from commercial pressures. The motivation now was somewhat different. There was no challenge to the notion of cinema as a socially engaged activity, but it was desired that the control and administration, as much as possible, be in the hands of film directors, writers, and cameramen. In short, filmmakers were looking for relief from government officials. The government accepted the idea. On May 1, 1955, the Creative Film Unit system came into being, a system that has survived various political vicissitudes and still functions.

Under the system directors, script writers, cameramen, production managers, and assistants come together into companies, discrete separate organizations. These film units are under the charge of an artistic director (almost invariably a renowned film director) who is supported by a literary director responsible for script development and a production manager who does just what his job title says. At various times there were as many as nine such units, and a film person could attempt to affiliate with the group he chose to work with. Each unit constituted something like a cooperative which attempted to realize the projects of its membership.

Each project, at its inception, is discussed within the unit, which, if it warrants, will supply the seed money for the script. The unit-approved script is forwarded to the governmental authorities and, if it is not rejected, is budgeted by the government according to an agreement with the film unit. The responsibility for production remains solely with the unit. A director sets up a crew, selects a cast, schedules a studio, arranges for equipment and laboratories, and so forth. The completed movie, approved by the unit, is sent forward for approval by a commission appointed by the administration. At that point, the unit loses control over the product, which is to say over distribution and promotion. Under this system, the industry has averaged about thirty to thirty-five feature films per year for theatrical release and about twice that number made for television (productions made for one viewing, miniseries, television drama). Considering the size of the industry in Poland, the limited market, and the relatively modest technology, this is a significant accomplishment.

The Role of the State

The administration plays a key role in the process at two points: at the time of script approval and after the film is completed and delivered, when the administration becomes de facto distributor. Thirty years of experience has demonstrated that the authorities can and do eliminate some political movies whose message constitutes a confrontation with the authorities. Actually, clear-cut political film assaults are rare. It is also true that in some few instances projects sharply critical of the state were ultimately approved for viewing and distributed—for example, *Man of Iron*. Generally, it must be concluded from the long-term record of the industry that what was produced has mostly been determined by the units rather independently. Without the film unit system, semiautonomous and variable, the history and quality of Polish cinema would have turned out quite differently.

This certainly does not mean that tranquility and harmony is constant within the units and between them and the administration. There are disputes continually about projects and trends, but the system has been sufficiently institutionalized to afford a very workable mode of operation. Occasionally the system has faltered, though. It worked well from 1955 to 1968. After the 1968 political crisis the system was dismembered at the order of the authorities. A different organization was put in its place, the most distinguishing feature of which was that the people in charge were selected for reasons other than their competence. This lasted for three years. After the crisis of 1970 a liberalizing mood set in and the regular unit system was reestablished. This expert system has remained in operation since then, not however without problems. In 1983, during martial law, Wajda's unit, "X," and Ernest Bryll's unit, "Silesia," were disbanded.

Along the way, throughout the tense periods and during all the many debates about artistic autonomy and integrity, an important role was played by the Polish Filmmakers Association, the guild representing the directors, cameramen, and others, a guild headed by Kawalerowicz, then Wajda, and now Majewski.

Studios

The units themselves, unlike the Hollywood companies of old, do not own studios. They make use of the three studios owned by the government. The oldest of them is in Lodz, about one hundred miles from Warsaw, in operation since 1945. Another is in Wroclaw in southwest Poland. The third, smallest, and busiest, is in Warsaw. All three studios are fully equipped and have the usual workshops and necessary laboratories. They are state-owned enterprises, made available on a rental basis to the units.

Distribution

Movies finished by the artistic units and accepted by the administration are put into distribution by a state monopoly, which has its branches in all big cities. It would seem that, for financial purposes, optimum and maximum distribution would be a goal. Actually, some films that gain less than complete approval from the authorities are limited as to distribution by limiting the number of prints, directing them to some movie houses rather than others, and so on.

The distribution organization also controls the dissemination of foreign films with the aid and counsel of a Repertoire Council, consisting of critics, various film experts, and state authorities. The result of all the distribution activity is that 50 percent or more of the films viewed in Poland are Polish or from another Eastern European country. The balance are mainly from France, Italy, and the United States. The choices seem logical. Artistic productions are screened often and as a matter of course. Any production by Fellini, Antonioni, Bergman, or Bunuel is sure to be screened, as are big box office hits, for example, the works of Coppola, Spielberg, and the like.

As was the case elsewhere, the coming of television led to the reduction in the number of movie houses in the country. There are now only about one thousand well-equipped theaters. After being shown on theater screens, films are made available for television viewing. In terms of financial returns, the limited market and dissemination on noncommercial television make it impossible for the industry to be a profitable one. It has become necessary to live from subsidies. The Ministry of Culture supports this industry as it does art museums, drama houses, operas, and other cultural activities.

The Film School At Lodz

Certainly this complex expert organ could not function without its trained and skilled personnel. The source of personnel was very much on the minds of those who pioneered cinema just after the war. A training institute, which was established in Crakow, moved to Lodz in 1948. There generation after generation of film people were educated who took into their hands the shape and fate of the art. For quite a number of years now, almost all directors, cameramen, production managers, and many writers have received training there. It functions according to three branches of filmic art: direction, camera work, and production management. The course of study is complete and arduous, taking five years. During that period, each and every student, under very real conditions, makes a certain number of films of varying complexity and scope—documentary, short feature, and a more ambitious diploma film. Since the late seventies, a script studio has been added to the other three specialties. Also since that time, a somewhat competitive institution has existed in Katowice, brought about by suggestion of the television industry.

It is appropriate to mention the considerable and interesting production in Poland of documentary films. Besides those that were simply utilitarian, like instructional pieces, there evolved over the years a great interest in the documentary as an analytical tool and in the esthetics of the form. Themselves influenced by the English thirties (Grierson, Rotha, Wright), they in turn influenced the nature of Polish feature filmmaking. Likewise, at least passing deference is due to the considerable achievement of the makers of animations, such as Jan Lenica, Walerian Borowczyk, Mirosław Kijowicz, Witold Giersz, and Daniel Szczechura, who made reputations for themselves far beyond the borders of their country.

This book deals only with narrative, feature film, the main thrust of any film industry, and the way that form articulated Polish consciousness.

The Modern Cinema of Poland

I

Postwar Beginnings

World War II was an immense event for every country in Europe, the historical perception of which varies among the nations. In France, England, and Italy, for example, it is seen as a profound episode that had its beginning, cul-
mination, and finale. With the passage of decades, it has been absorbed into
the past. The Polish reaction is and was different. World War II in Poland
barely receded into history. It was and is present and formative. There are
reasons. Those reasons have been as influential in the evolution of Polish
cinema as in Polish political and social life.

The war and occupation visited upon Poland a period of cruelty and ruin,
extreme even in that context. Seven million Poles were killed, cities and
towns literally leveled to bare ground and rubble, industries destroyed, forests decimated. Warsaw suffered four separate waves of destruction: one
during the blitz in 1939, the second during the suppression of the ghetto uprising in 1943, the third during the general uprising in 1944, and the fourth
during the winter of 1944–45, when it was meticulously and carefully demol-
ished by German military engineers, house by house and block by block. In
January 1945 when the first Red Army units entered the city, Warsaw was a
surrealistic desert of smashed stone and shattered glass, cannon-wasted
fragments of buildings, with little trace that there had once been streets and
boulevards. This image is useful in helping to understand what happened in
the country after the war, what climate there was for social and political life,
what the possibilities were for themes and subjects to dominate postwar
thinking, what was in store for culture in general and film art in particular.

Survival within this landscape after battle was attended by the memory of
six years of ineffable terror, the remembrance of days and nights when at any
hour, any man, woman, or child could be arrested, tortured, killed, or hurled
into the camps without pretext or cause. This was the trauma that brought
about a certain kind of consciousness.

Apart from war at its most drastic, there was another principal reason
World War II would not recede into history. That was the political change that
came in the aftermath. What occurred was a transformation of political and
social governing principles as well as a new set of names for the personae of
power. The assumption of power by the Communists and their allies meant
change of the essence: new social structure, different economic system, re-

jection of many former ideas and ideals, change in the scale of values. Some of the ideas put forward and the changes that were being made were reluctantly accepted by a large part of society. The destiny of every Pole was caught, for good or ill, in a different mechanism that would regulate from that time on his aspirations, successes, failures, and expectations. All culture was not simply to be rebuilt but built new, including cinema.

What was the situation within the film industry in 1945? There remained 230 theaters in the entire country. Of these, one-third were in a single province of which Lodz is the main city. Of film studios not much remained, but they had never been important. Distribution companies no longer existed. In any case, there was nothing to distribute. In what theaters there were, an audience might find odds and ends of prewar films for which there no longer existed any system of distributive rights, or the viewers could watch Soviet films brought in by the Red Army. However sparse the fare, the public did have a craving for movies.

Before the war this had been one of the main forms of entertainment, just as it had been throughout the rest of the developed world. During the occupation there must have been a yen for films as evidenced by resistance movement efforts to keep people out of movie houses where they were subjected only to Nazi propaganda. A boycott was implemented by the use of social pressure and the slogan "only pigs watch flics" (*tylko świnie siedzą w kinie*). It was no surprise, then, that right after the war young and old alike were starved for some film entertainment and expression. This desire was enhanced by the expectation that new films would treat with the experiences of recent history. Who was to make these movies, and where?

Ruins of a Film Industry

The filmmakers who had been active in the thirties were scattered. Some few lived through the occupation in Poland—scriptwriters Ludwik Starski (b. 1903) and Anatol Stern (b. 1899); directors Leonard Buczkowski (b. 1906) and Jan Fethke (b.1903); and a group of popular prewar actors. Others from the industry had made their way to the West, among them some of the best-known directors, like Michał Waszynski (b. 1904), Józef Lejtes (b. 1901), Ryszard Ordyński (b. 1878), and the avant-garde figure Eugeniusz Cękalski (b. 1905). Some were found in the Soviet Union during the war, where they organized a film unit attached to the Polish army that was being put together in Russia. For the most part these had been members of the loosely structured avant-garde, those whose work was unconventional, noncommercial, new in theme and technique, usually identified with leftist causes and sympathies, for example, Jerzy Bossak (b. 1910), Stanisław Wohl (b. 1912), Ludwik Perski (b. 1912), and the leader of this contingent, Aleksander Ford (b. 1908). They were the first to return, coming as they did in the wake of the Soviet and

Polish armies as a military film unit equipped with cameras as well as basic sound and lighting equipment. During the latter part of the war they produced some newsreels and documentaries. When hostilities ceased, they were at home and ready.

This cadre was to dominate film life over the first postwar years, which was not surprising since they were on location and had the initiative. In the first peacetime months there were two parallel temporary film administrative units, one military and the other civilian. The chief of each was the same man, Aleksander Ford. On November 13, 1945, the provisional government, leftist oriented, decreed the establishment of Film Polski as a state enterprise. The effect was to nationalize the industry in its entirety. Film Polski was awarded a monopoly in all film activities including production, distribution, and exhibition. It was even given the authority to administer the entire phototechnical industry. The first head of this consolidated entity was Aleksander Ford.

The first actions of Film Polski were aimed at increasing the number of theaters. By 1947 there would be 599. At the same time, a distribution system was put into place to serve the theaters. This system had available in 1946 individual film titles numbering 158. Of these, 53 were prewar Polish films, 84 Soviet, 16 English, and 5 French. Discussions were begun regarding the possible distribution of 65 American films through the Motion Picture Export Association (MOPEXAS), but only a fraction of these were ever shown on Polish screens. The Cold War had begun. There was little political room for American productions.

The shortage of filmmakers was greater than the shortage of films. That was a problem that needed to be addressed by the new administration. Two years after the end of battle, in 1947, an organization of film people came into being that included directors, producers, even make-up technicians. There were fifty-six members, and of these only twenty-eight had any prewar professional experience. It was clear that the education of young filmmakers was essential. That realization had already resulted in the 1945 formation of a Young Filmmakers Workshop in Crakow. From it came some who would be quite notable in the future, among them, Jerzy Kawalerowicz (b. 1922), Wojciech Has (b. 1925), and Jerzy Passendorffer (b. 1923). By 1948 this embryo evolved into an ambitious institute and was reconstituted as the Higher School of Film. A decision was made to relocate it in Lodz. Eventually its graduates exercised profound influence on the shape and future of the industry.

Lodz is an industrial city about one hundred miles from Warsaw. It had not suffered devastation comparable to the capital's, so there were physical facilities available. Film Polski borrowed a covered sports stadium from the municipal government, the property to be returned at the end of the year . . .

then the next year ... and the next. To this day, the Lodz studio, previously a sports center, continues to be the principal film production facility for feature films. In fact, the production of feature films was one of the reasons for its establishment.

Before the war Polish features were not much noted outside the country; however, within Poland they constituted a very popular form of recreation. About thirty to forty feature films were made yearly in the 1930s. Given the number of theaters and the relatively weak export market, this was enough. With few exceptions they were purely commercial artifacts resembling the productions done in Vienna, Berlin, and Budapest at the time. Polish movies were generally a bit lower than these others in artistic and technical merit, partly because the industry was financially frail. Big investors in the country had never seen great possibilities in the movie-making business. (Ironically, some of the great fortunes in Hollywood were made by Polish immigrants.) Financial backing was mostly piecemeal, for example, theater owners funding movies they could show in their houses. Few companies had stability. Nevertheless, this old repertoire, full of patriotic cliché, romantic complications, comic situations, and the like, maintains to this day a surprising popularity. They are still presented on television from time to time to a ready audience.

That amounts to a kind of contemporary nostalgia. The public of the postwar period waited for something different, something relevant. They wanted and needed art that would confront the fresh, painful experiences of war and occupation.

Wartime Memories

The first feature fiction film to come out was *Forbidden Songs* (*Zakazane piosenki*), which premiered on January 8, 1947. It was originally conceived of as a documentary of medium length about the songs sung in the streets during the Nazi occupation. Ludwik Starski, a popular prewar screenwriter, saw in it the possibility of a good feature film. The premise is that a musician collects such songs. The memories they evoke appear on the screen as flashbacks that depict wartime Warsaw. Through the songs a dramatic time is recaptured. The lyrics exemplify the indomitable nature and tough humor of the common man. In spite of this rather flimsy framework, the director, seasoned prewar professional Leonard Buczkowski, managed to capture an authentic mood and portray something of the folklore of occupied Warsaw. Curiously, given the painfulness of the subject, there is a certain sentimentality throughout the film that surrounds its dramatic moments. The mixture was a success but also created some problems.

On the one hand, newspapers reported that the queues were Dantesque in length at the entrances to the theaters. On the other hand, just after it premiered in January 1947, it came under attack on the critical front. Marxist principles and plain patriotic sensibilities generated the accusation that the film forgave or condoned German crimes. Allegedly, the film portrayed German soldiers and even the Gestapo in a "manner contradicting their brutality." For many the film offered a picture that did not accord with their impressions. The film was withdrawn from circulation and a new version issued which included scenes emphasizing German brutality, at the same time accentuating the role the Red Army played in the liberation of Warsaw. That version came out in 1949 and was as popular as the first. *Forbidden Songs* is a thin film and is even somewhat primitive in technique, but it was one of the most popular of those filmic endeavors that opened the postwar period of cinema. To this day it is sometimes revived. In all, it has played to an audience in Poland exceeding fifteen million viewers.

Experiences of war and the occupation were likewise central in Wanda Jakubowska's *The Last Stage* (*Ostatni etap*) [1948], but were handled in a completely different way. Jakubowska (b. 1907) was connected with prewar circles that were esthetically progressive and politically left-wing. She was coorganizer of "Start," a group of film artists with these affinities. In 1939 she made *The River Niemen* (*Nad Niemnen*), all the prints of which disappeared during occupation. In 1943 she was arrested by the Germans and shipped to Auschwitz, then Ravensbruck. With a companion from Auschwitz, a German prisoner named Gerda Schneider, she wrote a screenplay based on extensive documentation—German records, memoirs of prisoners—and her own experience. Its form was idiosyncratic, quite unusual for the time. At the expense of story unity, it was a weave of strands, a number of these snapping in mid-pattern quite unexpectedly. It did not seem a faulty story but rather as if someone were narrating in a voice choked with emotion, not able to tell something in a linear way. No documentary could possibly equal this authenticity. This piece is far from perfect in form and occasionally offensive with cant and pathos, but on the whole it is in subject matter a moving testimony and in form a preview of a new language for cinema. *The Last Stage* was generously acclaimed when it was shown in 1948. That year it won the Grand Prize at the Marienbad Film Festival. Since then it has been screened in scores of countries. It helped emphasize that there was something to notice in this industry striving for a new start with some old hands, some new young ones, and under a completely changed system.

The administrative head of the system was, of course, also a director and brought out his own contributions in time. Aleksander Ford had been a left-wing activist in the thirties. During that decade he made documentaries and feature films, all with clear leftist messages. He avoided, indeed attacked the commercialism of those times in form as well as substance. All his work was a statement in opposition to the professionals of the industry, as well as in opposition to the political establishment of the country. He made, among other things, an interesting film about proletarian youth, *Legion of the Streets (Legion ulicy)* [1934], a lively, realistic portrayal that anticipated and in a way predicted neorealism. It was one of his many challenges to orthodoxy and professionalism. Paradoxically, when he became the authority over all Polish cinematography after the war, he learned to appreciate conformity and professionalism.

His own first postwar project was conceived in 1945, but was not made and shown until 1949. It was done in association with two prewar professionals, scriptographers Ludwik Starski and Jan Fethke. In making the film he used two veteran professionals from the Czech industry, cameraman Jaroslav Tuzar and art director Stepan Kopecky. Much of the movie was made in the well-equipped Barandov studio in Prague. Ford's antiprofessionalism did not survive in the war, as this project clearly reflects.

Border Street (Ulica graniczna) [1949] is a story of several Polish families, some Jewish and some gentile, living together in one building. The adults are generally friendly; the children play together in the streets. War and occupation come. The Germans establish the wartime ghetto of which this street is the very border. Jews are moved to the other side of the border to the ghetto. The liquidation of its inhabitants begins. Then comes the ghetto uprising of 1943. Against this historical and dramatic background, Ford sketches the relationships among the young people, adding a personal dimension to a production whose larger subjects include the suffering and determination of the ghetto fighters, the noble relationships that can exist in horrendous times. This was an ably realized film, successfully emotional partly because of a good cast of actors, especially Stanisław Godik, who created a memorable character in the role of the Jewish tailor. Looking at it today, *Border Street* seems conventionally linear, quite ordinary in the telling of its story in comparison with *The Last Stage*, for example. One also perceives the kind of staging techniques characteristic of studio work as well as character conceptions that are very traditional. Not quite what one might have expected from an avant-gardist, the film is nonetheless quite important for its gravity and careful realization, and indeed it had much appeal to the audience of its time.

That same year *After You Come Others (Za wami pójdą inni)*, also on the subject of the occupation, was brought to the screen by Antoni Bohdziewicz (1906–1970). It is about an episode in the history of the resistance movement (Communist branch) involving a secret printing press and the people who worked it. The story is a bit thin and the characters not fully developed, but the background is effective. The depiction of wartime Warsaw has a feeling of actuality. The film came along exactly at a time of ideological readjustment in the industry, and it is impossible to say which of its faults may be the result of bureaucratic meddling and pressure. More important than the film itself is the director. Before the war, Bohdziewicz was a successful radio producer. He did some film training in Paris and made some short avant-garde works. During the occupation he was in the resistance (non-Communist branch). He created an underground film squad that shot excellent footage of the Warsaw Uprising, 1944. Through the whole postwar period he was an indefatigable advocate of creative freedom in film art. At the Higher Film School in Lodz he was teacher, guardian, inspiration, and friend to many. Wajda, Munk, Polański, Skolimowski, all remember Bohdziewicz with respect and even reverence. His name is not very well known because, candidly, his films were not very good. But behind the scenes, he exercised considerable influence.

The war with its abundantly varied experience was to serve as a subject of films for many years to come. It is understandable that it needed attention at the outset of the postwar period. Equally understandable was the need of the public to come to terms with the changes that were taking place in Poland. Something was expected of the film industry that would give expression to contemporary life. The country was, after all, undergoing a profound reorientation. Socialism had been introduced. Political and social emotions were elevated. Then, as now, all the issues surrounding political and economic life in Poland were sensitive, given to rhetorical tendentiousness. This was so no less in film than in any of the other areas of expression.

Films about Today

Addressing themes of the quotidian on screen began at least in 1947, as far as feature fiction cinema was concerned, when Eugeniusz Cękalski and his wife Krystyna Swinarska, newly returned from America, made *Bright Fields* (*Jasne lany*). They wrote the screenplay about current events in rural Poland. The story was tendentious and propagandistic, or what is called in Poland "schematic." (Schematism is the application of doctrinaire, flat formulas to narrative.) Such was this tale: A progressive teacher wants to bring electrification to the village. The miller and richer peasants, portrayed as local reactionaries, sabotage his plans, but a member of "the People's security" intervenes and brings everything to a happy conclusion. The product was lamentable, with heavy characterizations, incredible story, awkward dialogue, and melodrama. It seemed to please no one. The Peasant's Party saw it as a false picture of the peasants. The Communists complained that there was no representation showing the role of the party itself in solving the crisis. The general public was disappointed, even frustrated, because they were anxious to see contemporary problems sensibly handled by filmmakers. *Bright Fields*, planned as a serious attempt to take the measure of a serious problem, ironically became an example of schematic cliché and artistic failure. The deficiency was so marked, it may have discouraged other projects.

It took two years for the next feature focusing on contemporary life to appear: *Treasure* (*Skarb*) [1949], a comedy by the director of *Forbidden Songs*, Leonard Buczkowski, from a script by Ludwik Starski and Roman Niewiarowicz. *Treasure* is an unpretentious work about two separate pairs of lovers in ruined Warsaw looking for living quarters just after the war. Their story links with another, the search for an alleged treasure to be found in the wreckage of a certain building. The narrative is skillful and augmented by good humorous writing and fine comedy performances on the part of Danuta Szaflarska (b. 1915) and Jerzy Duszyński (b. 1917) as one couple, and Alina Janowska (b. 1923) and Adolf Dymsza (b. 1900) as the other couple. Dymsza, a very popular prewar stage comedian, appeared on screen for the first time in this film to an enthusiastic reception. This ordinary comedy retains its effect even forty years later. Buczkowski presented the audience with good composition and sympathetic, positive, slightly naive characterizations. One is reminded of René Clair's *Quatorze Julliet* or the comic pieces of Monicelli.

Treasure remained popular for years, although it had some political trouble at the outset. After the premiere the film was attacked by the "official" critics. It was accused of "imitating prewar comedy" and even of being "petit bourgeois." "There is something quite offensive in the solidarity among some people toward the end of getting rich without working" (Grzelecki, Stanisław. *Odrodzenie*, no.9, 1949). So wrote one critic resenting the notion of buried treasure as a comic device. The complaint was ridiculous at face, but it was an unpleasant augury. There were dismal clouds on the political horizon. The first postwar chapter in society and in cinema was coming to a close.

So far the balance sheet for filmmakers was modest: a handful of feature films of which only two or three were noteworthy. But due credit has to be given for other kinds of progress. Hundreds of new movie theaters were opened. A film studio was created. Surviving filmmakers had been brought together to work. Scores of documentaries had been assembled. Probably the accomplishment that was to count for most in the long run was the establishment of the film school that was to play such a great role in the future, a future that at this moment did not look so bright.

Wisła

The dismal political clouds sailed in from the horizon and settled over the country. In 1949 the social atmosphere was charged. Following the elimination of the Peasants Party and the merger of the Communists (Polish Workers Party) with the Socialists (Polish Socialist Party) a purification of the ranks had begun. A monolithic political entity was the goal. The leader of the Communists, Władysław Gomułka, was himself removed and then arrested. Together with his closest allies, he was charged with "rightist-nationalist" deviationism. Ideological paths were closed off, restricted. The first political and spy trials began. Stalinist theory and militant stands against the continuous threat of imperialism dominated all official thinking. An intensification of the class struggle was officially declared. What tolerance there was came to an end. The Third Plenum of the Central Committee of the Polish United Workers Party, the new monolith, took up questions of ideological error in all aspects life including the cultural.

In just this kind of atmosphere a fractious congress of filmmakers was held in the resort town of Wisła in southern Poland. The film community was joined by high-ranking political leaders. The mood was accusatory overall. Why was there so little progress in advancing the class struggle? What was the role of the working class in regard to cinema? What about manifestations of bourgeois and petit bourgeois thinking in films? Who was responsible for cosmopolitanism (i.e., an insufficiently narrow point of view)? What was the proper line on national unity?

This last question is especially interesting. According to new doctrine, the nation was not united in its struggle against the Germans during the war. Allegedly the working class (or the Communists representing them) struggled heroically, while the other classes (or the *Armia Krajowa*, that is, Home Army), did not. This was an attempt to aggrandize the role of the Communist underground resistance and minimize, even cancel, the role of the Home Army. Given the size and widespread participation of Poles in the resistance work of the Home Army, such a position was offensive and potentially inflammatory. In any case, the unity question became an issue of long duration as well as a theme for literature and film.

Whatever the theme or subject matter, there were approved approaches. These were described under the rubric "socialist realism," the principles of which were clarified and promulgated at the meeting in Wisła. Socialist realism obligates art to do special things in the reeducation of society. Art that does not fulfill its task, as defined, is inferior and possibly even unacceptable, that is, it might be banned. The task can be fulfilled if the artist comports with some basic rules. In filmmaking it works like this: 1) There must be a portrayal of a positive hero in the leading role, a person without fault, who struggles ceaselessly for socialist ideals and who is victorious. 2) The class struggle must be illustrated by showing a confrontation between the new socialist order and the old capitalist order or its remnants in which the new wins out. 3) It must be demonstrated that in this confrontation the party plays the crucial role, that is, it organizes, mobilizes, and leads the masses. 4) There must be a correct examination of the character and behavior of social types, that is, not empirical or statistical types but a description of a type that enhances the schematic message.

It was clear that films made up to that time did not fit this pattern. Implicitly there was a general failure to be charged against the industry. Naturally the meeting generated hostility and resentment. Antoni Bohdziewicz, sharply criticized for *After You Come Others*, challenged the model of the positive hero and the whole idea of ideologically overloaded films, speaking in defense of artistic freedom. Not until 1957 was he allowed to produce another film. That was one specific result of the meeting. There were a few others.

At least two existing films were altered and issued in their new manipulated versions. One of them had had the title of "Robinson Warsaw," an allusion to Robinson Crusoe. It was based on a script by the prominent Polish novelist Jerzy Andrzejewski (b. 1909) from an idea allegedly said to originate with Czesław Miłosz and directed by prewar filmmaker Jerzy Zarzycki (b. 1911). The premise was unusual but not unrealistic. After the failure of the uprising, Warsaw is reduced from a city of a million inhabitants to utter ruin. The only people left are groups of German military engineers who are demolishing what little remains. Somewhere in this wasteland a person is hiding. In that desert of rubble, he imitates for four months Defoe's Robinson Crusoe, surviving until liberation in January 1945. It is not possible to recapitulate the fortunes of what seemed like a likely film premise, or to detail the film's many versions, cuttings, editings, and trials, all of which resulted from the sharp criticism and attacks made at Wisła, where among the kinder criticisms it was said that the film had "false ideological-esthetic overtones." Eventually it emerged anemic and all but unrecognizable with the title *Unconquered City* (*Miasto nieujarzmione*) [1950]. Robinson Crusoe ended up as a minor motif. The main narrative was a story concerning resistance fighters and Soviet paratroopers.

A similar fate befell the debut of Jan Rybkowski (b. 1912). He began his work before the war on the experimental stage as a set decorator and a novice director. In 1949 he attempted to make his first film from a script and story by Jarosław Iwaszkiewicz (1894–1980). The title was *A Home in the Wilderness* [1950]. Here again there was an interesting premise. Somewhere near Warsaw there is a solitary house, inhabited by two single women. The actions and moods connected with the occupation scarcely reach there. In a deliberate, measured dramatic way the story of Warsaw unfolds as different people come and go. The whole concept and execution were changed. A gallant officer is introduced into the story. He organizes underground activities. One of the women is drawn into a love involvement with him, but more important she is drawn into the struggle. At the end something was added:a depiction of liberated Warsaw, rebuilding activity, children at kindergarten, and the like. Another casualty of the conference.

This meeting can be considered a turning point. It brought to an end the explorations toward an industry and an art form. At the same time it established the theory of socialist realism as a doctrine, an operational set of rules. Indeed, films were now to be made according to these rules. The film most often cited as heralding this new mode is *Two Brigades* (*Dwie brygady*) [1950], based on a play by the Czech writer Vasek Kania, originally titled *The Brigade of Karhan the Grinder* (*Brygada szlifierza Karhana*). The subject is a kind of Stakhanovite competition set up by the workers in a factory. In a second and parallel thematic plot, a group of young theater people dispute the proper way in which to present this competition as a stage subject. The message of the movie is framed within the cooperation that comes about between these two centers of work. The factory people better understand their activity and its meaning as a result of the stage presentation, and of course the actors better understand the meaning of their art by their involvement with the factory hands. The film was directed cooperatively by a group of students from the film school, among them Wadim Berestowski, Janusz Nasfeter, Marek Nowakowski, and Silik Sternfeld, all under the supervision of Eugeniusz Cękalski, whose film *Bright Fields* was an early example of doctrinaire schematism. *Two Brigades* was, to put it bluntly, a total failure. The premise was flimsy and the story anemic. There was not a single character developed in a believable way. Everything about it was artificial and false. Since its production it has stood as the perfect example of socialist realism. Perhaps it was useful in showing directors what they should avoid, or avoid insofar as they could.

Films about youth undertook the burden of socialist realism in large part over the next three years. *First Take-off* (*Pierwszy start*) [1951] was written by Ludwik Starski and directed by Leonard Buczkowski. A similar film, *Crew* (*Załoga*) [1952], was written by Jan Rojewski and directed by Jan Fethke. The first takes place at a youth camp for glider training, the second at a school for sailors and aboard a ship.

Three Stories (*Trzy powieści*) [1953] was made under the direction of Antoni Bohdziewicz working with his students Czesław Petelski (b. 1922), Konrad Nałęcki (b. 1919), and Eva Poleska-Petelska (b. 1920). This is a three story film presenting episodes about young volunteers. More believable than the attempts cited above, they also depended on shallow tendentious themes: a girl has a positive change of attitude under the influence of the collective; young people are won over to socialism; young people learn to fight sabotage; and so on.

As meager as the years were esthetically, there was here and there a promise of something good to come in the future. Jerzy Kawalerowicz's name was noted and emphasized for the first time. He had been assistant to Wanda Jakubowska during the shooting of *The Last Stage*. Kawalerowicz (b. 1922)

and Kazimierz Sumerski won a competition for scripts about life in rural Poland. They also codirected the film *Community* (*Gromada*) [1952], which
was the story of a grain mill being built by the efforts of poor farmers working
cooperatively in the face of opposition by Kulaks (rich farmers) and capitalist
millers. This story too was schematic and formula-bound but the finished
movie had more artistic merit. It is discussed in chapter 6. From a modern
perspective, *Community* seems tied down by a simplistic plot. Nonetheless,
something more credible, more authentic emerges than in, say, *Bright
Fields*.

These doctrinaire projects were inescapably handicapped by the distor-
tion socialist realism wrought upon facts and current perceptions. The past
is easier to make into fiction that is different from reality or what reality supposedly was. Because of this, at least partly, the films made in the early fifties
that went to the past for their subjects were better. It is also true that the older,
more experienced directors chose subjects from the more remote past to
work with, making choices that were wiser than those made by their younger
colleagues. And it is useful to add something obvious: mature, experienced
directors working with less constrained themes are bound to make better
films. Some of the works that emerged were surprisingly elaborate esthetically.

This is true of Aleksander Ford's *Chopin's Youth* (*Młodość Chopina*)
[1952], Poland's first postwar monumental production: 30 sets, 21 locations,
138 actors, 2000 costumes. Ford's intention was neither to do a strict biography nor a romanticized life. Along the model of Soviet epics, he intended
to present the Romantic period, and, using it as background, portray the
composer as he came to manhood during the 1820s. Chopin's inspirations
were mainly to come from Poland's history, her suffering, and her folklore. It
was his desire to link these to the revolutionary tide sweeping Europe during
Chopin's life. All were to be reflected in his music. The finished film was carefully crafted and not without beauty. It seems slightly forced when the director pushes the connection between Chopin's art and the fight for progress
and revolution. The connection is valid, to be sure, but Ford's treatment of it
is not deft. In the film's favor, it is totally free of those stereotypes abounding
in Western commercial films about artists. *Chopin's Youth* was praised by
critics and prized by the government, and it made solid Ford's position as the
foremost man of film in the Polish People's Republic.

In richness, acclaim, and artistic accomplishment, *Chopin's Youth* passed
a quite successful film made just one year earlier, a film with which it had a
number of points in common. Jan Rybkowski's *Warsaw Premiere* (*War-
szawska Premiera*) [1951] was a biographical film of another nineteenth century composer, Stanisław Moniuszko. Like *Chopin's Youth* it was not meant
to be a close biography but the rendition of an epoch. The setting was 1857

in the Russian sector of partitioned Poland, a time and place buffeted by cultural and political currents. Moniuszko, too, articulated the folk undercurrent in Polish music, and Rybkowski, like Ford, strained that theme at the expense of dealing more with the artist as individual and his creation. This was in some degree rescued by the warm characterization of Moniuszko achieved by actor Jan Koecher, who captured the composer's plain, simple personality and gave depth to his life as a relatively poor organist and music teacher.

Not every large historical project was a success. Perhaps Wanda Jakubowska did not go back far enough in history to get distance and perspective. Perhaps she simply did a miserable job. In any event, her *Soldier of Victory* (*Żołnierz zwycięstwa*) [1953] was an esthetic travesty. It would not be worth discussing except that it is a curiosity that illustrated the problems of the period of socialist realism. The story subject is General Karol Świerczewski, a person who was indeed quite fascinating. He was a Pole who lived in the Soviet Union, a Communist, a soldier. He rose to the rank of general in the Red Army. In 1936 he was sent to Spain, where he commanded the international brigades for the Republican cause. During World War II, Świerczewski commanded the Polish units in the east. He was assassinated by Ukrainian nationalists in 1948. Around this character Jakubowska constructed a film that was, to be charitable, multithematic, to be candid, out of control. She included all—almost literally, all—the themes of the 1940s: fascism, armaments manufacturers, imperialism, Trotskyism, spy networks, and more. She even dealt with the recent "traitors" Gomułka and Spychalski, both at the time under arrest but fated to return to power in just three years. As one might imagine, the result was an incredible cinematic fiasco. Even the bitter-end defenders of socialist realism were unreceptive. It was shown in May and June 1953 when there were as yet few signs that Stalinism would soon pass away.

That same year two incidental comedies made on socialist realist principles reached audiences. Rybkowski did *Matter to Be Settled* (*Sprawa do załatwienia*) and Buczkowski did *Adventure in Marienstadt* (*Przygoda na Mariensztacie*). They are of no interest historically.

The last notable production belonging to this school of esthetic philosophy was *Not Far from Warsaw* (*Niedaleko Warszawy*) [1954], by Maria Kaniewska (b. 1911), an actress by profession but the director of this work. The script was by Adam Ważyk (b. 1905), a prewar leftist poet, who was at this time an oracle in questions of socialist realism, which he renounced in 1956 in his strident "Poem for Adults." The film was a political banality, a composition of stereotypes. We have a courageous party secretary in a factory, imperialist spies, saboteurs, a militant female comrade, an awakening to the loathsomeness of reactionaries. It all went too far. That fundamental fault plus the fact that things had already begun to change a little and a certain freedom was now possible brought upon this film a torrent of condemnation. Pent up critical frustrations were vented and *Not Far from Warsaw* was forced to pay for sins committed by other movies over the past several years. Bolesław Michałek wrote, "This film is such a cripple it is an act of cruelty to criticize it" (*Przegląd Kulturalny*, no. 44, 1954). Another critic, Krzysztof Teodor Toeplitz wrote that "this is a bastard of a film, an ugly cinema foundling which even its putative parents wouldn't defend. Whoever receives it should do so with a healthy dose of contempt and not be deluded that other people will not turn their eyes away" (*Nowa Kultura*, no. 45, 1954). Notice that it was already possible in 1954 to write such things about work which conformed to the official esthetic code.

Change

The political climate was changing perceptibly. After the death of Stalin on March 3, 1953, the political ice began to break. It broke up faster in Poland than elsewhere, particularly in the areas of culture and literature. Objections were raised against schematism and the objections were tolerated by the authorities. The effects were felt in film studios as well. Two films came to the screen that prefigured what was to come. Aleksander Ford made *Five Boys from Barska Street* (*Piątka z ulicy Barskiej*) [1954], from a script by Kazimierz Koźniewski, a journalist and writer. There was still a touch of cliché—a group of neglected boys led astray by the fascist underground—but in all, the movie was credible and vigorous. The characters of the boys, particularly the two leads, were full of life and interesting. These were not two-dimensional figures made only to carry a message. The narrative moved with the pace of a thriller. There was little propagandistic dialogue. *Five Boys* received a good press and was sent to the festival at Cannes where it took the award for directing. The French critic Jean de Baroncelli wrote, "an affectionate and tender work, important and beautiful, whose merit is in the fact that it does not seek to prove anything" (*Le Monde*, November 26, 1954). Perhaps in this there is some slight overstatement, but it is still clear that films had changed and obviously for the better.

The other important work of 1954 that evidenced political and esthetic change was a two-part opus by Kawalerowicz with the titles *A Night of Remembrance* (*Pamiątka z celulozy*) and *Under the Phrygian Star* (*Pod gwiazdą frygijską*). The two-film project was based on a story published a year earlier by Igor Newerly (b. 1903). The background is set as a workers' strike in the 1930s. In this context, which would seem to be appropriate for schematic development, the unexpected occurs. Strong individualistic traits come out among the characters. The film seemed in every way different from the pamphlet films of the previous five years. The project is discussed in detail in chapter 6. Suffice it to say at this point that Kawalerowicz advanced the view that destiny can be depicted as something different from and more than an illustration of ideology. He reasserts autonomous values. The project also advanced the art form by bringing to the screen craftsmanlike execution up to this time seen only in the work of Ford. This work had visual coherence and, more than that, cultural depth in rendering a people and an epoch.

Once put to retreat, socialist realism, "schematism," disappeared quickly. It was in full operation in 1949. The turn came in 1954. Stalinism in Poland did not have the staying power it had in Czechoslovakia or even Hungary. In 1954 and 1955, when the neighbors to the south were still caught in a cultural impasse, the mood in Poland supported a new liveliness in the arts. The real milestone year was 1955.

Examining a list of films from 1955, many of course would not command one's profound attention. Certainly not Jakubowska's *Atlantic Story* (*Opowieść atlantycka*); nor *Three Starts* (*Trzy starty*), a film about sports made by Czesław Petelski, Ewa Petelska, and Stanisław Lenartowicz (b. 1921); nor *Irene Go Home* (*Irena do domu*), remarkable only because of the performance of the comedian Adolf Dymsza.

More to the point, one notices an impressive list of accomplishments. Jan Rybkowski, after a false start and some moderate success created something significant in *The Hours of Hope* (*Godziny nadziei*). Here he found a subject so clearly interesting to him that he was inspired to advance a changed and distinctive point of view. The story takes place in Germany at the pivotal time when war is about to become peace. Other changes will come in the wake of this one. Freedom is approaching but there is an imminent threat to that freedom. Rybkowski presents excellent characterizations involved in a fascinating clash of customs and mores. He creates a climate of hope as well as one of disillusionment. In this full, rich work, one senses a fresh wind blowing. There is still some small residue of propaganda, but it is unimportant compared to Rybkowski's new and different reality.

Munk and Wajda

The documentary *Blue Cross* (*Błękitny krzyż*), came out in 1955, made by Andrzej Munk (b. 1921), who had made himself known the year before with *The Stars Must Shine* (*Gwiazdy muszą płonać*). A graduate of the film school, he made this feature/documentary by reconstructing events that had taken place during the war in the High Tatras on the Polish-Czech border. A full discussion of this is in chapter 7.

Perhaps most important to notice with regard to the year 1955 in Polish cinema is that in January of that year Andrzej Wajda's first film premiered, *The Generation* (*Pokolenie*). Wajda had been Ford's assistant (second di-

rector of *Five Boys from Barska Street*), and was helped by Ford in getting
the chance to do his own feature. *The Generation* is discussed in detail in
chapter 8. Here it is useful to note the role it played in the changing scene.
The subject was not unique, youth in the time of the occupation, but it was
immediately evident that Wajda gave it new dimensions. Instead of the usual
pathos, there was a deliberate creation of a sense of tedium and fatigue.
Whereas optimism in adversity was the prescription in the past for depicting
the occupation, Wajda projected anxiety. There was a different texture and
tone to this reality.

Both *The Hours of Hope* and *The Generation* were accused of imitating
Italian neo-realism. This brought an old argument to a head. The debate
about neo-realism had been going on for several years. The controversy is
somewhat difficult to comprehend because some elements of the debate are
contradictory. Neo-realism was closely linked to Italian antifascism and most
of its promulgators were leftists. It drew much from Soviet cinema, particularly Pudovkin. It was critical of the social structure and system in capitalist
Italy. One might have expected there to have been an affinity between neo-
realism and socialist esthetics. How then account for this opposition?

Explanations like this, of which there were many, hardly help. "Nihilism
and catastrophism which are the results of formalism do not suffice imperial-
ists in their active mobilization of volunteers. . . . Aid comes as well from naturalism, which they call in the west neo-realism." So wrote Włodzimierz Sokorski (*Sztuka w walce o socjalizm*, [Warsaw, 1950]), a most authoritative
cultural politician, as early as 1949. In the early fifties neo-realism was accused of deep pessimism because it did not foretell the victory of the prole-
tariat in the class struggle. Challenged also was the tendency to naturalism,
the propensity to dwell upon the grimness of life, to observe and describe at
the expense of creating the kind of drama that would contribute to victory in
the class struggle.

Actually this was not an abstract argument concerning the art of another
country. The debate about neo-realism was a disguised debate over Polish
art. The filmmakers and critics in Poland who defended it were fighting for
freedom of expression in their own country, for a cinema that was closer to
actuality, for a more honest observation of the world they lived in. The doctrinaire opponents intended to keep Polish film in the straitjacket designed in
1949. The establishment was not comfortable in having society depicted accurately.

In this context *The Hours of Hope, The Generation,* and Kawalerowicz's *A
Night to Remember* were drawn into the squabble. They were seen as being
under the influence of neo-realism. That would have been a dangerous condemnation just a couple of years earlier, but in 1955 criteria were in flux. New
ways of thinking about film, art, and even society were coming about.

In 1954 and 1955 certain expressions were to be found with increasing frequency in public discussions and in print, expressions such as: "democratization of public life," "battle with bureaucracy," "decentralization of authority." In December 1954, at the plenum of the Central Committee of the Polish United Workers Party—even there!—criticism was voiced gainst the diseases of "dogmatism and schematism." A short time later, the writer Leon Kruczkowski (b. 1900), a prominent party member, carried this message and its tone into cultural discussion by condemning schematism and the art of "illustration," that is, art that illustrates ideological theses. He denounced any tendency to disguise truth and reality with ideological or artistic "lacquer," and he rejected the tendency on the part of zealous party hacks to reduce every kind of controversy to class conflict.

The idea grew that cultural and artistic life could be separated from the restraints and constraints of administration. Minister of Culture Włodzimierz Sokorski, who previously led the campaign for socialist realism, wrote in 1955, "We are believers in socialist democracy in which collective groups make decisions and the constituted political apparatus carries out the actions. We accept the notion that artists ought to decide about art without questioning, however, the rationality of the existence of administration" (*Przegląd Kulturalny,* no. 5, 1955).

Another high level administrator, Leonard Borkowicz, president of the Central Bureau of Cinematography, the office in charge of the whole industry, wrote in March 1955: "[In film] not considering the artist, controlling the artist, or attempting to control the viewer, all lead in a straight line to the inevitable collapse of art" (*Film,* Nov. 16, 1956).

The Production Units

Given the transformation of the climate it would be surprising if there were no alterations in the organization of the film industry, thus far rather strictly and centrally ruled. Indeed, an important change did occur, the introduction of separate film units for production, each one headed by a leading director. The notion actually existed before the war among the members of the "Start" group. A number of people associated with that group were now leaders of the industry, including Ford, Jakubowska, Jerzy Toeplitz, and Jerzy Zarzycki. The idea became a fact on May 1, 1955 with the institutionalization of an entity with the slightly pompous name "Creators Film Units, a voluntary association of filmmakers brought together to produce movies."

This was a significant event in the history of Polish cinematography and perhaps in the history of all state-owned cinema. The units fostered mutual dependence among filmmakers and their staffs, and relative independence from the administration. The point here is that the state was prepared to return a measure of responsibility and autonomy to the filmmakers. The state officials had also become convinced that the overly centralized method of controlling production was inefficient, slow, and costly.

Gains in efficiency had the quickest and most visible results. Up to this time there had been only four to eight features produced per year. By comparison, in 1957 there were sixteen features made, in 1961 there were twenty-four. Eventually the schedule showed thirty to forty features produced per year. This occurred within the limits of the same infrastructure, the same technical facilities, studio, workshops, cameras, and other equipment. The change was that there were now decentralized units run by and for experts. In addition, production costs per project were on the average going down. Eliminating some of the noxious effects of government bureaucracy proved a remarkably beneficial prescription.

Such an increase in production required a host of new directors, cameramen, assistants, and production managers. Fortunately, the Higher School of Film at Lodz, eight years old, was in full operation, turning out each year a fair number of graduates from three departments: directing, camerawork, and production management. They were easily absorbed into feature work and also into documentary, television projects, and instructional production. At the end of 1955 it was calculated that 158 out of 228 professionals working in the film industry were film school graduates. Among assistants working in production, 93 percent of the directors' assistants and 74 percent of the cameramen's assistants were from the film school. Little by little Polish cinematography was coming under the domination of the Lodz film school alumni. Because of that it was also seeing a change in its character and identity. A new generation was being heard, a generation with a different outlook on reality in an industry that offered a lot of upward mobility for the talented, and certainly the graduates from the period around 1955 included more than a few whose talents were extraordinary, among them: Andrzej Wajda, Andrzej Munk, Janusz Morgenstern, Stanisław Lenartowicz, and Kazimierz Kutz, to name only a handful.

So in that memorable year, 1955, there came a confluence of three developments. First, a more open atmosphere made it possible to reject many stultifying ideas and some restrictive methods. Second, the reorganization of the industry enabled quantitative as well as qualitative expansion. Third, the film school was fortifying filmmaking with its preparation of well-trained professionals. These three elements created conditions extremely conducive to intellectual ferment, artistic adventure, and critical attention. The first results of all this are the films and directors that came to be called the Polish School.

II

The Polish School, 1956-1962

The cultural events of 1955 portended political transpositions shortly to come. Far-reaching political shifts occurred in 1956 that had been evolving since 1953. Early in 1956 Khruschev denounced Stalin's abuse of power at a closed meeting of the Soviet party hierarchy. Soon, this information was made available to the upper echelons of the Polish party and the news circulated. Against that background the Poznan riots broke out in June 1956, manifesting political and economic discontent. The riots were suppressed by force of arms. Some people were killed, others arrested. The accusation was made that the riots were of "foreign, Western inspiration." Many disagreed, including a good number of influential people in the party apparatus. Importantly, Władysław Gomułka did not agree. The former party secretary had been released from imprisonment and his return to the ranks of the party was being negotiated, even his return to authority.

In October, in an atmosphere of debate which involved the entire nation, the Central Committee of the party met, dominated by the supporters of Gomułka. It was decided to give Gomułka the highest position in the country, First Secretary of the Party. Khruschev and the leadership of the Soviet Union were disturbed by the events in Poland. Various responses were contemplated, but eventually the Soviets decided to accommodate themselves to the situation, perhaps because simultaneous developments in Hungary seemed more serious, even dangerous.

Gomułka returned to power under good auspices. He enjoyed broad national support, which gave him a freedom of action not available to previous administrations. Himself a victim of Stalinism, he set about undoing its harm. Among his first acts was calling a halt to the collectivization of farms. In an agricultural country, this was a decision of profound consequence. Against the strong opposition of the farmers, the government began collectivization in the early 1950s. Gomułka, understanding how inflammatory this was, stopped the process. Within months 90 percent of the collective farms that had been formed dissolved. A dramatic gesture was made toward the Roman Catholic church with the release from confinement of Stefan Cardinal Wyszyński, Primate of Poland, and with the settlement of a general accord. He carried to conclusion the process of rehabilitating those who had been imprisoned for political reasons.

There was still the sensitive issue of the large number of people who, during the war and occupation, were connected with the non-Communist resistance movement, directed from London by the government-in-exile. During the Stalinist period this movement was attacked. The *Armia Krajowa* or Home Army (often referred to simply as the AK), a powerful anti-German underground organization, was unjustly accused of cowardice, even of having been in league with the Nazis against the Communists. Home Army leaders were denounced as traitors and criminals and some ended up in prison serving long sentences. The condemnation of the Home Army and actions taken against its former members caused harm to hundreds of thousands. With the return of Gomułka, the whole thesis was rejected. "Blood spilled for Poland, no matter by whom, is precious," said Gomułka. The reverberations found their way into literature and movies.

In fact, it was now possible to do much in the cultural area that was not permitted before. Social criticism of an authentic kind spread throughout the arts. In the mass media one saw negative depictions of things that up until that time had not been admitted as existing in socialist Poland: squalor, crime, waste, bureaucratic idiocy, numbing official propaganda, and cant. Cabarets and satirical theaters sprang up like mushrooms after rain, the most prominent being the Bim-Bom in Gdansk, Warsaw's Student Satirical Theater, and the Cellar Under the Sign of the Rams in Crakow. Following the annual art exposition in 1955, there was a clean break in painting away from socialist realism. In literature ferment had been encouraged with the appearance in August 1955 of Adam Ważyk's "Poem for Adults."

All of this was not taken as a departure from socialism. It was popularly understood that Stalinism had been full of mistakes and distortions, but the socialist system was reformable. The belief was that it would suffice to eliminate errors in order to secure new, wholesome social conditions. Optimists foresaw a good "Polish road to socialism." This state of flux was encouraging in both politics and culture.

In the arts, no discipline was more profoundly affected than cinema. The system of film production units worked increasingly better. Bohdziewicz, Jakubowska, Bossak, Zarzycki, and of course Ford all headed their own units, as did Jerzy Kawalerowicz, the youngest among them, who would make some of the most important new films in his unit, "Kadr." The total number of films grew and the response from the public was inspiring. Cinema came to the center of public discussion as a catalyst for lively debates about contemporary life and recent history.

The audience became more active. There was an impressive expansion of the phenomenon of film societies, which were organized to foster discussions of individual movies as well as general developments, esthetic questions, and so forth. They were somewhat patterned after the French cineclubs and the British film societies, and included students, the intelligentsia, many ordinary workers, and even military personnel. The societies were successful in nurturing serious engagement with film as an important art form and recognizing as well as promoting work of quality. Changes in the criteria of censorship abetted the climate thus created bringing more foreign work to Polish screens. A relatively independent body called "Repertoire Council" was formed for foreign film programming. There was a new wealth to choose from among films from France, Italy, and the United States and an audience for it that possessed growing critical perception.

If perception was fresher so were the ideas and concerns that now permeated film criticism. The principles of socialist realism that were so stridently asserted in 1948 at the meeting at Wisła were now rejected and ridiculed. In contrast to other countries where schematism lasted much longer and even yet broods over the work of artists, in Poland it was dead in 1956. The problem now was to determine the standards and values that should apply. What should films be about and how should they be made?

The answers were formulated, and a cinema was born with its own style, its own themes, its own spiritual and esthetic identity. "The Polish School" came into being. This was a film movement that comprised three separate trends. First, a canon of critical realism appeared determined to present life as it truly was in Poland's society. Second, films were made about recent history, the war, occupation, the immediate postwar period. They involved sensitive and emotional themes, like the Home Army. Third, a number of filmmakers turned away from socialist realism so far as to concentrate on psychological and literary quality in movies, on inner reality instead of outer reality.

The Black Series

The spirit of critical realism began at the documentary studios in Warsaw under the leadership of Jerzy Bossak, prewar journalist and publicist who returned to Poland with Ford in 1945 to assemble and direct documentaries and establish the Documentary Studio. Shoved aside in the early fifties, he returned in 1956 as a leader in the industry. A number of young graduates from Lodz gathered around him to develop the documentary as an instrument for social analysis. But there was already some momentum in the new documentary awakening. A year earlier Jerzy Hoffman brought out *Attention Hooligans! (Uwaga chuligani!)* [1955], which he made with the collaboration of Edward Skorzewski (b. 1930), both men graduates of the Moscow Film School. From today's perspective the film seems banal, a straight presentation of certain facts, one of them that in big cities there are groups of young people who do not behave well. Certainly nothing electrifying here. But it must be remembered that the mode up until then had been to idealize, to build optimism. In contrast, *Attention Hooligans!* said outright that all was not well, and perhaps we were not in the best of all possible worlds.

A similar theme was developed in *Where the Devil Says Goodnight (Gdzie diabeł mówi dobranoc)* [1956], about lower class street kids. The directors, Kazimierz Karabasz (b. 1930) and Władysław Ślesicki (b. 1927), who were later to be quite notable among European documentarists, achieved something beyond reportage by dealing sharply with bureaucracy and by pointing out the cultural facades that hid malfeasance. The next year the same directors made *People from an Empty Place (Ludzie z pustego obszaru)* [1957], on the same theme but deeper in its analysis. Bossak, with Jarosław Brzozowski, directed a documentary characteristic of the Black Series, *Warsaw 56 (Warszawa 56)*[1956], in which beneath the surfaces of new, seemingly pleasant homes there is dilapidation. In such a house, on a broken staircase, we see a very small child at play, attached by a security cord to a balustrade because any extensive movement would be deadly. This filmic device is most effectively used to capture a complex feeling, frustration emanating from seeing pathetic danger caused by incompetence.

Examining reality in a different area, Włodzimierz Borowik (b. 1915) made *Paragraph Zero (Paragraf zero)* [1957], on the spread of prostitution in the city, not the kind of prostitution depicted sometimes as elegantly corrupt or piquante, but the kind that exists in seamy misery, meanness, and ugliness. Since according to official doctrine there was no prostitution in Poland, not even the most elementary ordinances and regulations existed in the public code. Hence the title, *Paragraph Zero*.

There were about twenty of these "Black Series" films made between 1956 and 1959, constituting critical realism in a documentary mode. Not an overwhelming number to be sure, but they did contribute to establishing a new relationship between cinema and reality.

Toward a Truer Picture

"This is atypical: old engineers are not regularly lost under the wheels of locomotives." That was reportedly the response to Jerzy Stawiński's proposal for a feature film originally to be titled "The Case of Engineer Orzechowski." It was about the death of a railroad engineer under strange circumstances in which suspicions of sabotage were raised in a novel way. Andrzej Munk, fresh from directing *Blue Cross*, got interested in the script and so was born *The Man on the Track (Człowiek na torze)* [1956], which had quite a role to play in the way film style and content evolved. The movie disclosed what sort of truth is hidden by old conspiracies. It is discussed fully in chapter 9.

At the Lodz school, under the tutelage of Bohdziewicz, a young group pro-

duced *The End of the Night* (*Koniec nocy*) [1957]. They were Julian Dziedzina (b. 1930), Paweł Komorowski (b. 1930), and Walentyna Uszycka (b.
1931) as directors, with Jerzy Wojcik (b. 1930) as cameraman. The acting
parts were taken by some of their Lodz colleagues and by young unknown
actors, among them Zbigniew Cybulski (b. 1927), Roman Polański (b. 1933),
and Ryszard Filipski (b. 1934). The story is placed on the same social landscape that served the "Black Series" so well, the world of young people on
the margins of society, whose lives are neglected and ignored by the official
social system. The film examines their games, unfulfilled aspirations, and
frustrations. It culminates in a grand, brutal scene, when the boys, after
shooting the proprietor of a shooting gallery, steal a car and in a reckless escape drive into a crowd of pedestrians. On the whole, it was an immature accomplishment, not well structured, lacking continuity, and psychologically
inconsequential. However, given the standards of the time, it was shocking
for its violence and arresting for the sincerity of its social analysis, in spite of
an ending that is less than credible in which a policeman gives a moralizing
speech. It was well received by the critics upon its release but largely ignored
by the public. Its significance is in the illustration it provides of young filmmakers searching for new perceptions and portrayals of reality. What part
were the veteran filmmakers taking in this search?

Jerzy Zarzycki, whose *Unsubdued City* was so badly treated in 1949,
made two sharply critical films in quick succession. The subject of *Land*
(*Ziemia*) [1957] was the now discontinued collectivization of farms. A land-
owning farmer refuses to turn his property over to the collective. With brute
stubbornness, against all persuasion, he desperately desires to stay on his
own plot. The attachment to the land is the strength of this warm, humane
man. What a change we have here! A landowner, a "Kulak," who would have
been excoriated if this film had been made according to socialist realism ten-
ets, is portrayed sympathetically along with his cause. But the film has faults:
the characterizations are muddled; the terms of the conflict themselves are
not clear. Apart from its ideological digression, it remains in the memory
thanks to its good visual quality, its rendition of a gloomy, gray, cloud-laden
landscape, against which we come to appreciate the ascetic and stubborn
face of the farmer, played by Janusz Strachocki.

The second film Zarzycki made that year carried the understated title, *Lost
Feelings* (*Zagubione uczucia*) [1957], based on the script by Hanna Mort-
kowicz-Olczakowa and Jerzy Andrzejewski. We follow a day in the life of a
woman laborer living in the new model city of Nowa Huta. She has been
abandoned by her husband, is inhumanely overworked, and struggles emotionally with her fourteen-year-old son, a delinquent who runs away. It is not
a well-wrought work, suffering from what appears to be a rushed production
and dramatic truncation, but it has power in its raw presentation, in its direct-

ness. One senses sincerity and a feeling for the lot of common people caught up in bad circumstances. After a few weeks the film was removed from the screens in spite of the fact it shared the critics award with *The Man on the Track* as best Polish film of the year.

Another veteran, the redoubtable Ford, found relevant new material in the work of a singular young talent nearing maturity, the writer Marek Hłasko (b. 1934), a literary phenomenon still under-appreciated. Hłasko came to manhood during Stalinism ("I learned to write by composing denunciations," he joked.), and when that period passed his talent exploded in a series of innovative stories that were nothing short of a rediscovery of the Polish people in their milieu. With unvarnished realism he wrote of the lives of people outside the mainstream. He wrote energetically and even harshly but at the same time with twilight lyricism. Hłasko emigrated in 1959, after which he wrote little. His life ended in uncertain circumstances, reportedly by suicide, in his thirty-fifth year. In the late 1950s he was at the peak of his creative drive. Given the drift of the times, it was natural that Hłasko's subjects and moods would be attractive to filmmakers.

Aleksander Ford, doyen of directors but less and less an establishmentarian, wanted to make something contemporary, sharp, and critical. *The Eighth Day of the Week* seemed like the answer. It was the story of a pair of lovers who wander about in a city of shared rooms and flats, trying to find a place to consummate their passion. The method of film narrative is to evoke realism and lyricism at one and the same time. The city is rendered as repellent, cold, gray, its citizens sunk in alcoholism. There was simply no room in it for two people in love. The movie came out in two versions, Polish and German, since it was a coproduction with the West Berlin company CCC Filmkunst and starred the German actress Sonia Ziemann opposite the Polish actor Zbigniew Cybulski. Polish authorities were skittish about approving it; the portrayal of life was so forbidding. There were also anxieties that the film would awaken feelings of enmity and contempt in Germany against modern Poland. Nevertheless, it did open in Germany but got no special attention at all. It was banned in Poland. Even a film made by the most powerful personality in the industry could not absolutely count on the tolerance and cooperation of the state.

Another film based on Hłasko's work also ran into problems the next year. Czesław Petelski made *Damned Roads* (*Baza ludzi umarłych*) [1959] from Hłasko's short story "Next One for Paradise." It is probably the most important of Petelski's films. The story takes place in the mountainous, gorge and ravine scarred, forested, unpopulated region in extreme southeastern Poland. The land seems forsaken except for a brigade of trucks and their drivers, a group of desperadoes from who-knows-where, men with cloudy pasts, no homes, no future. All they have is a pool of old, dangerous trucks in which they drive their timber through the hills. Now and then one of them perishes: "Next One for Paradise." The story concentrates on several characters reminiscent in their ways of the rootless, lost men in the movies made about the French Foreign Legion in the 1930s. Conflicts develop among them, especially after the appearance in this men's camp of a woman, the wife of the new chief. In an alcoholic stupor, an atmosphere of profanity and baseness, a game of life is played out. There is no touch of light or hope until the last scene when new trucks are heard coming. Only this suggests the possibility that anything will change for these lost people. This small hint of optimism added to the end of the film by administrative order so offended Hłasko that he had his name removed from the credits.

Did this film succeed in capturing reality as interpreted according to the climate of the times? One irritated critic wrote, "Reality is carried past believable truth. In these [hills] there are only blizzards in the winter and torrents in the summer. Not for a moment does the sun come out, because only fools believe there is a sun" (Jaszcz [Jan Alfred Szczepański], *Trybuna Ludu*, no. 222, 1959). The criticism might have been both unjust and valid at the same time. *Damned Roads* was a good film with unified visual qualities, clear characterizations, incrementally rising tension, and psychological heft. But the critics and the public expected films relevant to their own lives and not abstract dramas played out by people from nowhere.

Damned Roads was the last expression of what might be called dark realism, the realism of shock. By 1960, corrosive bitterness was less and less acceptable to the official sponsors. Four films appeared in 1960 that involved themselves in realism but depended less on heavy impact and passion for exposé. Stanisław Różewicz made *A Place on Earth* (*Miejsce na ziemi*) about the life of a youngster who simply cannot come to terms with his mother. In effect shoved aside from society, the boy is sent to a correctional institution. The vicissitudes of failure and then the slow successful rehabilitation are presented with psychological credibility and without didacticism. Nonetheless, the film did not meet with much enthusiasm. "A good-natured film, clean ... positive and constructive, but perhaps a bit obvious, a bit spare, even dry," wrote critic K.T. Toeplitz (*Świat*, no. 15, 1960).

The Little Realism

One film that did cause a good deal of discussion was *Small Town* (*Miasteczko*) [1960], made by a group of recent graduates from the Lodz school: Romuald Drobaczyński, Julian Dziedzina, and Janusz Łęski. A portrait of a small town at the end of the fifties sketched out by using several story lines, the film was loose in structure, more descriptive than dramatic, and not noteworthy for keen observation. It took as its theme the need to be liberated from a suffocating atmosphere. In spite of its weaknesses it did make an impression, perhaps because it exemplified so well, along with the other films from 1960, a current to be called the "little realism." This was a realism of customs, manners, small gestures, milieu, and climate, not a realism that induces social diagnosis and criticism. In this vein Bohdan Poręba (b. 1934) made his first feature *The Moonwalkers* (*Lunatycy*) [1960], another film about erring youth—five young people existing in a boring, hopeless environment who are on the verge of crime and delinquency. The coauthor of the script was Stanisław Manturzewski, a sociologist researching youth. *The Moonwalkers* spelled out effectively the detailed texture of the lives of these young people, their rules, their norms of behavior, their hopes (such as they were), their fads and fashions. It was devoid of a strong sense of drama. Like *Small Town* it was a piece of work that enriched the general picture of society without discovering anything unique.

The last of this group from 1960 belongs only partly to the "little realism." While it surveys the contemporary scene, it is done in a completely different spirit and with different intentions. Janusz Morgenstern's *See You Tomorrow* (*Do widzenia, do jutra*) [1960] is warm, not critical, delicate and sympathetic rather than grim and pessimistic. It is the story of a romance between a young man and a foreign girl depicting sentimental and fragile feelings as they wax and wane among young artists associated with the Bim-Bom cabaret in Sopot. Their personal answer to problems of Stalinism was to search within themselves for good feelings and sensibilities so that they might not be squandered.

So ran the course of realism in the 1950s. The country was presented to the public in ways very different from earlier films. The picture presented was shocking to many, but it was a shock of recognition and was basically welcome to a public needful of honest statements and believable representations. Tough-minded realism and the little realism remained prominent in the pattern of cinema within which there were other equally important designs.

Curiously, the stimulus for the grandest polemics came from recapturing the past, more than from exposing the truths of contemporary life. Even the very recent past was open for deep interpretation; in fact it was treated as an index of Polish history, especially World War II. The theater of reality made room for the theater of legend.

Recent History as Drama

We have mentioned that in 1956 the wartime services of the Home Army were finally recognized. With the end of Stalinism, charges of treason were abandoned and praise was given, even officially. The legend of the Home Army—especially of the Warsaw Uprising of 1944—which had been suppressed in the early 1950s, grew and flourished. A debate was generated. On one side were those who admired all patriotic heroism, on the other those who saw in the rising (and other such events in Polish history) only an irrational gesture of heroism devoid of sense. There was more here than two points of view about the uprising. The contrasting attitudes have been part of a dialectic going on in Polish culture for two centuries.

The opening event for the renewed round of debates was the release of Andrzej Wajda's *Canal (Kanał)* [1957], made from a script by Jerzy S. Stawiński, which offered an interpretation of the role of the Home Army and the theme of heroism. Wajda's film poses key questions: What is the sense of fighting on when defeat is inevitable? Do heroism, suffering, and death serve the nation in a real way? Do these constitute a set of gestures that build legends and have meaning only to a future generation? While Wajda had doubts about the good sense of the Warsaw Uprising, his romantic temperament, his tendency to favor the dramatic act gave the inference that he stood for heroism to the last, true to the tradition favored by romantic Poles. The public perception for a brief period differed from this. All Wajda's films are discussed in greater detail in chapter 8.

Ambivalence also played a role in the acceptance of another of his films, *Lotna (Lotna)* [1959], about the outbreak of war in 1939. The tale summons up something deeply nostalgic in Poles and those familiar with Polish history, its symbols and legends: the white horse, the cavalry, the charge and attack. But assaulted by tanks and planes, as they were in 1939, this cavalry seems like an apparition from some older war. Is there heroism here or just quixotic gesturing done in the pursuit of legend? Wajda's depiction finds value in the heroic.

Munk or Wajda?

There were films made to represent the opposite idea, made to throw a different light upon the romantic heroism that was so much a part of the Polish literary and dramatic culture. Andrzej Munk, whose *The Man on the Track* broke new ground as filmic social criticism in 1956, produced *Eroica (Eroica)* one year later and placed it before a dumfounded audience. The film has two episodes, the first of which is entitled "Scherzo alla polacca." It is a comedy about the Warsaw Uprising (yes, a comedy!). In contrast to the tragic and trapped heroes of *Canal*, Munk gives us a rascal. *Canal* is serious, somber, full of gloom. *Eroica* is comedic, almost farcical. *Canal* is set in a visual frame of reference that is Dantesque. *Eroica* depicts backyards in the countryside, chickens scattering, children playing at war. If "Scherzo" offers contrast, the second episode gives us a sort of inadvertent reply to *Lotna* and a direct rejoinder to any promoter of legend. "Ostnanto lugubre" shows a group of officers in a prisoner of war camp who treat their failing spirits by resorting to a legend of one of their own who had the will and strength to es-

cape. Actually, the legendary officer is hiding in the attic of the same barracks! So much for the stuff of legend.

It must not be suggested that Wajda and Munk were clear and uncompli-
cated polar opposites on the theme of heroism. *Canal* and *Eroica* were even
written by the same writer. The premises were not clearly opposing to each
other. Wajda was not absolutely affirmative about the heroism of 1939 or
1944, nor was Munk absolutely negative; but they both had a tendency to
lean in one direction or the other, so their films serve usefully as examples
of filmic approaches to a central Polish theme, romantic heroism.

The Polish Dilemma

That theme is central to the many questions raised by the films of "the Polish School." Are the Poles to live by accepting rationally and calmly the
course of history, no matter what it may bring? Should they stand in the way
of historical force with little chance of bringing about any ultimate changes?
Should the nation's existence—not only in history but also today—be understood as the sum total of daily affairs, small events, compromises? What of
the tradition of heroism and its legends? Which is the right way to reach the
old dream of national independence, by heroism or prosaic everyday
work?

This was a renewal of the ideological questioning that infused Polish intellectual life throughout the nineteenth century and divided the intelligentsia.
The same questions were asked at each crisis, 1794, 1830, 1848, and 1863.
The literature of the times is rich in discussion of this Polish dilemma. It was
nothing less than this that cinema took up in the late 1950s. It is what gave
the Polish School its strength, passion, and energy. The dilemma and questions arising from it were never abstract, not in the nineteenth century, not in
the 1950s, not later in the 1970s and 1980s when a new generation reframed
it thus: Should we be satisfied with little favors, small advances, the permissible? Or should we go after everything at once, now?

One might arbitrarily state, simply to make a point, that Wajda and Munk
bracketed the dilemma, first with *Canal* and *Eroica*, then later with *Ashes
and Diamonds* and *Bad Luck*. *Ashes and Diamonds* compressed within itself all the relevant questions and problems in the light of duty and a certain
heroism. Munk, the ironist, in his *Bad Luck* (*Zezowate Szczęście*) [1960]
played the dilemma with comic, almost farcical interpretation. This arbitrary
assertion of a kind of dialogue between Munk and Wajda is instructive; however it omits too many who were working with the same material.

Members of the Polish School

For instance, Jerzy Passendorffer (b. 1923) made his best film in 1958.
Answer to Violence (*Zamach*), a reconstruction of an event that took place

in the center of Warsaw in 1944, the assassination of Gestapo General Franz Kutschera. The script was by Jerzy S. Stawiński, who wrote *Canal* and *Eroica*. The assassination was a Home Army action, famous in the history of the occupation. The movie is conventionally made with classical structure (preparation, act, escape), lacking the artistic maturity and sophistication of a film like *Canal*. But in spite of stereotypic characters and situations, it succeeded with the public and was effective in developing the question regarding the rationality of heroism, and the role of legend.

This was also true of *Pills for Aurelia* (*Pigułki dla Aurelii*)[1958], directed by Stanisław Lenartowicz. Actually it had been the intention of Lenartowicz and his writer Aleksander Ścibor-Rylski (b. 1928) to narrate an "ordinary day during the occupation," hence make a film implicitly without heroism. Nevertheless, when finished, it did get involved in the debate over heroism. The story was about a unit of the underground that acquires weapons and rescues one of its men—certainly not an "ordinary day." Its retelling was supposed to suggest the commonplace, perhaps even with comedic overtones, but when finished it took on the heavier tones of tragedy.

Stanisław Różewicz made his best film, *Free City* (*Wolne miasto*) [1958] from a script by Jan Józef Szczepański, recounting another episode of desperate heroism, the defense of the post office in Gdansk (then Danzig) on September 1, 1939. On that morning the Germans invaded in force, and in Gdansk, besieged the post office as one of the locations controlled by Poles. For fourteen hours a garrison of a handful of mailmen held out stubbornly against the invaders. Eventually they capitulated, were taken prisoner, trucked to the outskirts of the city, and shot. Again the debate on heroism: "*Free City*, carrying as it does the memorialization of the heroes of the Gdansk post office, popularizes the false idea that heroism is important above all considerations." So wrote K.T. Toeplitz (*Kwartalnik Filmowy*, no. 2, 1959). Indeed, the idea of a group of postmen holding out against Hitler's army is unrealistic, maybe even unreal, but the event and its story is indelibly marked in the history of the country.

There were two contributions to the theme by Witold Lesiewicz (b. 1922), former documentary-making partner of Munk. He made *The Deserter* (*Dezerter*) [1958], about Poles in the western territories conscripted into the German army, a subject of exceptional sensitivity, and later *April* (*Kwiecień*) [1961], a drama of war and the moral choices it presents. The husband and wife team of Czesław and Ewa Petelski joined the debate with *A Sky of Stone* (*Kamienne Niebo*) [1959], followed by *Sergeant-Major Kalen* (*Ogniomistrz Kaleń*) [1961].

One of the more interesting figures to be associated with the Polish School and to participate in the debate on honor and heroism was Kazimierz Kutz (b. 1929), who debuted with *Cross of Valour* (*Krzyż walecznych*) [1959]. He had been in the industry since 1955, serving on the set of *Generation*, and as second director for *Ashes and Diamonds* and for Passendorffer's *Answer to Violence*. *Cross of Valour* was a movie of three stories by Józef Hen. The first and second parts especially applied to the Polish School in an emotional as well as philosophical way. In the first, a country boy is honored for his bravery with the Cross of Valour. He is anxious to appear with his medal in his village and gather the glory he has earned; this was the motivation for his act of heroism. When he arrives home he finds that the village no longer exists. What good was his medal? When it comes to more fighting he no longer volunteers. The second story is even more simple. A man gives shelter to a stray dog. A warm man-dog relationship develops until the man learns that this dog had been an SS canine, a prison dog. The man must decide if the dog is to survive. Kutz introduced the common man as protagonist to the canon of the Polish School. He did so with a warmth and directness rare in Polish cinema, a warmth that compares to the films made a bit later by the Czech directors Forman, Passer, and Jasny.

The older generation of filmmakers, those from the generation of Ford, Jakubowska, and Bohdziewicz, did not, by and large, join in the themes of the Polish School. An exception was Leonard Buczkowski who made a craftsmanlike film about a submarine that escaped from the Germans on the first day of war, *The Submarine "Eagle"* (*ORP Orzeł*) [1959]. And on the periphery, Jerzy Zarzycki made *White Bear* (*Biały niedźwiedź*) [1959], based on an odd premise: a Jew during the occupation escapes discovery by putting on a bearskin and working as a prop for a photographer. Artistically the film was a failure.

The New Auteurs

These films that dealt with the national dilemma and the concurrent group that developed cinematic critical realism were not the only components of the Polish School. They sparked the most heated controversies, to be sure. It was also characteristic of the period and the school that new talents came to the fore with their special personal styles, themes, and moods. It can be said that *auteur* cinema was the practice in Poland, closely conforming to the descriptions that were to be written a few years later when *auteur* theory became an esthetic and critical issue in Paris and New York.

Wajda and Munk were *auteurs* in the full sense of the word and the theory, although the messages they were communicating were so startling that this new quality, *auteurism*, escaped special attention. However, the films of the *auteurs* did indeed win ample notice, and such directors as Tadeusz Konwicki (b. 1926), Jerzy Kawalerowicz (b. 1922), Wojciech Has (b. 1925), and Tadeusz Chmielewski (b. 1927) took their places within the definition of *auteurism* and as members of the Polish School. Kawalerowicz is discussed in chapter 6. For continuity we simply note here his exceptional productivity during the years 1955 to 1960. During that time he made several films that were to become classics. There were *The Real End of the Great War* (*Prawdziwy koniec wielkiej wojny*) [1957], *Night Train* (*Pociąg*) [1959], and finally, the famous *Mother Joan of the Angels* (*Matka Joanna od Aniołów*) [1961], a sophisticated work visually, and modernistic in its visionary ambiguity.

Konwicki

Tadeusz Konwicki is quite unique. He came from Wilno, a cultural and historical center for Poland, now a part of the U.S.S.R. The peculiarity of this region has left a mark on his biography and on everything he has done. One of the outstanding writers in Poland to appear since the war, Konwicki began his writing during the trough of socialist realism. As the rules softened and his work ripened it was evident that here was a most unusual writing phenomenon, witty, intelligent, sensitive to paradox, cruelly skeptical. As he recalls it, "Some time in the fifties, I was invited to an office, and in very distinguished circumstances over a cup of coffee, I was offered a career as a screenwriter. I remember resisting, but I gave in. I wrote the piece, which I rewrote endlessly until I felt confused and numb, but finally the cameras did their work. I'd rather not mention the title" (*Film*, no. 28, 1964). The title was *The Career* (*Kariera*) [1955], directed by Jan Koecher. It was indeed not worth mentioning for its intrinsic merits. But two years later Konwicki would redeem himself with a screenplay for Lenartowicz's film *Winter Twilight* (*Zimowy zmierzch*) [1957]. It drew public attention by portraying subject matter that was quite original, subject matter from Konwicki's own fictional (and perhaps once real) world, the world of a provincial town somewhere in the east of Poland, inhabited by small-town people sunk in resignation but with keen recollection of old, trivial disputes. The evocation of mood and the somewhat unique background were effective, but the film was far from perfect. The characters were sketchy, the piece lacked drama, and the action— if, in fact, one can characterize anything in this movie as action—lacked continuity. It is mainly significant as the film that introduced Konwicki's universe, something that would become increasingly interesting.

The first film he directed, actually codirected with Jan Laskowski, was *The Last Day of Summer* (*Ostatni dzień lata*) [1958], an undertaking so modest as to be almost in the amateur category. It was made on a miniscule budget that was simply tacked on to the costs of a different production; it had no crew, one cameraman (Laskowski), and two actors (Irena Laskowska and Jan Machulski). There is nothing in it except for the beach, the sea, an occasional airplane overhead, and two people unsuccessfully searching for mutual understanding. On the surface the film's main idea was lack of communication. But there was also another, deeper theme, one which was to become central to Konwicki's later work: the emotional destruction wrought by war upon people who are fated never to find peace and harmony, the kind of people the writer Tadeusz Borowski described as "contaminated by death."

In 1961, Konwicki made his first full-scale film, *Halloween* (*Zaduszki*—literally translated the title should be *All Soul's Day*). The same themes and character types appear but in a more significant context. A man and woman arrange a date in a small hotel. It should be a typical rendezvous, but it turns out badly. Instead of passion and desire the two people bring with them their memories of war and death. Both people are burnt out, dead souls as it were, devastated, incapable of love. Their meeting leaves them unmoved. Nothing has happened.

Has

Contemporaneously, another quite individual talent emerged as a maker of feature films, Wojciech Has (b. 1925). He had been making documentaries and educational films for eleven years without remarkable achievement. At thirty-three he made the feature *The Noose* (*Petla*) [1958], based on a short story by Marek Hłasko. The plot concerns an alcoholic who follows a path toward suicide. He transformed Hłasko's realistic prose into a visual style that approaches surrealism: empty streets with no destination; strange, fleeting figures; a clock counting off the remaining hours of life; a scene in a funeral home with a mourner looking suggestively at the hero. This is more a projection of the hero's states of mind than the world he inhabited according to Hłasko's story. When *The Noose* was screened it was not surprising to note that critics referred to Has's "expressionism." While he did not play with perspectives in the manner of Robert Wiene, nor fashion sharp, distorted characterizations, he did treat the world of his hero as a drama of hysterical annihilation.

He made his second feature the same year, *Farewells* (*Pożegnania*) [1958], another adaptation, this time from a novel by Stanisław Dygat (b. 1914). Dygat wrote in a literary mode within which story and characters are less significant than the author's personality, his ambiguous, ironic tone, and the game he plays with the reader. In this novel, the hero is an intellectual who wants "to be somebody," "do something," "experience something," but has neither the strength nor the patience and covers up his failure with a grimace of boredom. With surpassing verisimilitude Has captured the tone of false nonchalance conceived by the author. It is the story of a young man whose love affair with a dancer takes place first before, then after the war, when conditions had changed considerably. More so than in *The Noose*, with the help of Dygat, Has fashions a vision of the world that is to become essentially his, a world of past things, objects covered with dust and cobwebs, things once treasured and now forgotten. It is a storeroom, as it were, of the past winning sidelong glances of nostalgia. Against the background of a somewhat capricious story, Has fashioned a special visual style.

In a departure from tragic expression (*The Noose*) and irony (*Farewells*), Has made his third movie, a psychological piece directed in a straightforward way, *Two-Room Tenants* (*Wspólny pokój*) [1960]. Again a literary work was the basis, this time a biographical novel from the thirties by Zbigniew Uniłowski (1909–1937), a study of bohemian life in prewar Warsaw. Has tried to make it into a mood piece, developing a lost generation atmosphere. The plot was devoid of sharp and focused events; the film depended on depicting people living together in psychological emptiness. Clearly Has was not going to be involved in the main themes of Polish cinema. His material was his own. Unlike Wajda, Munk, Kawalerowicz, and others who were quite in the center of intellectual currents, Has, like Konwicki, chose a separate and private route for his expression.

Eve Wants to Sleep

Poland's most renowned director of comedies, Tadeusz Chmielewski (b. 1927), also chose a private route for his expression. *Eve Wants to Sleep* (*Ewa chce spać*) [1958] reached the public with éclat. It was a surprise to all including the critics and other directors. Chmielewski made a mad comedy out of a fantastic and grotesque world, which nonetheless resembled the country in which he lived. The story concerns a young girl who is looking for a place to spend the night in a strange city. She gets involved in a series of hilarious situations, which are depicted sometimes in the style of Rene Clair and sometimes in the slapstick mode. Comic inventiveness goes off pyrotechnically producing absurdity, paradox, and irony, all in a basket of warm humor. *Eve Wants to Sleep* ends with the camera turning suddenly upon the crew, including the director, made up to look like that father of Polish cinema, Aleksander Ford, then a quick cut to a pickle jar exploding. This is comedy that swings somewhere between Lubitsch and Monty Python.

It was a complete novelty to its audience, of course, whose viewing had been dominated by a rather serious repertoire; at least it was a novelty with respect to film. But this kind of humor—absurd, ironical, slightly bitter—was characteristic of the Polish intelligentsia. One thinks of Witkacy, Gombrowicz, and Mrożek. Chmielewski tried the formula again in *Jack of Spades* (*Walet Pikowy*) [1960], but not with equal success.

This introduction of comedy into the repertoire serves as a convenient point for recapitulations. What has happened so far? By 1962 an important growth period that had begun in 1955 was concluded. From the small parochial industry, Polish cinema developed into an original, artistic, intellectualized, and stylized formulation that began to perform a new role in society, perhaps even to the surprise of the film people themselves. "The Polish School" was the first and most lasting cinematic movement in the eastern block as well as the most influential.

Quite simply, the industry came under the influence of creators in their thirties, born in the 1920s, most of whom had graduated from the film school in Lodz: Wajda, Munk, Lenartowicz, Lesiewicz, Has, Morgenstern, and Kawalerowicz. The previous generation, those who had begun their work in the prewar period and who recreated the industry after the war were no longer in control. Those included Ford, Buczkowski, Jakubowska, Starski, and Zarzycki. The new generation brought with it a different point of view. They had not been adults during the war. Coming of age during the war created a different cast of mind. The past endured as an adult was different from the past endured when young. Different questions are asked. How does one come to terms with such a historical moment as the war? What is the role of the individual in the tide of history? Does heroic gesture provide redemption from defeat? These were not questions separable from contemporary life either. In any case, the approach of the new generation was less burdened, more searching.

The younger group also brought with them new styles of presentation. One-dimensional characters were passé, as was simplified bombastic acting. Characters were closer to everyday experience. Staging was less stilted and studio-bound. Narration ceased being obtrusive and didactic. The result was a new and original identity enhanced by an enthusiastic response from the public. The movies became a topic of public discussion and indeed of vigorous public debate, especially concerning the themes of Polish identity and the course of recent history. Cinema clearly emerged as central to the cultural and intellectual life of Poland. This was important since the pendulum was about to swing again, toward conformity.

III

Stabilization

The extraordinary excitement generated after the political events of 1956 began to wane in the sixties. In the meantime, the government strengthened its position and moved away from reformism. It rejected Stalinist conservatism on the one hand, but on the other hand was even stronger in fighting off "revisionism." After a period of activity and hope society was returning to greyness. To be sure, there was no attempt to return to the models of the early fifties. Private ownership in agriculture continued. Investment excesses were curbed to protect consumer standards. Life in Poland was indeed better and quieter than during the fifties. Harsh methods of repression did not return. There were no mass arrests, epidemics of false accusations, or manipulation of charges. The public was calm. The poet Tadeusz Różewicz, with some slight irony, named this period, "our small stabilization."

There was still room for freedom of expression; not as much as in the period around 1956, but certainly much more than was allowed in the early fifties. In the world of stage-theater, avant-garde developments were under way and continue even to the present. Literature was dominated by the mature work of Jerzy Andrzejewski (1909–1982), Kazimierz Brandys (b. 1916), Tadeusz Konwicki (b. 1926), and Jarosław Iwaszkiewicz (1894–1980). There was no return to socialist realism. The term was laid to rest permanently, at least in Poland. Normative esthetics, defined "types," Stalinist standards— none of these had a revival. This does not mean that the authorities became indifferent to cultural activity. They simply ceased to be sensitive to violations of various esthetic principles and showed signs of obvious irritation only when portrayals became too bleak or negative, or when content seemed clearly politically antipathetic.

The film unit system was operating successfully. In the 1960s more influence and responsibility rebounded to a group of vigorous unit production managers. Year after year the annual production of films increased. At the same time the individual films diminished somewhat in ambition and seemed less and less to constitute important social events to the extent that they had from 1956 to 1962. (This would change again in the late 1970s.) They became at this time simply films, stories about various things depicted in various ways. This was part of "our small stabilization."

One exception deserves mention. Janusz Morgenstern's *Life Once Again* (*Życie raz jeszcze*) [1965] was politically sensitive and stirred up interest. Written by Roman Bratny, it pictured with courage and intelligence an episode from the Stalinist years. Set in the gloom of that period, it tells of the experience of an innocent man jailed and sentenced for political reasons. Even though a happy ending was imposed on the original version, the film was allowed a run of only a few days before it was removed and shelved. It languished in storage until the fall of 1986 when it was broadcast over television to a very large audience. But as we have indicated, Morgenstern's film was an exception, and things were relatively peaceful from the political angle of vision.

Other developments need elaboration. Coming to terms with the past, the fate of the individual caught up on the current of history, the destiny of the Poles—all these faded a little. But in another way there was an important strengthening of a key aspect of cinematic evolution, the further development of the *auteurs*: Wajda, Kawalerowicz, Has, Konwicki, and others. In the mid-sixties their ranks were enriched by the addition of some important young individuals: Polański, Skolimowski, Majewski, and Kluba. At the same time one notes a turn toward more distant history, history less immediately relevant.

War as a Subject

This is not to say that the Polish interest in depictions of World War II waned. The war continued as an important subject, but it was treated in a less grim way, with greater stress upon victory rather than upon sacrifice in the face of defeat. Jerzy Passendorffer, who debuted with *Answer to Violence*, made several films about fighting the Germans and also about the battles with Ukrainian nationalists that took place in the eastern part of Poland just after the war: *The Broken Bridge* (*Zerwany Most*) [1961], *Christened by Fire* (*Skąpani w ogniu*) [1964], *Scenes of Battle* (*Barwy walki*) [1965], and his triumphal *Direction Berlin* (*Kierunek Berlin*) [1969]. These were characteristic of the new way to treat war in films. Czesław Petelski added to his *Sergeant-Major Kaleń* with the movie *The Beater* (*Naganiacz*) [1964], a story about a hunt for Jews in hiding. Finally, Petelski made *The Rowan Tree* (*Jarzębina czerwona*) [1969], a film that closed his series of war pieces.

Stanisław Różewicz made his best film in 1961, *The Birth Certificate* (*Świadectwo urodzenia*), three stories about children during the German occupation. After several other good films on different themes, he made *Westerplatte* [1970], about the defense of the Polish garrison in Gdansk (Danzig) in September 1939. It was a pathetic event but a heroic one; a small unit of soldiers successfully resisted the entire German attacking force.

Różewicz used a calm, narrative, nondramatic, quasi-documentary style, admirable for its cool objectivity.

Jan Łomnicki (b. 1929), maker of outstanding documentaries, made his first feature, *Contribution* (*Kontrybucja*), in 1967, a typical example of the war movies of this period.

If tragic dilemma and moral perplexity were less stressed in the somber treatment of the war experience, there was room for these elements in comedy. In a country scarred by war and the occupation as Poland was, it was something of an act of courage to attempt comedy on the subject of World War II. Stanisław Lenartowicz made *Giuseppe in Warsaw* (*Giuseppe w Warszawie*) [1964], a hilarious story about a fugitive Italian prisoner of war caught in the turmoil of the occupation.

Tadeusz Chmielewski, a bit quiet since the artistic and popular success of *Eve Wants to Sleep*, solidified his reputation as the chief of comedy directors with *Where Is the General?* (*Gdzie jest general?*) [1964]. He turned to the war again in 1970 for his successful comedy, *How I Started World War II* (*Jak rozpętałem II wojnę światową*). It is the episodic tale of a somewhat slow-witted young man who becomes involved, unwillingly and unwittingly, in all the important events of the war in Europe, Africa, and Asia.

This second wave of war films was quite different from the first, which featured such films as *Eroica* and *The Canal*. Here, rather than perplexity, we have ordinary patriotic reflex, and instead of defeat we have vigorous optimism. We even have laughs. But mainly there was a return to simple story treatment without philosophical and historical reflection about the course of Polish history. In place of the agonized protagonist, intellectual and ruminative, a different hero was depicted, a folksy character, usually of peasant origin, guided by common sense and peasant wisdom, who views war as a sort of necessity rather than as an apocalypse. This was a significant change. In fact this was a wholesome addition to the store of characters, albeit often suffering from simplistic presentation. Oversimplification was accompanied by deterioration of narrative quality. There was a tendency toward stereotypes. Even the visual quality of filmmaking did not live up to its earlier promise.

The Historical Spectacle

Something new appeared, however: large-scale historical epics. Their genesis may have owed something to the fact that the film units were trying for financial success. Their popularity was to some degree insured by virtue of the fact that the projects were based on very popular novels that were prescribed reading in schools. It is to be praised that these popular—or intended to be popular—films were not rendered simply and crassly in a commercial way. They were not merely costume movies but carried a burden of history and historical interpretation. Each of them was more than a story of adventure; each of them was serious about history.

As we have already seen, the way events of the past are viewed and understood goes to the core of any discussion about Polish culture. History in Poland has never been a record, pure and simple; it has always involved subjective philosophy. Consequently, the historical novel looked for the contemporary relevance of past epochs and events, much in the way the Elizabethans rendered history of present significance when they changed and shaped it to suit their dramas. To suit the emotional and intellectual needs of a nineteenth-century audience, Henryk Sienkiewicz (1846–1916), Stefan Żeromski (1864–1924), and Bolesław Prus (1847–1912), as well as some lesser lights, wrote their historical but pertinent novels. One must remember that there had been no political entity known as Poland since 1796 when the country was dismembered and its several parts incorporated into Prussia, Austria, and Russia. Sienkiewicz admitted that he wrote of Polish victories in the East and against the Swedish "deluge" in order to help mend the broken heart of the nation. It is a truism that more or less, for better or worse, every nation writes itself the history it needs. This is nowhere more true than in Poland, given its peculiar history of glory, dismembered longing, resurrection, destruction, nationalism, and pride. This special creation of history is reflected in the grand historical epic films of the sixties.

The first of these, a truly monumental project, was Aleksander Ford's *Teutonic Knights (Krzyżacy)* [1960]. Ford had already proven his ability to deal with large-scale productions in *Chopin's Youth*. *Teutonic Knights*, based on the Sienkiewicz novel, depicted events from the fifteenth century when Poland, with other Slavic allies, defeated the army of that order in battle. The book was written about the year 1900 when there was an intense Germanization program under way in that part of Poland under Prussian sway. It helped raise morale and enhance national feeling. Ford's movie was accurate with respect to avoiding anachronisms, and it was skillfully staged. Its chief weakness was in the relatively flat portrayals of the main characters.

A similar but much more modest project was Jerzy Hoffman's *Pan Michael (Pan Wołodyjowski)* [1969]. Hoffman (b. 1932) adapted this from the third book of Sienkiewicz's trilogy, literature that is indeed well known to the Poles. The main character was one of Poland's favorite literary creations and his portrayal by actor Tadeusz Łomnicki added to the popularity of the persona. In general the film was not nearly as good as *Teutonic Knights*; it simply lacked Ford's mastery. Nevertheless it remains one of the most popular of all film productions and is regularly revived.

The Auteurs and Historical Spectacle

The *auteur* directors also were attracted to the historical format as a means of contemporary comment. In 1965 Wajda made his significant

Ashes (*Popioły*), based on the novel by Żeromski, written in 1904, about the odyssey of Poles who participated in the Napoleonic wars. This extremely influential film is discussed in chapter 8. Kawalerowicz was another to join the historical lists with his *The Pharaoh* [1966], from the novel by Prus, a story about power, cynicism, immorality, and manipulation. Wojciech Has was attracted to this format.

Has

The sixties were the most prolific period for Has, an individualist not associated with any group or movement. He had generally been indifferent to political and social subjects. He tried like almost every other director to tackle contemporary times, but he did it by making films with a present-time focus and a past-time perspective. In *Gold* (*Złoto*) [1962], the subject is ostensibly modern construction. Has imposes upon this his favorite motifs: old-fashioned interiors, attics full of junk, unusual landscapes. The construction workers are strange creatures who read Jack London in the workers' hostel and Villon at the construction site. Has did not feel it was a successful mix.

A year later he made a beautiful and careful film entitled *How to Be Loved* (*Jak być kochaną*) [1963], based on a short story by Kazimierz Brandys (b. 1916). It was psychological cinema in which an actress on a flight to Paris reflects on everything she had experienced during the German occupation: suffering, love, disappointment, disaster. From this personal biography composed of subjective scraps and shards there emerges a historical picture comparable to those of the Polish School. It was made an outstanding subtle piece of artistry by the consummate acting of Barbara Kraft. In 1964 Has wanted to break into the grand historical mode with *The Saragossa Manuscript* (*Rękopis znaleziony w Saragossie*).

Like *The Teutonic Knights*, *The Saragossa Manuscript* was a superproduction in every way. As a period piece it was original and unprecedented. The literary source was an eighteenth-century novel written in French by a Polish aristocrat, Jan Potocki (1761–1818). He was a most unusual man, a traveller, an eccentric, something of a scientist, a man who viewed literature as an intellectual game, not as a vehicle for a message. This is reflected in the structure of his tale in which one story is built into another as in *The Thousand and One Nights*. There are natural consequences to such a technique, a changeability of tone, improbability of situation, indistinct characters. But would Has try to change this into some sort of conventional film? According to Has, "Intricate plots that overlap are meant to be a joke on the forms and types of narration. Can't we too have this kind of fun at the cinema? Must we treat the work so seriously? I am delighted with the charge that my film is not homogeneous, that it presents a mix of various conventions ..." (*Film*, no. 10, 1965). That is indeed what Has's film was like. It is a story that appears to be taking place in the Andalusian Mountains around 1739. The protagonist is a captain of the Royal Guard, Alfons von Warden (Zbigniew Cybulski), who meets with unbelievable adventures and incredible characters. Really, the story takes place nowhere except in the tale. It stays a kind of joke full of charm, intelligence, and sophisticated effects. Actually, only by stretching the definition of the genre can it be said to be a historical film. A grand spectacle it was, nonetheless, and no doubt it was inspired by the other films of the grand spectacular historical mode just then being made.

Later in the sixties, Has made *The Code* (*Szyfry*) [1966], a psychological piece made from the story and screenplay by Andrzej Kijowski (b. 1928). It takes place both in current times and during the German occupation. Then he made *The Doll* (*Lalka*) [1968], an adaptation of a very popular novel by Bolesław Prus. In this he executed a rather faithful version of the novel without offering any experimental device or new insight.

Salto

Making his solitary artistic way, Konwicki eschewed the grand spectacle and made no effort to join this mode. This was just as well, for his own devices led him to make his magnum opus, *Salto*, in 1965. In this single film, Konwicki brings to mind much of the tradition of Polish literature—*The Wedding* (*Wesele*) [1901], by Stanislaw Wyśpianski (1869–1907), *Kordian* by Juliusz Słowacki (1809–1849), and perhaps above all the modern work of Witold Gombrowicz. In the story a middle-aged man wearing dark glasses (played by Zbigniew Cybulski) arrives in a small town. Is he some advocate for some cause? A prophet? A healer? A victim? He is surrounded by ambiguity. He has a different story for everyone. He introduces himself to some as Malinowski, to others as Kowalski (these are the Smith and Jones of Polish names). The town is full of characters who connect themselves in some vague way with Kowalski-Malinowski. There is a landlord, a good man who dreams of being a villain; a poet; a Jew named Blumenfeld, a holocaust survivor. Speaking of himself Blumenfeld says, "As a child I was very delicate. Only during the war I became someone. For five years I was hiding under a sofa or behind a wardrobe. That was something!" Malinowski-Kowalski seduces a girl, searches for alleged treasure (no one knows quite what the treasure is), and talks about his strange and illogical life. He succeeds in getting everyone involved in mystifying problems, and it all climaxes in a strange dance, the "salto." In the morning it will prove that he is a nobody, a man who is running away from his wife and children, from the monotony and misery of existence. Or is that another mystification? The tale is both tragic and comic. Irony becomes lyric, the trivial seems lofty. One thinks sometimes, by way of comparison, of Hickey in *The Iceman Cometh* but with exaggerated expressionistic overtones.

While some of the themes are similar, *Salto* offers more than *Halloween*. It is a mix of myth, motifs, and themes from the literature of the nineteenth century, and some twentieth-century allusions are involved as well. From the nineteenth century he takes the theme of Polish fate, usually tragic, from Gombrowicz and the twentieth century he borrows frustration, defeat, and what Gombrowicz called "Polish helplessness." Konwicki at once used all this even while he derided it. This film was truly a Polish complex.

Still Another Generation

By now it is commonplace for us to think that people only ten years apart can have completely different outlooks, but this is not such an American nor such a completely contemporary phenomenon. Ten years seemed to be the margin of separation between philosophical generations in the development of the Polish film industry. There are reasons. The older generation, born in the 1920s, matured during the war and the German occupation. That was their point of reference. Those born in the 1930s were still more or less children at the end of the war. They came of age after the war. The choking obsession of the war years was strange for them. They perhaps remembered the war, even suffered because of it, but they were not of the age of choice and responsibility. This is important to keep in mind for the group of directors who now enter the scene, who were beginning their work in the 1960s.

Polański

Roman Polański was a child actor, practically by accident. While taking different routes through his adolescence and teens, all his paths seemed to cross through the theater. Polański (b. 1933) started his postprimary education in the Krakow School of Arts where he started out successfully but then ran afoul of the school authorities. His on-again off-again acting connections took him out of town to do a bit part. There he met a young senior student in film from Lodz, Andrzej Wajda, who gave him his first orientation to film work. When Wajda was ready to make his first feature, *Generation*, he was looking about for young actors and thought of Polański. Shortly thereafter Polański entered the Lodz film school and began his career. His love of being in front of the camera as well as behind it never went away. He often took minor roles.

But it was his inventiveness and practical intelligence as a student of directing that surprised and impressed his professors. During his second year he made a short film, *Two Men and a Wardrobe* (*Dwaj ludzie z szafą*)

[1958], which won an award that same year at the Brussels Exposition, and which quickly earned worldwide recognition. It was a surrealistic farce about two young people who emerge from the sea carrying a huge old-fashioned wardrobe. They drag it around and about the city unable to find a place for themselves. This simple idea opened a series of unusual, uncommon, and funny situations and reactions, all of which gave Polański's film its sparkle and originality. A year later he made his graduation film, *When the Angels Fall* (*Gdy spadają anioły*) [1959], a thin story about a woman who is a lavatory attendant and who remembers the times of sweet, romantic, and pure youth. The role was played by Polański's wife, Barbara Kwiatkowska-Las who was discovered by Chmielewski for his picture *Eve Wants to Sleep*. Polański and his wife then left for Paris. At the beginning of 1962 he returned to Poland. A young writer (later to be director) had written a screenplay for him, and the film unit "Kamera," managed by Jerzy Bossak, one of the professors at the film school, was ready to produce it.

The film was *Knife in the Water* (*Nóż w wodzie*) [1962], Polański's first feature and the only feature film he made in Poland. Within the bounds of a totally realistic style, Polański develops an abstract power struggle between three people sailing on a small yacht in the Mazurian lakes. He (Leon Niemczyk) is a mature, self-confident, dominating person, clearly accustomed to authority. She (Jolanta Umecka) is his girlfriend or wife, resilient in the face of male domination. Finally, there is a hitchhiking stranger (Zygmunt Malanowicz), a young boy, timid at first but later a threat to the older man's domination. Indeed this is a psychological duel between the two who gradually unmask each other and themselves until the only person left with integrity seems to be the woman. Apart from the psychology there is an attendant social theme: the generation gap, which is to say the attack by the young on the entrenched generation just ahead of them. The story unfolds with precision, steady drama, and situational inventiveness. It is a remarkable film, perfectly executed with excellent character development, psychological subtlety, and spare simplicity in the major theme.

The film at first had trouble with the censors who challenged the image of the younger generation, who were not represented as the officials thought they should be. But the objections were raised under different pretexts. Finally, approval came through, and the movie went on to financial and critical success, including extraordinary attention in Western Europe and in the United States, where it became the cover story for a popular American journal. So began Polański's remarkable career, which matured mostly in the West. *Knife in the Water* brought instant success and promise for more.

Skolimowski

The screenwriter of *Knife in the Water*, Jerzy Skolimowski (b. 1936), was to play a part in Polish cinema of the sixties also, and, again like Polański, his career matured in the West. He began as a student of ethnography, became an amateur boxer, a poet, and in general carried with him a high ambition in intellectual and artistic life. As a student in the Lodz school he cowrote the script for Wajda's *Innocent Sorcerers* before writing *Knife in the Water*. He was thought something of a wonderboy. For his diploma work, he assembled many fragments he had shot over the years (all along having in mind that they would fit a unified project) into a feature film that he wrote, acted in, and directed. It was called *Identification Marks, None (Rysopis)* [1964]. In it Skolimowski plays the part of a modern young man looking for his niche in society. The narrative is weak but the character very clear. That, plus touching simplicity and charming original visual style made it evident that a promising new talent was at hand.

On the strength of this, Skolimowski was given an immediate opportunity to make a full-scale feature, *Walkover* [1965], a movie about boxing. In a way it was an extension of the theme of *Identification Marks, None*. A young man faces some critical choices when he embarks on a career as a boxer. *Walkover* has the same charming directness, the same stylistic freshness, and the same keen sense of observation that characterizes *Identification Marks, None*.

A year later he made the startling film *The Barrier (Bariera)* [1966], full of unusual visual language, symbolic and brief like the lines of a modern poem, possessing all the intensity of modern graphics. The symbols express the major themes of the film but in themselves are quite precise and specific. They are introduced in a realistic context, a simple situation, but as things unfold, the new and larger meaning emerges. When a bloodmobile calls upon students to give blood, it is a simple situation; but as it develops we key into the larger thematic play, namely, are the students willing to "give blood" for their country and people as their fathers were, or are they too selfish and egoistic? To give another example of Skolimowski's emblematic technique, it is worth noting that the film is set at Easter, which in Poland is an eating holiday, a feasting time. At such a time it would not seem odd to see ducks hanging here and there waiting to be prepared and consumed, but another meaning deftly emerges from this triviality. The duck is a bird with no ambitions, it prefers to gain weight rather than fly. It is a bourgeois bird!

With such expressions of symbolic language, the story of a young graduate who has no taste for working up the ladder of success in the usual way unfolds. He looks for shortcuts and would gladly marry a rich girl to get a nice house and car. In an odd and unexpected way he meets a girl streetcar driver whom he tries to intrigue and seduce in a complicated game. He loses the game (or wins it?) because he gives up his tawdry ambitions for this simple girl. It was a Skolimowski theme, this challenge to the cynical conformity of ambition on behalf of fundamental personal honesty.

This theme had already shown itself in his script for *Knife in the Water* and appeared again in *Hands Up!* (*Ręce do góry!*) [1968], the last film he made in Poland. It was not as provocative in an esthetic way as *Barrier*, but it was still far from conventional and was based on an unusual premise. It deals with mature, fat, lazy conformists, who were once spirited young members of student organizations in the fifties. They meet after a number of years at a party where a dance takes place, a strange stylized dance in which one of the movements is the raising of hands, as if in the classical gesture of surrender. We observe in a series of extravagant situations the anatomy of Philistinism, conformism, the devaluation of once proud ideals. It is to these surrenders that the phrase "Hands up!" is addressed. The film is laced with ironies. For one, the idealistic past is linked with Stalinism; for another, their enthusiasm was always accompanied by fear. There is a telling episode which the people recollect during this reunion. There was, years before the meeting, a state celebration for which these people, then young, prepared a huge portrait of Stalin. It was to be assembled from parts of the portrait cut into horizontal strips, much as billboard pictures are pasted up from vertical strips. Absent-mindedly a boy repeats one of the parts. When the portrait is raised there is a tremor in the crowd. Stalin has four eyes! He sees everything!

Although at the time of the filming Stalin had been dead for fifteen years and had even been condemned by the Soviets in 1956, a thick political atmosphere still surrounded the image of the man, and this scene caused *Hands Up!* to be kept off the screen because Skolimowski resolutely refused to cut that part of the movie. The film was scheduled to be shown without major change in 1982, but the events of December 1981, interfered. Finally in 1985, seventeen years after the film was made, it was shown unedited and recognized as an uncommon film, startling in its originality, content, images, editing, and music.

Skolimowski's anti-philistine message had its sincere doubters. An attack upon the get-rich-quick mentality and materialism in favor of ideals seems appropriate in an affluent society. In the Polish context, it was somewhat questionable. In the sixties in Poland there was a shortage of consumer goods, with little chance for many to develop a penchant for excessive consumerism. Except perhaps for a handful of the politically favored, the material ambitions of most people were very modest: a small refrigerator, an old used car, a brief holiday. To be sure, greed and materialism can thrive in circumstances of poverty and often do, but an attack on the relatively modest desires of ordinary people can be construed as less than authentic criticism. That aside, it is clear that Skolimowski was a unique artist, full of invention and surprising ideas, whose persistence in elaborating those ideas must be admired.

After *Hands Up!* Skolimowski worked in West Europe mainly, although he maintained residence in Poland. He had worked in the West before. In Belgium he made a film called *Le Départ* (*The Start*) [1967], which won him a prize at the West Berlin Festival. Later, in England, he directed *The Adventures of Gerard* [1969] and *Deep End* [1970]. In Germany he made *King, Queen, Knave* [1972], based on a novel by Nabokov. Again in England he made *The Shout* [1975]. In 1982, still in England, he returned to a Polish subject in *Moonlighting* which had some success at the Cannes Film Festival that year.

Moonlighting is about a crew of Polish guest workers, in the fall of 1981, a home renovation crew who come to England to completely rebuild a house on the inside. They speak no English at all, except for their boss, played by Jeremy Irons. While working on their project—living, eating, sleeping, and working in the gutted house—martial law comes to Poland, but the men do not know it, nor are they told by the boss, who feels that they will abandon the job if they learn of the crisis. The workers are nonentities. No relationship and little interaction has been worked out between them and the boss. This makes the film somewhat weak insofar as dramatic quality is concerned. The project was a reaction on Skolimowski's part to the psychological heaviness of martial law, which had its effects on Poles outside of Poland as well as inside. Dramatically, it remains more of a sketch than a film. Many western viewers added another dimension to the film and saw it as an allegory with the boss representing the Polish government and the absentee landlord suggesting the Soviet Union. Beyond these suggestive points the notion that it is an allegory doesn't hold up very well.

Majewski

Janusz Majewski was a contemporary of both Polański and Skolimowski. A graduate of the School of Architecture, he worked as a production art director before he entered the film school at Lodz in 1960. After his graduation from Lodz he worked in documentary filmmaking and as a TV film director. For a TV series entitled "Fantastic and Amazing Stories" Majewski demonstrated a gift for creating uncanny effects together with a deep sense of visual taste. *The Lodger* (*Sublokator*) [1969] was his first screen feature, although his experience was already deep and wide. In *The Lodger* he manifested a remarkable sense of the absurd and a talent for subtle black humor. The tenant in the film struggles with several women of different ages in a fresh situational comedy devoid of stereotypes, vulgarity, and stock devices. Majewski then made a most intricate crime movie, *The Criminal Who Stole a Crime* (*Zbrodniarz który ukradł zbrodnię*) [1969]. At the end of the decade he directed the fantasy, *Lokis* [1970], a film based on a short story by

Prosper Merimee. Through the seventies, Majewski remained interested in complicated, sometimes stylized, psychological films, unfailingly brought off with good taste and exceptional craftsmanship.

Kluba

The last of the notable young directors who emerged in the mid-sixties was Henryk Kluba (b. 1931), whose path to film work, as with so many of the other directors mentioned, was indirect. After graduating from acting school, Kluba went to work as a journalist, then ended up at Lodz, graduating in 1957, a bit earlier than the others. For some years he played minor roles as an actor. (He was one of the two men carrying the wardrobe around in Polański's classic short film.)

Kluba's first independent feature film was *Skinny and Others* (*Chudy i inni*) [1967]. It brought him notice. The story is about a group of construction workers at the site of a dam, differing personalities from different places, mostly small towns and villages. They enter into relationships with each other as they face their common task, a situation that is uncomfortably reminiscent of some of the formulas of socialist realism. Kluba, however, broke through any shadow of a stereotype, making his characters genuinely individualized, with psychological traits that are not at all trivial or shallow, evincing all the while the director's genial sense of humor.

His next film, *The Sun Rises Once a Day* (*Słońce wschodzi raz na dzień*) [1967], was more ambitious. It is a story of peasants in the Podhale region in the mountains of southern Poland who are taken by surprise by the political changes of 1945. The mountaineers' expectations of independence and socialism were strikingly different from the reality they faced. Their attitude is portrayed as somewhat anarchical (which in reality is not far from the truth, knowing the people from that area) and they were dissatisfied with restrictions being placed upon them. The film, told in the form of a folk ballad, gets its texture by rich representation of the folkways and art and the somewhat wild traditions of the people of the Carpathians. The supporting music, composed by Zygmunt Konieczny, is vivid and powerful. The movie is rich but not excessive, humorous and pathetic, stylistically one of the most original films of the period. The film, however, ran into the bad luck of 1968, another political crisis, so because of its anarchical tone it was not allowed on the screens until 1970.

IV

Crisis and Autonomy

The year 1968 was marked by student demonstrations throughout the United States and Europe, and Poland was no exception. In Warsaw it started in a simple way. The authorities suspended a theater run of a Polish classic, *Forefathers' Eve (Dziady)* by Adam Mickiewicz (1798–1855). The allegation was that some lines and some of the play's intentions might incite enmity against Russians, albeit the work was 136 years old. In truth, there were audience manifestations of feeling during the play corroborating that the enmity was already present. Student response to the closing of the play was hostile, provoking demonstrations that spread to other campuses and inspired anger in intellectuals all over Poland. Poland is precisely the kind of country that can be led into crisis by a piece of classical literature, but we must realize that there was much more in the background. The economic situation was strained; there were strong factional disputes within the party; and of course there was the tense political situation in neighboring Czechoslovakia, brought on because of liberalization within the Czech Communist party, a phenomenon called the Czech Spring, crushed by a Soviet invasion in August of that year.

Besides condemning rebellious students, the authorities resorted to an ugly ploy: they blamed "Zionist elements" for inspiring the provocations and events. The Israeli campaign of 1967 and the official Polish reaction to it made this tactic convenient and timely. Elements within the party found it opportune to call for a purge to clear the party of an ineffectual older generation of Communists, many of whom were of Jewish origin. Clearly, a measure of plain anti-Semitism was involved that took on a virulence of its own, some say in spite of Gomułka's efforts to contain the excesses. In any case, the result was that many people of Jewish origin were cashiered and relieved of positions in government, at universities, at scientific and cultural centers, in the press and the other media, and of course within the ranks of filmmakers.

In the film industry, the purge was not openly anti-Semitic. Rather it was directed against "commercialism." The accusations meant that the industry had abandoned socialist ideology. They were directed most sharply toward production managers in the film units, who, it was alleged, had usurped control. The unit system was changed, the existing units dissolved and replaced by reorganized units. They were no longer autonomous entities responsible for the whole process from idea to finished movie. Instead they became something like clearinghouses for scripts which were forwarded to the administration, after which the units had little control over what happened. Most of the new unit directors were not even members of the film community. The basic idea of self-management was abrogated. Another chapter in the history of the Polish cinema was about to begin. The transition was graceless to say the least.

Emigration

As the "anti-Zionist" campaign continued from 1968 into 1969, a number of filmmakers of Jewish origin, both from the older as well as the younger generations, emigrated. One of those was Aleksander Ford, the founding father of postwar cinema, maker of outstanding films, and a Communist. He moved first to Germany, then Switzerland, and finally to the United States where he died, a probable suicide. Among those who departed with him were Władyslaw Forbert, cinematographer in many important films and another camera specialist, Jerzy Lippman, who worked on Wajda's *Canal*. Two young and talented documentarists, Marian Marzynski and Tadeusz Jaworski soon left, as did Helena Lemańska, animator and producer of a very popular and rather good newsreel. Especially hard hit were the ranks of the production managers. Among those who left were Józef Krakowski, Ludwik Hager, Zygmunt Szyndler, and Roman Hajnberg (Harte).

Films, in Spite of Everything

It was an agonizing period for the film community, among whom only a very few participated in the attacks. Clearly, the independence of the film units and of the entire industry was in jeopardy, but after a short while the ugly campaign abated. The core of the industry survived, albeit with scars. While the new units were not very effective, their operation was not paralyzed. The *auteurs* continued to make films. Kawalerowicz made his subtle, psychological *The Game (Gra)* [1969], not altogether a successful venture. Andrzej Wajda spent the difficult months of 1968 doing his only autobiographical film, *Everything for Sale (Wszystko na sprzedaż)* [1969], and then *Landscape after Battle (Krajobraz po bitwie)* [1969], which, like his *Ashes* and *Ashes and Diamonds*, aroused interest and discussion transcending the frame of reference of the movie.

A young, surprising, and interesting talent emerged in Witold Leszczyński (b. 1933), debuting with *The Life of Matthew (Żywot Mateusza)* [1968]. An acoustical engineer by training, he became interested in technological innovations. This led him to the Department of Camera Operation at the Lodz school and then to a second graduation this time from the directing department. He made some documentaries in Norway, and this connection brought him his first script idea, which came from the writing of Tarjei Vessas, a Norwegian novelist. It was a rarity in that it involved no Polish themes nor did it touch any of the sensitive social points. It was simply a beautiful, poetic film about an over-sensitive eccentric who lived outside society, a mix of madman, saint, and primitive, who related mystically to nature. The story was set in the nostalgically beautiful landscape of the Mazurian lake district. Simplicity, freshness, and a remarkable feeling for the regenerative strength of nature won Leszczyński note in Poland and abroad. His film won prizes at Chicago, Valladolid, and Cannes. Unfortunately, he would not make another noteworthy film for some years.

Another Crisis

The events which took place in the port cities of Gdansk and Szczecin in December 1970, would make history and have a permanent effect on the evolution of events in Poland. It all started simply. The workers protested against rising prices, particularly meat prices. Following strikes and demonstrations the authorities decided on a hard-line course of action. In the face of military force, there were riots, which led to the burning of some government buildings. This in turn led to a military assault by security forces against a crowd of workers, which resulted in a number of wounded and dead. The shock affected not only the populace of the two cities but the nation as a whole, not excluding the highest councils of the Party. Gomułka and his team were ousted and replaced by Edward Gierek, party chief of Silesia, former miner. The Gomułka years, calm except for 1968, came to an end.

The new team took over in an atmosphere of economic expectation. Gierek was given great credit for promoting the welfare of Silesia, governmentally and economically. The period of Gomułka's secretaryship was looked upon as a time of lag, of recession, a time when Poland was outperformed by most European countries. The leaders were prepared to take new measures and change emphases. Importance was given to consumer standards and the quality of everyday life. "For a better life" was a slogan of the early 1970s. After five or six years it would begin to be evident that the new policy of consumerism coupled with heavy investment made possible by foreign capital would fail, largely because the investments were mismanaged. Economic failure led eventually to the Solidarity crisis of 1980, which in many ways was a replay of 1970, magnified.

But in the meantime, people did lead better lives for a while after 1970. Cars, television sets, other major consumer items became available, almost commonplace. Even the weekend retreats so beloved of Eastern Europeans, the summer cottages, the dachas, were no longer rarities. Gigantic projects under way in the metallurgical, chemical, and mining industries were supposed to promote economic abundance in the coming years. Official propaganda was very optimistic; success was at hand and inevitable. It seemed that all the reasons for frustration and failure had been overcome. Misfortune, almost a tradition to the Poles, had seemingly departed. Poles wanted to believe in their own success story. Posters with the slogan "A Pole can do it!" were ubiquitous. This was the principal theme for the mass media: success at last!

This more or less official optimism was not obligatory in literature, theater, and cinema, where the tone was quite different from the newspapers and television. In cultural matters the state's policies were quite pragmatic; it did not have the same hold on intellectuals as on media servants. There was compromise. The effect of this compromise was to open doors previously closed to writers, filmmakers, and dramatists. It seemed that for the moment, the authorities were feeling that more was to be gained by avoiding direct confrontation.

Such was the situation in early 1971 when filmmakers initiated attempts to recreate the film unit system, supplanted in 1968. The government proved amenable. On January 1, 1972, the imposed structures were dissolved and the former system of film units reintroduced with broader freedom and more extensive production prerogatives. The new units now had the theoretical right of approving screenplays and of making production decisions. The Committee for Screenplay Evaluation, a body that had often exercised its right to reject and change film projects, was dissolved. The government maintained only the right to veto scripts, a right that it used sparingly in the seventies.

Changes in personnel were significant. Managers from the older generation like Jakubowska, Bossak, and Wohl, stepped aside. The next generation stepped into the system, which called for an artistic director and a literary director for each unit. They were as follows, with the name of the unit given, then the artistic director, then the literary director: "Kadr," Jerzy Kawalerowicz and Ryszard Kosiński; "Iluzjon," Czeslaw Petelski and Lech Bach; "Profil," Bohdan Poręba and Wacław Biliński; "Pryzmat," Aleksander Ścibor-Rylski and Tadeusz Konwicki; "Silesia," Kazimierz Kutz and Ryszard Klys; "Tor," Stanisław Różewicz and Witold Zalewski; "X," Andrzej Wajda and Bolesław Michałek. Top management was composed of—miracle of miracles in any country or field—people of genuine professional accomplishment, who enjoyed the confidence of the cinema community. This was indeed why the seventies became such a thoroughly successful time for Polish film, why just at this time there began the extraordinary series of films, wave after wave of accomplished pieces in a succession not yet broken and only somewhat interrupted by the martial law events of 1981 and 1982. Some changes occurred. Ścibor-Rylski and Konwicki were dismissed and their unit dissolved under questionable political circumstances. Other, more ordinary, changes also occurred. Janusz Morgenstern was made head of a newly cre- ated unit; Kutz was replaced by Ernest Bryll; and Stanisław Różewicz was replaced by the brilliant young Krzysztof Zanussi. For the most part, rela- tively normal working conditions—one can even say favorable conditions— existed for the decade of the seventies, an examination of which breaks into two coherent parts. The first half of that decade is discussed in this chapter; the second half of the period, the time of the "cinema of moral concern," is treated in the following chapter.

What did this decade accomplish? For one thing it built well on what had come before. For instance, the literary adaptations that had attracted viewers continued to attract makers. *The Deluge (Potop)* [1974], the second part of a great literary trilogy by Sienkiewicz, was made by Jerzy Hoffman, who in the sixties had made *Pan Michael*. Daniel Olbrychski, in the meantime, had be- come a kind of Polish superstar helping make this production an incredible box-office success with an audience of twenty-five million.

A different, off-beat presentation based on readings from literature was Walerian Borowczyk's *Story of Sin (Dzieje Grzechu)* [1975], from a 1908 novel by Stefan Żeromski, a story quite different from his epic, *Ashes*. Żeromski, a patriot and social activist, expressed the aspirations and frustra- tions of turn-of-the-century society in most of his novels . But *Story of Sin* was different, a sensational and melodramatic tale of a kind-hearted young girl who slides into crime and the gutter. A careful reading of this neglected book reveals that behind the sentimental facade the tale is redolent with so- phisticated eroticism. Borowczyk was a director capable of adapting this kind of new reading. He began his career as a painter and graphic artist, made modernist short films, and moved to Paris where he made *Goto, L'isle d'amour* [1969], *Blanche* [1972], *Contes immoraux* [1974], and *La Bete* [1975]. These were sophisticated films of modernist visual composition and boldly erotic, films to be disassociated from some of his later work which was simple soft-porn. In 1975 he returned to Poland to make *Story of Sin*. In the novel there are sentimental and didactic elements that Borowczyk succeeds in dissolving in his marvelously constructed and visually beautiful, erotic drama. It is worth noting for itself and its literary roots, although it is quite atypical and difficult to categorize among these other films.

More typical was Jerzy Antczak's *Nights and Days (Noce i dnie)* [1975], his most ambitious work and a project that took him years to complete. Antczak (b. 1929) was originally an actor as well as a theater and television director. He served for years as chief director for television theater in Warsaw. In 1971 he made the extraordinary, grim, fictionalized documentary, *The Nuremberg Epilogue (Epilog norymberski)*, a reenactment of the trial that was tense, dramatic, and concise. *Nights and Days* was based on Maria Dąbrowska's (1889–1965) popular novel in four parts (1928–1934) about life at the beginning of the twentieth century. It is a colorful family saga, with rich atmosphere, well-drawn characters, and a sentimental look at the impoverished nobility, the genesis of the intelligentsia. The movie is charming and decorous. During the course of this work, Antczak filmed a fifteen hour version for serial viewing on television, reshot it as a film for the big screen, eight hours long, then compressed that version for more generalized viewing. It was a popular success, in some part due to the inspired performance of Jadwiga Barańska as the main character. In most ways, the film is conventional, but it is craftsmanlike, ambitious, and beautiful.

Has's Experiment

Quite different, quite unconventional, but perhaps one of the more interesting films to emerge from this literary trend was Wojciech Has's *Hospital under the Hourglass* (Sanatorium pod Klepsydrą) [1974], a single story from two short stories by Bruno Schultz (1892–1942). Schultz's prose leaves us a dreamlike, poetic picture of the hermetic world of a Jewish community in southern Poland. It is on the edge of reality where fears, anxieties, and obsessions thrive. Schultz was known only among a few avant-garde intellectuals before the war. He lived in a small town, which may have contributed to this anonymity. His life ended with a bullet from a Gestapo trooper who shot him in the street. After the war Schultz's strange prose was rediscovered, and a number of directors thought about adapting it to the screen. That was a heavy challenge. How was one to make a picture out of fog and shadow? What dramatic shape could be given to imagination flowing freely in words? Wojciech Has succeeded in something that seemed impossible. He created a film that was at once dreamlike and real, lyrical and dramatic, surrealistic and disciplined, a sort of visual poem evoking the life and dreams of an extinguished Jewish tradition in Poland. The film was not for a general audience, so it was not energetically distributed, yet it is an exquisite work of art full of surreal charm bringing back in its way the lost eastern European world of the Jews.

Wajda

Wajda, by now Poland's preeminent director, made four literary films in the early seventies. First he made a nostalgic scenic film from an existentialist short story by Jarosław Iwaszkiewicz, *Birchwood* (*Brzezina*) [1970]. Then he made a film which must be called unique in every sense of the word by adapting a magical, symbolic play by Stanisław Wyspiański, *The Wedding* (*Wesele*) [1972]. He attempted, not successfully, an adaptation of Joseph Conrad's *The Shadow Line* (*Smuga cienia*) [1974], and he directed a monumental historical and social fresco, *Land of Promise* (*Ziemia Obiecana*) [1975], based on a novel by Stanisław Władysław Reymont. This prolific period in the director's work and career is evaluated in detail in chapter 8.

Another *auteur*, Tadeusz Konwicki, made *How Far, How Near* (*Jak daleko stąd, jak blisko*) [1972]. Konwicki, an outstanding novelist, turned to cinema from time to time because of sudden need or whim to make films that were personal confessions about the times in which he lived and people whom he loved and hated. This piece was a strange, somewhat fantastic story of a man who is to die in ninety minutes, the screening time. It is an unrestrained stream of memories, associations, and anxieties, a dialogue full of bitterness and existential sadness, laced with sarcastic humor. Before making this movie, Konwicki had already written the novels, *A Dreambook for Our Time* (*Sennik współczesny*) [1963], *Ascension* (*Wniebowstąpienie*) [1957], and *Nothing or Nothing* (*Nic albo nic*) [1971], which had fully established him as a major writer noted for his expression of reality as at once dreamlike and real and for his range of talent. Later, in *The Polish Complex* (*Kompleks polski*) [1977], and in *Minor Apocalypse* (*Mała apokalipsa*) [1977], the element of the grotesque in his work would shape itself as truly apocalyptic.

Two other notable *auteurs* contributed to this literary mode of filmmaking. Janusz Majewski made *Lokis* [1970], already cited, as well as *Envy and Medicine* (*Zazdrość i medycyna*) [1973], from a psychological story by Michał Choromański, and *Hotel Pacific* (*Zaklęte rewiry*) [1975], based on a 1930s novel by Henryk Worcel (b. 1909). These films proved Majewski's literary and psychological mastery of the medium and demonstrated his interest in subtle, psychological paradoxes. In a sense he can be characterized as the most "European" of the literary filmic *auteurs*. All of these movies were skillful in narration, well acted, and directed with great care for detail. The only lack was in creating dramatic intensity, strongly visualized characterizations, the qualities that marked the films of Wajda, Has, and Konwicki. This fault was also characteristic of films by Stanisław Różewicz during these years, all based on very valuable literary material: *The Romantics* (*Romantyczni*) [1970], *The Glass Ball* (*Szklana kula*) [1972], and *Passion* (*Pasja*) [1978]. These were intellectually substantial, even well-made, but they lacked dramatic strength.

Directly or indirectly, in one way or another, literary cinema dominated the first half of the decade of the seventies. It was said that these films reflected artifacts rather than the life of the country with its problems, dangers, and emotions. The subject gave rise to some controversy. The charge was that movies used literature as the man in the circus uses stilts. Cinema on its own was, because of this dependency, smaller, less significant, ordinary. The allegation was not without merit, for this period at least, but on the whole the re-

sult of literary influence was positive. Neither Wajda, Has, Konwicki, nor the others ever practiced literal adaptation. Mature literature offered them a dynamic impulse, an esthetic genesis. They were launched on a search for new visual language and rhythm, for elaborate compositions and structures capable of expressing ambiguous and rich themes cinematically. Thus the dependence of filmmakers upon literature during the early seventies contributed considerably to the development of the language of film.

It should be noticed that these filmmakers were attracted by mature, serious, complex literature which offered dignity and a range of topics and thereby a range of human experience not common in movies. It brought out deeper reflections with regard to a number of themes: man in relation to death (Wajda, Has, Konwicki), the individual in relation to history (Wajda, Różewicz), and psychological and moral tensions (almost all the directors). The literary influence resulted in a dignified and intelligent cinema, charming and/or reflective, and not simply imitative. It is true that literary influence in some cases reduced vitality by treating subjects less given to topical polemics. It focused more on inner experience than on social experience. Films made in the first half of the seventies, therefore, were less reflective of social crisis than some previous series.

Not each and every *auteur* participated in the cinema of literature. Kazimierz Kutz and Bohdan Poręba were notable exceptions. Kutz, whose first two films gave promise of an extraordinary career, made relatively insignificant films toward the end of the sixties, but in 1970 he directed *Salt of the Black Earth* (*Sól Ziemi Czarnej*), and in 1972 *Pearl in the Crown* (*Perła w Koronie*), composing a Silesian working-class saga. Kutz, son of a Silesian miner, found in these films his great theme after some less successful projects. Upper Silesia was his home, a land of mines, heavy industry, and working-class people. In its gloomy landscape, coal-dusty and grime streaked, Kutz found bleak charm, and in the Silesians, a hard-working, tough, and awkward people, he found human sympathy, intelligence, and a special sense of humor. *Salt of the Black Earth* recounts the industrial strikes of the 1930s, while *Pearl in the Crown* takes for its subject the uprising in Silesia which occurred during the confusion of the first years after World War I, when the people of the region declared war upon the Germans and forced the incorporation of Upper Silesia into the newly created Polish state.

Hubal and Echoes of the Polish School

Bohdan Poręba is best known for *Hubal* [1973], a controversial film that seemed to be a delayed commentary on the Polish School of the late fifties. It was based on the true story of a Polish commander of cavalry who took the name Hubal. When the campaign of 1939 was ended, Hubal declined to surrender and, instead, went into hiding in the forests of central Poland, where he led his men in a desperate private war against the Germans. The film was extremely popular, which is not surprising given its romantic content, the desperate charges, the bold cavalry with swords, and the stubborn patriotism. Hubal had something of the spirit of the Polish School without the latter's sense of failure. It provoked criticism esthetically, largely because the director employed all the hackneyed clichés of patriotism indiscriminately.

Comedy was never a strong suit in the Polish cinema. Quite the contrary, film was dominated by serious moods, solemn subjects, and sometimes gloom. All the more, then, each attempt at comedy met with a welcome reception from the public. Sylvester Chęciński (b. 1930) made *Among Ourselves (Sami Swoi)* [1967], *None Who Are Strong (Nie ma mocnych)* [1974], and *Love It or Leave It (Kochaj albo rzuć)* [1977], all of which were from screenplays by Andrzej Mularczyk and all of which were related to one another in their contents: clear, likeable characters from two peasant families constantly feuding within the warm atmosphere of a rural community somewhere in western Poland. Tadeusz Chmielewski made another successful comedy called *I Hate Mondays (Nie lubię poniedziałków)* [1971]. Jerzy Gruza, in cooperation with Krzysztof Toeplitz (b. 1933) made two: *The Woodpecker (Dzięcioł)* [1970], and *I Am a Butterfly (Motylem jestem)* [1976]. Stanisław Bareja (b. 1929) was a special kind of contributor in this genre. He is gifted with an exceptional inventiveness, but is a careless scriptwriter and without any great talent at directing. His productions therefore suffered, although they abounded in excellent ideas that combined satire with absurdity. Most notable of the several comedies he directed in the seventies was *What Will You Do with Me When You Catch Me? (Co mi zrobisz jak mnie złapiesz?)* [1975]. This was also his harshest satire, in which the country is presented as a mixture of absurdity, stupidity, and ill-will.

Young and Atypical: Piwowski, Żulawski, Królikiewicz

The early seventies likewise found some atypical and fresh talents making their mark, such as Piwowski, Żuławski, and Królikiewicz. Marek Piwowski is one of the most original people in the industry. In the the early sixties he was known for short films made with imagination and laced with absurdist ironies. In the late sixties he made a full-length comedy called *The Cruise (Rejs)*, released in 1970. The story of the making of that movie would make a funny book on its own merit. Piwowski packed a film crew, a few actors, and some friends (together with scriptwriter Janusz Głowacki) onto a pleasure boat on the Vistula River. He proceeded to shoot a film based on a very vague and thin story line, seemingly directing incidents among the voyagers rather than building any coherent narrative. Presumably something was supposed to happen on the ship that would constitute a movie. What emerged was a hybrid production without much coherence, but one that was remarkably funny, fresh, shrewd, and intelligent. Piwowski went under the surface of his characters to expose falseness, posturing, stupidity, and conventionality. Not even the captain and first mate were exempt. It was more a big joke than a coherent film, and it received official disapproval. Questions were raised. What is that Ship of Fools supposed to signify? Does it symbolize the country? Who does the captain resemble? It was because of such quasi-paranoid suspicions that the film was not released until 1970, and then only in a very limited way, with few prints made available. The film was received enthusiastically, especially by the younger movie-goers; indeed it had a much larger audience than many other films that were more widely distributed. Piwowski continued to make short films, including the caustic *Hair*, about a competition of hair stylists from socialist countries. In 1975 he directed his second full-length feature, *Foul Play* (more accurately, *Pardon Me, Do They Beat You Up Around Here?—Przepraszam, czy tu biją?*), which is perhaps less imaginative and extravagant than *The Cruise* but more substantial on a number of levels. It is a detective genre game of wits between the police and a gang, as well as an examination of the limits of unethical conduct and deliberate provocation that police may use. It is also robustly entertaining. There are exaggerated criminal characters, con games, ingenious knavery, and a fast-paced heist caper. Piwowski's flamboyant approach was bound to ruffle some feathers among authorities. Cautionary signals were raised with respect to his future projects. He proposed many, but they never seemed to get to production.

Andrzej Żuławski (b. 1940) is another unusual young director who made his talent known in the early seventies. Żuławski had been an assistant to Wajda with whom he worked from *Samson* and *Love at Twenty* through the making of *Ashes*. He was also a writer of screenplays and novels, and in the sixties made several television pieces, which he directed faultlessly. His first full-length feature was *Devil* (*Diabeł*) [1970], from his own script. It was an unusual, indeed radical, period film, the action taking place in eighteenth-century Poland just as the Polish state seemed to be dissolving, a baroque panorama embellished with depictions of extraordinary violence: rapes, executions, castrations, suffering, and pain. People are nothing more than the subjects of sadistic manipulation, while relationships are reduced to the most basic reflexes. From these scenes emerges a horrifying and appalling depiction of a society in disintegration, an intense visual expression that is more like a transformed scream than a narrative. It was obvious that Żuławski possessed a special, powerful talent. Unfortunately the Ministry of Culture did not permit distribution, a ban that has never been lifted. For the authorities, *Devil* was a work that went too far beyond any acceptable moral standards and would, if anything, enrage the public. Żuławski, however, maintains that the decision to shelve the film was political rather than moral.

In 1972 he made his second feature, *The Third Part of the Night* (*Trzecia część nocy*) under the auspices of Wajda's newly formed film unit, "X." It was based on a short story written by his own father, an excellent writer, which described an episode from the occupation in which people had fleas bred upon their bodies in order to manufacture typhus vaccine. It is a hallucinatory film with reality and nightmare interwoven. Human values are shattered; barbarism is triumphant. The film earned critical acclaim. Żuławski moved to Paris where two years later he made his next film, *L'Important c'est d'aimer* [1974]. In 1976, back in Poland, he began a project he had had in mind for years, an adaptation of a philosophical science fiction novel written by his ancestor Juliusz Żuławski, *Na srebrnym globie* (*On the Silver Globe*).

Given his strong new international reputation, he was accorded abundant resources—a huge crew, expensive sets, crowds of extras. The production was a complicated one and went beyond deadline. In the meantime, a new minister, Janusz Wilhelmi, had taken over the operation of the film industry bringing with him a great antagonism toward artists. Żuławski was the first target of his animosity. Citing delay and overexpenditure, he gave orders to halt production and to haul down the sets. The existing footage was to be sent to the archives. Next he dissolved the unit, headed by Ścibor-Rylski, in which the film was being made. This whole affair became an issue and was the subject of petitions, protests, and pronouncements. The issue dragged on for months, never reaching a conclusion. A great deal of unedited material remained, unusual, beautiful, and imaginative, but given the frustrations, Żuławski returned to Paris permanently. One unreleased film and one aborted film out of the three he made in Poland seemed too much to take. Finally, in 1986, a decision was made to resume work on *On the Silver Globe* and Żuławski returned to complete it.

Another unusual personality was Grzegorz Królikiewicz (b. 1939). His first film *Clear Through* (*Na wylot*) [1973], was a surprise and created quite a stir. It purported to be the tale of an ordinary murder that had been chronicled in the thirties, but it had few characteristics of a regular crime film. Obsessively and relentlessly the movie gnawed at the psyche of the wife of the murderer as well as the murderer himself and at their lower-middle-class social background, all this by way of looking for a motive, which may have been in their mediocrity, their pettiness, their neuroses slowly turning into madness. The visual work was expressive, violent, provocative. Every take was an assault on the audience. In fact, scandalized spectators left performances during the showing, but Królikiewicz claimed this was what he was trying to do, lay bare the mediocrity in each of us to the point of being offensive. In his second film, *Eternal Resentments* (*Wieczne Pretensje*) [1975], he went even further in his experiment in style and extravagance. This time the content and the message of the movie remained unintelligible even to his enthusiasts.

In this same film unit ("Profil") was a young director, Krzysztof Wojciechowski (b. 1939), who was influenced by the French movement, *cinema verité*,and made some intriguing quasi-documentary features in the seventies. He used real people whom he entangled in some vague story, as in *Loving Each Other* (*Kochajmy się*) [1974], his first film in which he illustrated how an argument suddenly divides a rural community. His second, *Stress at the New Address* (*Róg Brzeskiej i Capri*) [1979], presented a Warsaw district and its wonderfully colorful criminal characters and mores.

Who among these rising directors would exert a decisive influence on the course of Polish film? It turned out to be none of these at all. The person who would have the most profound effect was a man who was educated in physics and philosophy, who became an amateur director, then later graduated from the directing section of the Lodz school—Krzysztof Zanussi. A separate chapter is committed to Zanussi, but it must be mentioned here that it was he who started a new style and introduced the most effective new themes into cinema. After his fascinating debut with *Structure of Crystal* (*Struktura kryształu*)[1969], followed by *Family Life* (*Życie rodzinne*) [1971], and *Illumination* (*Illuminacja*) [1973], and several television films, he made *Camouflage* (*Barwy Ochronne*) [1976], which like Wajda's *Man of Marble* (made the same year) was an exceedingly important event.

That year, 1976, marked a breakthrough in the industry. Young filmmakers were pressing the studios. *Man of Marble* and *Camouflage* led them to new, more daring approaches to social and moral issues. In the background was the presentiment of an economic, social, and political crisis, one which indeed occurred in 1980. These artists, together with their older colleagues, created the extraordinary period during which Polish cinema matured into a new and vibrant personality.

V

The Cinema of Moral Concern

In the winter of 1975–1976, after fourteen years of repeated attempts to procure approval for the project, Wajda was finally allowed to proceed with plans for the production of *Man of Marble*, to be made the following summer. At the same time, Zanussi was at work on the final version of what had at first seemed to be a modest film about a summer camp for students, namely, *Camouflage*. In the studios optimism prevailed, and young people were invading the offices of film units with new projects. Signs pointed to a revival. Many young directors were awaiting their debuts, and the situation was not dissimilar to that twenty years earlier when the Polish School came into being. Just like the fifties, most of these young directors were graduates of the Lodz school. They gathered around two units: Tor, whose director was Stanisław Różewicz (eventually succeeded by Zanussi), and "X," Wajda's unit.

Tor

In Tor, Andrzej Krauze (b. 1940) produced *The Finger of God* (*Palec Boży*) [1973], an agonizing and dramatic film about a young nonconformist. The picture was violent and desperate, like the cry of a rejected man withdrawing from the world into madness. The main theme was the widening abyss dividing the nonconforming individual from a society ruled by routine. Likewise in Tor, Edward Żebrowski (b. 1935) produced his first work, *The Rescue* (*Ocalenie*) [1972], a film suggestive of Zanussi's thematic and moral approach. It is a psychological study of a shrewd intellectual, terminally ill, who wants to evaluate his own life against others and to assess his chances and conditions of survival—an intelligent, tough piece of cinema, unadorned by any embellishment. After this project, Żebrowski did not direct again until 1978, in the interval dedicating himself to screenwriting.

Another strong, young personality in Tor was Krzysztof Kieślowski (b. 1941) who had done some documentaries and had produced for Tor two famous TV movies, *Underground Passage* (*Przejście podziemne*) [1973] and *Personnel* [1974]. The latter gave evidence of Kieślowski's approach and his biting sense of observation as he dissected theater life off-stage—the social connections behind the scene, the forming of cliques and elites, the leadership. This subject was to recur for Kieślowski. In his first full-length feature, *The Scar* (*Blizna*) [1975], Kieślowski demonstrated again his gift for incisive revelation and illustrated the kinds of changes beginning to occur in the consciousness of the film industry. It is a story about the director of a large, new factory (many were being built in the seventies) who was well-meaning and honest in contrast to a mendacious local official. As the story unfolds, the good man turns out to be weak, helpless, indeed worthless. He does not understand the moods of the people he is in charge of and renders himself ineffective. Although the story is placed in the late sixties, the film is more suggestive of the situation in Poland exactly contemporaneous with the making of the film in the mid-seventies.

Mention should be made of two young artists who, in the in the mid-seventies, were making television films for Tor. Wojciech Marczewski and Filip Bajon would make a more strident mark a few years later with significant feature works.

Unit "X"

In addition to working with its own members, Wajda's unit "X" made some attempts at coproduction with directors from other countries, but with little success. The Czech director Jiri Menzel failed to obtain his government's permission to work with Poland and the Hungarian director Miklos Jancso backed out of a planned film about a Polish-Hungarian hero, General Józef Bem. Finally, in the late seventies, Marta Meszaros from Hungary made a film for "X."

But whatever its success or lack thereof in stretching cooperation on the international scale, "X" was abundantly fortunate in the results of its investment in talented young directors. Among the most accomplished of them was Feliks Falk (b. 1941), author of several plays, who made his first feature film from his own screenplay in 1975, *In the Middle of the Summer* (*W środku lata*). It was a psychological study of a relationship between a woman and a man at a moment of growing but ambiguous menace. Menace had been a theme Falk used in his theater plays. There was something in the film of Zanussi's subtle psychological analysis that intellectualized the atmosphere suggesting imminent catastrophe. The piece was insufficiently appreciated and received little attention.

A number of directors got a chance to work at "X" by using the device of the medley production, that is, several short stories within one feature title. There were three such experiments. The first, *Portraits from Real Life* (*Obrazki z życia*), was based on journalist Jerzy Urban's ironic, critical column. It was a relative failure, lacking coherence of any sort, using material of uneven quality. The second medley, *To Be Continued* (*Ciąg dalszy nastąpi*) [1976], was made in co-production with the Lodz school, and included directors Zbigniew Kamiński (b. 1947), Paweł Kędzierski (b. 1946), and one

Radosław Piwowarski (b. 1948), whose work was eventually excluded from the film. This was an interesting work, particularly Kamiński's subtle, psychological story about a lonely woman, played exquisitely by a theater actress from Crakow, Teresa Budzisz-Krzyżanowska. Kamiński also managed to make his own full-length feature, *Madame Bovary, That's Me (Pani Bovary, to ja)* [1976]. Like his shorter piece, it was a study of a young married woman who seems to be happy and content, but who—like Flaubert's heroine—is bored with the monotony and mediocrity of everyday life and so seeks adventure. Another project carried out after several unsuccessful efforts was *Screen Tests (Zdjęcia próbne)* [1977], consisting of parts written and directed by Agnieszka Holland, Paweł Kędzierski, and Jerzy Domaradzki (b. 1943).

June 1976

Not without their effects upon developments in Tor, "X," and all the other film units were the events unfolding during 1976. As usual the trigger of events was a rise in meat prices: workers in Radom and at the Ursus factory in Warsaw reacted. Militance prevailed, especially in Radom, in the form of strikes, marches, and a siege of a party committee building. The authorities responded immediately to head off graver actions and withdrew the decision to raise prices. Simultaneously, actions were taken to suppress manifestations of dissent in Radom. There were arrests and jail sentences. Some workers were fired. Given the decision to rescind price increases, one might have thought the incident would pass. But the failure of the government to invent new economic policies, and the growing lack of confidence in the government on the part of the workers contributed to a brewing and simmering situation. This was exacerbated, not alleviated, by an official intensification of the "propaganda of success," as if the good news could obscure the reality and the looming crisis.

During 1976 and the beginning of 1977 it did not seem that the film industry would be much affected by events. In one related incident, a television film *Peace (Spokój)* [1976], by Kieślowski related a story that pictured contemporary occurrences. It was never broadcast. The energy for change and development in cinema came from two films just completed, both already mentioned several times, *Man of Marble* and *Camouflage*. Production and distribution details about these movies are discussed elsewhere in this book; the point here is to stress the impact that both of these films had on the industry. Wajda's *Man of Marble* had its effect by presenting a vivid, skillfully constructed, retrospective evaluation of the era of Stalinism, an era previously off-limits for serious portrayal (except for *Life Once Again*). Zanussi's *Camouflage* elaborated cynicism, degradation, conformity of the establishment versus the idealism of students, all behind a seemingly innocuous presentation of activities at an academic summer camp. Both films touched very sensitive spots in Polish life. Both set strong examples: cinema could and should take up these questions and must speak directly about those things that had been proscribed. Filip Bajon, then a young director and writer, put the new responsibility succinctly: "Cinema and not fiction has become the answer to the public's feelings, needs, and expectations. It may still not be perfect, but one can clearly see that direction it is taking and what it is trying to achieve. The public feeling of our time is best recorded by film and that is what gives film its significance" (*Kino*, no. 4, 1976). A new esthetic perception had been reached by this generation, and a certain tough-mindedness had come to the art.

Screen Tests

This was evident in the medley film by Holland, Kędzierski, and Domaradzki mentioned above, *Screen Tests*. The three wrote and directed, and what resulted was a simple, natural, and beautiful film. The first story, Kędzierski's, relates the story of an adolescent boy from an orphanage. In the second, Angieszka Holland depicts a young girl dreaming of a career. In the third part, the boy and girl meet during the making of some screen test shots, a meeting that becomes a parting with a ruthless twist. When the girl is chosen for a part, she turns away from the boy with whom she had just spent the night. Cynicism prevails. The movie expressed itself with basic authenticity and was both an artistic and popular success, especially among youth.

Top Dog

Indicative of both the changing esthetic tones and the breadth of expression being allowed and being practiced was Feliks Falk's *Top Dog* (more accurately, Master of Ceremonies, *Wodzirej*) [1977]. It was made in unit "X" in just a few weeks and turned out to be popular, tough, biting, and important. The hero is a young master of ceremonies who makes a living presiding over parties, shows, and fancy balls. The story begins when he learns about the most important upcoming ball, in his league a most prestigious event. He is obsessed with becoming the master of ceremonies for this grand ball, and for this he throws away personal loyalty, honesty, and truth and jeopardizes friendship. In a fervent but charming way he uses fraud, slander, blackmail, and every kind of deceit, all with a smile. He is surrounded by a panoply of mediocrity and sham in the form of show business hacks, local officials, and various authorities. It is not a subtle film and is not meant to be, in contrast to the same director's *End of the Summer*. Relationships are stark and the characters tend toward caricature. But it is perfectly constructed and the acting of Jerzy Stuhr is brilliant, losing nothing in the broad character he creates.

Top Dog portrays weak social structures, immoral arrangements that serve ambition, and cynical agreements. Yet the protagonist is not altogether a monster but also a creation of his environment in which he literally must lie, cheat, and betray if he wants to succeed. He must play a kind of daily politics to get along. It is impossible not to guess that the film indicts more than the small corner of show business controlled by masters of ceremony.

Certainly not all the young artists' efforts were or could be of the same caliber as Feliks Falk's *Top Dog*. Nonetheless, it was impossible to ignore the ferment, the activity, the search for challenges over the whole range of visual expression. The young people associated with unit "X," for example, came up with a project for a series of one-hour television films entitled *Family Situations (Sytuacje rodzinne)*. The title was liberally vague and the subjects universal enough to accommodate. The intention was to make a dozen or so films about conflicts and dramas in contemporary families. The project was approved, and in 1976 the films began to come out: *Sunday's Children (Niedzielne dzieci)* [1976], and *Something for Something (Coś za coś) [1977] by Agnieszka Holland; Rhythm of the Heart (Rytm serca)* [1977] by Zbigniew Kamiński; *Blindman's Buff (Ciuciubabka)* [1977], by Radosław Piwowarski; and others. This series was the start of a new trend, which was later to call itself the "cinema of moral concern."

It is, incidentally, clear from what precedes that production for television at this time in Poland was quite open to new ideas. For example, a new series was commissioned that was destined to be quite popular, called *Directors (Dyrektorzy)* [1975], a series directed by Zbigniew Chmielewski (b. 1926) that candidly and forthrightly portrayed a succession of factory managers, the pressures to which they were exposed, and the moral dilemmas they had to resolve. It was another paradox of this period of the mid-seventies, another bizarre turn and reversal in a strange mechanism, that television, which was engaged in the "propaganda of success," was at the same time a purveyor of realism in drama.

Within the ferment that affected the young television and cinema artists, there were also new brews for that older generation of directors who had labored so hard to bring visual and dramatic expression to this point. Jerzy Kawalerowicz, who had been more or less silent since 1969 when he made *The Game*, went to work on *Death of a President*, [1977], recreating the assassination of Poland's first president of the newly reconstituted Republic in 1922 by a fanatic nationalist. The film, which stressed the image of a liberal, democratic, and tolerant president in the face of dogmatic totalitarian challenges, was executed with the precision characteristic of Kawalerowicz. It made a deep impression, especially upon the young for whom the history of the period between two world wars was a blank. It is worth noting, parenthetically, that it marked the first appearance on screen of any representation of

Józef Piłsudski, Poland's twentieth-century founding father, patriot, chief-of-state, and finally dictator, a man whose name was, for many years, unmentionable and whose depiction was impossible.

Likewise, in 1977, Janusz Majewski, ever a master of psychological subtlety, made another period reconstruction with *The Gorgon Affair* (*Sprawa Gorgonowa*), a reenactment of a famous murder case from the 1930s. An attractive young woman was charged in the case, and although never proved guilty, she became an object of enmity for the petit-bourgeoise. There was another level to the film that dealt with an examination of the theme of justice, the pressures under which a court functions, and the concept of prevailing innocence without clear proof of guilt. These were topical issues for an audience in postwar Poland as well.

Joining those taking up the challenge of new issues and sensitive matters was the director Bohdan Poręba who consistently enjoyed the support and confidence of the authorities. In *Where the Water Is Clear and the Grass Green* (*Gdzie woda czysta i trawa zielona*) [1977], he addressed himself to the decay of the rules of social coexistence depicting strained relations in a provincial town. His perspective, however, was not new or reformist. A pristine party secretary puts things right and solves all problems with the help of the head office, and of course there is a happy, positive ending.

Tensions Mount

In the spring of 1977, both *Man of Marble* and *Camouflage* were shown with a sharp backlash. The vice-minister of culture responsible for production of films was dismissed, as were some members of his team. A campaign against these films and others was launched in press and speech. A new vice-minister of culture was appointed who took office with vindictive energy. Janusz Wilhelmi, a literary critic of substance and subtlety, brought to his task a reinforcing prejudice against cinema as an art form and the attitude of a ruthless politician, as mentioned above. He started his offensive by ordering a stop to the production of Andrzej Żuławski's *On the Silver Globe* (*Na srebrnyn globie*) on pretexts involving budget deadline and ordered that all sets be destroyed. In addition he ordered that Falk's *Top Dog* be sent "to the archives," a move that was tantamount to impoundment. More important, he threatened the entire film unit structure—which had been restored after previous tampering—either with depriving the units of any initiative and autonomy or perhaps even with dissolving them.

In the fall of 1977, at the annual film festival in Gdansk, this topic of crucial concern was addressed during the discussion forum of the Polish Filmmakers Association. Not surprising, the film community was united in its opposition to the actions of Wilhelmi and said so in an uncompromising report issued by the governing board of the association, a document written by

K.T. Toeplitz. Sharp, clear, individual positions were taken by directors Wajda, Petelski, and Kutz, as well as cameraman Krzysztof Winiewicz. The authorities proved intractable. They arranged that neither *Man of Marble* nor any other film by Wajda's unit "X" would receive any award. As a gesture meant to calm feelings and perhaps divide the membership of the association, the principal award was to be given to Krzysztof Zanussi for *Camouflage*, itself a controversial film. Presumably this largesse would ironically "camouflage" the intolerance of the ministry. Zanussi recognized the tactic and expressed himself by not showing up to receive the award.

The following months were dominated by political warfare between the Polish Filmmakers Association and the bureaucrats. The terms of service of some of the unit heads were coming up for renewal or for change. Rumor had it that some units, including Zanussi's Tor, Wajda's "X," and Kawalerowicz's Kadr were to be dissolved. There was some backing off on the part of the ministry in the spring of 1978, but the conflict was not resolved until Janusz Wilhelmi died in a plane crash during a trip to Bulgaria. With his death the stand-off was apparently over, the situation relaxed, and it was time for another step forward, especially for young directors.

1978

Janusz Zaorski (b. 1947) who had already made *Promotion* (*Awans*) [1974] and *Partita for a Woodwind* (*Partita na instrument drewniany*) [1978], made *Room with a View of the Ocean* (*Pokój z widokiem na morze*) [1978], a film that did not get much of a critical reception in Poland but was quite well appreciated abroad. In the film, a young man climbs to the top of the highest building in town with the intention of jumping to his death. After several hours of posturing himself to fall, he changes his mind. Zaorski's film records the fight for the man's life on the part of the representatives of society—policemen, medics, and so forth—who want to dissuade him by cunning, manipulation, perhaps even force. In contrast to these there is a single humanist who does not want to force the man to live, who wants him simply to take responsibility for whatever he will do, live or die. He is the one who succeeds. It was a modest, simple film with a clear message.

The same year saw the production of a most unusual and fascinating film, an experiment in mixing filmic modes, entitled *How Are We to Live?* (*Jak żyć*) [1978], directed by documentarist Marcel Łozinski (b. 1940). It was staged in free-form fashion in a summer camp for young couples, an actual summer camp run by an official youth organization. The characters were real people, campers, except for two people planted by the director. With their help he organized a kind of psychodrama in the form of a competition to determine the best married couple. The results were socially amazing and filmically effective. In this small hothouse community the worst vices were brought out from the individuals: hypocrisy, lies, perfidy, all within the framework of a bureaucratically run camp. As one might have expected, the film was regarded as more than a visual report about a camp; it was seen as a caricature of society focused through one lens. Officials did not want to release the film and this controversy lasted a long while. Finally *How Are We to Live* was released for a short time in the winter of 1980–81, the Solidarity period, but it was withdrawn again after martial law was declared in December 1981.

Also in 1978, Edward Żebrowski, after a long break from directing, did *Hospital of the Transfiguration* (*Szpital przemienienia*), based on a novel by Stanisław Lem (b. 1921), usually known for his sophisticated science fiction writing. This was not science fiction. The action takes place in a mental hospital at the beginning of World War II where, in addition to the inmates, a group of people from different walks of life and of different political persuasions have gathered. This very special society is threatened and meets the test. The characters reveal their true faces, and the concealed evil in individuals emerges. On a broader level, Żebrowski takes up the dilemma of the Polish intelligentsia: conformity or protest, helplessness or action, resignation or resistance.

After the crisis that began in 1977 when *Man of Marble* and *Camouflage* were shown was resolved, a generally more optimistic situation prevailed. In a discussion published by the monthly Kino (no.4, 1978), Feliks Falk said that what happened was the creation of "a new and unusual phenomenon, an unprecedented intensity and fresh perspective of the social themes that dominated Polish cinema in the late seventies." He credited his colleagues in the documentary field, like Kieślowski, Łozinski, Zygadło, and others who "without compromise were telling us as much as possible about Polish reality." With regard to this social orientation, Agnieszka Holland said, "We have to set our standards high because [*Camouflage, Man of Marble, The Scar*] have raised them considerably. Those films were the first to discuss certain issues concerning us in a manner which was honest and mature." Marcel Łozinski summed it up thus: "Who created this young cinema? Certainly, Andrzej Wajda, whose *Man of Marble* was his second debut, Krzysztof Zanussi with *Camouflage*, Krzysztof Kieślowski with *Peace*, and Feliks Falk with *Top Dog*, and other young directors, like Angieszka Holland, Janusz Kijowski, Pawel Kędzierewski, Laco Adamik, Tomasz Zygadło, and others." The age span among the lot was more than twenty-five years.

Generations

Indeed the young filmmakers had strong ties with their fellow artists of the preceding generation. In 1978, fresh from having made *Man of Marble*, Andrzej Wajda made another film that was just as outspoken, *Rough Treat-*

ment (more accurately Without Anesthesia, *Bez nieczulenia*) from a screen-play by Agnieszka Holland that had previously been rejected because of its frank examination of hypocrisy, conformity, and deviousness in institutional life. The same year, 1978, saw another important film by Zanussi, quite young himself but by now a seasoned filmmaker. *Spiral* (*Spirala*) was a film whose moral austerity and psychological honesty went beyond any other film he had made or was to make. An older hand, Tadeusz Chmielewski, veteran fabricator of comedies, made a penetrating psychological drama, *In the Still of the Night* (*Wśród nocnej ciszy*) [1978], a film that was at once a tragedy, a detective thriller, and extraordinarily evocative of mood and tension. Chmielewski surprised his audience with this seamless composition of hor-ror, pathos, and tenderness. In a natural way, the young were asserting a cer-tain sharp message about reality, but it is noteworthy that filmmakers of every age were feeling creative momentum and engaging in it.

1979

The year 1979 was a most abundant and valuable one. *Top Dog*, im-pounded since 1977, opened triumphantly. Wajda's *Rough Teatment* (*Without Anesthesia*) played to very large audiences. These were films made with emphatic realism, the vein in which other important developments occurred. This was not surprising since some directors, such as Kieślowski, Łozinski, and Zygadło, had been successful documentary makers before their feature projects.

Krzysztof Kieślowski made *Film Buff* (*Amator*) [1979], another landmark film of a banner year. It was a work of realistic analysis, a cold look at both personal and social motivations for behavior. A young worker, an amateur filmmaker, wants to make an honest and truthful film about his factory. The management encourages him and helps support the project. Then the young moviemaker faces the basic question, what does "honest and truth-ful" mean? By ordinary standards, of course, he can tell, but then he takes the measure of the intentions and desires of his sponsors, who thus become psychologically transformed into his censors.

Perhaps the whole truth is not desirable, not useful? Perhaps it is not fun-damentally and necessarily good for the people, the factory, or society. The film follows these complex considerations and the traps waiting for the truth-teller. Compromise appears as natural necessity; conformity seems like common sense. In a situation where truth and lie have many shades, the work he set out to do became impossible. *Film Buff* ends with a helpless gesture: the would-be filmnaker throws away his footage and turns the cam-era on himself. As is evident, *Film Buff* is about much more than its title and plot suggest. It is about the difficulty of creating art under moral and social constraints, under pressure of society and its demands. That is precisely how the audience viewed it. It was an unqualified success, even officially. It was chosen to represent Poland at the Film Festival in Moscow in 1979, and more important, it received a very impressive distinction, one of the top awards of the festival.

Falk, his spirits raised by the success of *Top Dog*, proceeded to make his next film, also based on his own script. *The Chance (Szansa)* [1979] has the same fundamental directness of message as *Top Dog*. In this story, two teachers become rivals in the struggle for their students' minds and souls. One is a noble, naive, humanist, an attractive but weak and ineffectual figure. The other is an autocrat, an advocate of order, based on discipline and re-pression if necessary, a strong man with the sensibility of a fascist. In this strange duel, neither man wins. The film ends with bitter ambivalence, the impossible choice between ineffective humanism and ugly, aggressive autocracy.

A young man who gathered more than a small amount of attention during this significant year was Janusz Kijowski (b. 1948), student of history, critic, and finally graduate of the Lodz school, where he made his first feature, *Index* [1978], a film dealing with the state of mind of the students during the student riots of 1968, a subject still tabu in 1978. Kijowski's treatment was mature and thoughtful but quite direct and realistic about unhealed wounds, about conformity and nonconformity that resulted from 1968 events. In 1979 he did *Kung-Fu* from his own script, a sort of continuation of his first film. Among all the films made at the time by the younger directors, *Kung-Fu* is surely the most "journalistic," topical, and directly social, to the point that it is lacking in any deeper exploration of psychological and moral motiva-tions. A group of young people fight to bring justice to a nonconformist who has been victimized by being set up, fired, and then accused of embezzle-ment. There are parallels to a film of Wajda's made a year earlier, namely *Rough Treatment*, but also some important differences. Wajda's protagonist bitterly accepts his defeat and inability to defend himself; Kijowski's protago-nist realizes a certain helplessness but refuses to surrender. To be sure, he places no faith in institutionalized justice, relying instead solely on his friends, who force a kind of justice for him finally, using force, cunning, and black-mail. The implications of Kijowski's film are that when legal and social rules which ought to defend human rights collapse, the only refuge is in informal connections among fellow humans, relations based on loyalty, solidarity, and friendship.

Piotr Andrejew's *Clinch (Klincz)* [1979], was another project oriented to straight realism. Andrejew (b. 1947) transcended the usual clichés of boxing films to show something of the questionable ethics and motivations of the sport. With linear clarity he depicts a story of two boxers, one of them an old prewar champ who is now a heavy-drinking manager and the other a young hopeful who slowly sinks deeper into a swampy business, an enterprise full of power games, connections, deals, and seamy influence.

Likewise related to the mood of 1979 was a film by Krzysztof Wojciechowski, *Stress at the New Address* (more accurately The Corner of Brzeska and Capri Streets, *Róg Brzeskiej i capri*), a semidocumentary of life in a decaying section of a city, the problems of its old and newer inhabitants, marginal people, drifters, dodgers, and dealers. As bad as life can be in this run-down neighborhood, is it not perhaps better than anonymity in one of the huge new housing projects? This question and its ramifications are addressed by Wojciechowski warmly and sympathetically within a style that is nonetheless relentlessly observational.

Such films owed a great deal to reportage, and documentary cinema. They had a social role to play, sometimes overtly political, sometimes sociological, and this was the import of their contribution. While they were skillfully realized, they added little to esthetic evolution, but others working at this time were indeed searching for new ways to make their statements. Among them was Filip Bajon, an unusual writer who had directed several television films. In 1979, he made his first feature, *Aria for an Athlete* (*Aria dla atlety*), a debut of great originality. On the story level it is about a man from the turn of the century, a world-famous wrestler hero in Europe and America, who listened avidly to opera. Woven into the complicated texture of the movie we find astonishing surprises of imagination through evocations of classical music, depictions of art nouveau, meditations on the crisis of the *fin de siècle*, a charming blend of ugliness and beauty, the sublime and the trivial. In this his first film, Bajon achieved a richness and depth, not to mention artistic flare, suggestive of Visconti.

Piotr Szulkin (b. 1950) is another director for whom imagination and fantasy have priority over reality. But his work was more straightforward, less elaborate, more coherently, coolly, and calmly shaped than Bajon, as in his first feature, *Golem* [1979], a tale based on a medieval legend of an artificial man made into a fantasy of the future. In it there is the aloof presentation of a world quite repulsive although peopled by creatures similar to us, similar but devoid of will and enthralled in misery. It is a film one watches with cold admiration, without emotion.

Great esthetic distinction belongs to a film that was among the most interesting of the year, a debut film in fact, *Nightmares* (*Zmory*) [1979], by Wojciech Marczewski (b. 1944). Of the films that were not social and topical in their orientation, *Nightmares* had the best reception critically. It was based on a novel by Emil Zegadłowicz (1888–1941), published in 1935, a story that created a scandal with its erotic scenes, anticlerical attitude, and semi-anarchistic reflections. Marczewski's adaptation fully lived up to its source in sensuality and in capturing a sense of intellectual awakening of an adolescent boy, the protagonist of the movie. But Marczewski surrendered nothing to literal treatment as far as his drama, picturesque visualization, and psychological analysis were concerned. His work was esthetically rich, psychologically sharp, and nostalgically evocative, all at once, in its depiction of spiritual, social, and sexual maturation of a boy.

Provincial Actors

Equally significant, a debut film also, was Agnieszka Holland's *Provincial Actors* (*Aktorzy prowincjonalni*) [1979], made in unit "X." It ranks among the outstanding films of this entire period. Neither topically realistic nor esthetically creative according to classification, it was actually both and something more. On the story level it is a lively depiction of a theater in the provinces, presented intelligently, accurately, and also subtly. An atmosphere of mediocrity prevails because of the unfulfilled aspirations of the players and the disappointments they have known in their careers. They wait for the big chance, but they are sure it will never turn up. Against this background, we follow the story of a young actor who cannot accommodate himself to this acceptance, dismal resignation, suffocating normality. His ambition has its release when a director from the capital chooses him for a stage production of Stanisław Wyspiański's *Liberation* (*Wyzwolenie*), an ambitious and mysterious play. The actor engages in a controversy over the production, an argument which he loses. Mediocrity prevails. There is no escape from this poisonous, stifling conformity. Thus the reference to Wyspiański's *Liberation* was not casual. The young man comes to represent more than himself. Wyspiański's play is full of meditations and reflections on the nature and fate of the nation. Holland turns this into a challenge through the actor who declaims, "Let us finally do something which depends on us," after Wyspiański. It is a protest against incapacity, against manipulation, and also against moral paralysis. Holland berates the same national trait that Gombrowicz called "Polish helplessness." The film calls for a break from an attitude that magnifies obstacles and makes them too great to be overcome by free will, aspiration, self-confidence. Partly because of the strength and relevance of its message, woven subtly and artfully into the film, *Provincial Actors* was one of the most valuable achievements in the latter half of the seventies.

An Extraordinary Time

1979 was an unusual year by every measure. In an industry producing around thirty films a year at the time, twelve directors made their debut feature films and almost every one of them was significant. What did they have in common? A portion of them were topical, social, contemporary, journalistic. Others were aesthetically elaborated period pieces. But all of them were authentically individual, subjective, personal expressions. They did all share one identifiable similarity: a distinct impression of moral stress and spiritual trial. Thus, this trend received the designation, "the cinema of moral concern."

The yearly festival at Gdansk was therefore especially interesting, given such remarkable new beginnings as well as contributions from veterans. To be sure it was one of the finest annual surveys ever held. Added to the films cited were Andrzej Kondratiuk's *Full Moon* (*Pełnia*) [1979], and Wajda's *The Maids of Wilko* (*Panny z Wilka*) [1979]. Both would have been important under any circumstances, but in 1979 they were adding to the riches at Gdansk. The forum of the Filmmakers Association that year was held in a mood of detente between the filmmakers and the administration.

The outlook was positive as 1980, destined to be a year of great events, approached. It began positively and effectively. Zanussi made two more films, *The Constant Factor* (*Konstans*) [1980] and *The Contract* (*Kontrakt*) [1980], both on moral and social issues. Emulation was apparent even among some who were antipathetic to the social and esthetic trends. Ryszard Filipski, actor and occasional director, made High Flights (*Wysokie loty*) [1980], a kind of social criticism he had not done before. Filipski, like Bohdan Poręba, represented views quite different from those in the films described above. Nonetheless, in *High Flights* he attacked moral decay among the elite of the "red bourgeoisie," drawing a picture that approached caricature (during an orgiastic party, officials were pictured throwing caviar at one another and dousing each other with champagne). But he contrasts these rogues by depicting an honest, if somewhat helpless, party secretary and his brave son, who it is suggested will eventually prevail over the corrupt officials.

Wajda, whose *Man of Marble* and *Rough Treatment* were scathing and searing revelations, followed his delicate esthetic piece *Maids of Wilko* with another nonsocial work, *The Conductor* (*Dyrygent*) [1980], starring John Gielgud, a film more successful outside Poland. To some it was simply one of his lesser works and intrinsically undeserving of great attention; to others it may have been disappointing simply because it was not another strong social statement.

New films from those directors who had debuted in 1979 were reaching the screen. Angieszka Holland made *Fever* (*Gorączka*) [1980], a gloomy picturization of life among revolutionaries in the aftermath of the abortive revolt of 1905, a portrayal of provocation, despair, doubt, but also of determination. The revolutionaries lived feverish lives, sick, heated, intense, and to make form match substance, Holland made her narration fitful, pitched, and frenetic. The movie was based on a rather forgotten novel from 1910, *Story of a Bullet* (*Dzieje jednego pocisku*) by Andrzej Strug (1871–1937), however Holland wrought from it a film that was violent and moving.

Not a debut but a reemergence caught the attention of critics, when Tomasz Zygadło (b. 1947) presented *The Moth* (*Ćma*) [1980]. In 1977, he made *Rebus*, a realistic piece about a group of young people living on the margin of crime. It was, however, only with *The Moth* that his esthetic and intellectual maturity was apparent. *The Moth* is a story about a radio announcer who hosts a nighttime call-in talk show. His callers are those who cannot sleep in the night, the worried, depressed, hapless, neurotic night-people, sometimes suicidal. As he clears them of their anxieties and fears, at least momentarily, he accumulates pain, anxiety, remorse, and anger in himself. The role was executed superbly by Roman Wilhelmi who maintained the pace of intense narrative fragmented from time to time by mad flashes. *The Moth* is one of the most mature manifestations of the cinema of moral concern.

Cinema of Moral Concern

The characterization "the cinema of moral concern" grew in recognition and eventually became a familiar epithet. What was it? From descriptions of films above, it is evident that it appeared most often in films whose content showed social orientation. Basically it was a concern for moral issues related to political and social problems and for the morality of politics and political decisions. While moral perturbation was not necessarily political, political decisions are always, at least in part, moral, therefore subjective, personal. In the seventies two politico-moral issues were reflected in films: corruption and social manipulation, both related. Manipulation according to the cinema of moral concern dislocated decent human relations and violated moral imperatives. Manipulation went hand-in-glove with what was euphemistically called "pragmatism," which meant the willingness to compromise always in all ways. It is important to note that the Polish cognate word *pragmatyzm* carries mostly negative connotations and is used quite differently from the American English words *pragmatism* or *pragmatic*, words which are ordinarily used positively. Pragmatism in the Polish pejorative sense means conformity, cronyism, servility, and corruption. The cinema of moral concern came to terms with these traits in Polish society.

While the official media organs were bragging about triumph in society, and art, and economic progress, these films were showing things people were talking about at home. It appears that moral consciousness had one safety valve, the cinema. It is significant that this approach was critical but offered the viewer a system of positive values. Indeed, at base there was a longing for elementary values like truth, loyalty, and tolerance. Things were often placed in a harsh light, but it was light, not darkness.

Esthetically this film movement was a dramatic departure from the cinema of literature of the first half of the seventies. These films were not "literary" in style, nor subtly psychological, nor extremely artistic. The style of the films of the movement was derived from the documentary tradition, thus the approach was quite direct. Drama was more important than nuance. The distance between the artist and the audience was shorter because the distance between the director and his subject was shorter, and the situation was as often as not an easily recognizable social situation.

Narrative and filmic dramaturgy shifted to fit this style. Literary cinema avoided clear-cut dramatic forms preferring to diffuse its material. The protagonist was not so much the subject of the story as the object, a witness, a pawn. By contrast the hero of a film of moral concern faces his problems, fights them head on. Actually, this comes closer to classical models of drama where the choices are clear as are the conflicts.

The movement met a mixed reception and a complex one. It did not, to be sure, enjoy the same large audiences as melodramas or films made purely for entertainment, but it did have a good audience, especially among the young. The critics, a majority of them, not only praised but critically supported the trend. But at the same time, these films constituted a challenge to the media, (mostly television) that had been creating a ballyhoo of success: all was better. Poles were now living in a harmonious society, free of conflicts and crises. To these circles the films were presenting an unreal world invented by "sick imagination" and "ill will." It was similar to the complaints made against realistic trends in the fifties.

Still, some valid points could have been made against the cinema of moral concern: to some viewers these films might seem monotonous, dull, lacking aesthetic sophistication, closer to journalism than art. All of this could be true to a greater or lesser degree depending on the film in focus. From the point of view of esthetically oriented critics, the films of, say, Szulkin and Bajon, in which the social content was absent, were the most valuable ones. This dialectic between social content and estheticism became an important topic in 1979 and 1980.

Critical dialogue notwithstanding, there was no holding back the wave of debuts nor the coming forward of new directors. Leszek Wosiewicz brought out *The Taste of Water* (*Smak wody*) [1980]; Jerzy Trojan made *Lost in the Sun* (*Ukryty w słońcu*) [1980]; Andrzej Jurga did *Bird Tango* (*Tango ptaka*) [1980]; and Andrzej Kotkowski finished *Olympiad 1940* (*Olimpiada 1940*) [1980]; all of these outside the trend we have been describing. There were two new films which stand out particularly, *Palace* (*Palac*) [1980], by Tadeusz Junak, and *The Knight* (*Rycerz*) [1980], by Lech Majewski. *Palace* was based on a novel by Wiesław Myśliwski (b. 1932), a writer of sophisticated, harsh rural themes. This film is not in the least topical but rather a deep and lovely picture of country people, their tales, legends, aphorisms, metaphors. *The Knight*, also a film of great visual charm, is a story about a medieval knight who searches for a harp with golden strings. It is a film about ritual and magic. In effect, a richly presented production dominates a rather feeble, if poetic, story. These films are quite far from the cinema of moral concern, perhaps even a challenge to that movement.

It was in fact so characterized by some. For example, Krzysztof Metrak, an intelligent younger critic, indicted the films thus: "Diverted from lively contemporary problems by 'good uncles', young directors rushed blindly toward some kind of search for their own style. But looking for originality, paradoxically they lost it, coming under the control of all sorts of art directors, cameramen, etc. These debuts illustrate a crisis facing the cinema of direct message. A luxurious cinema, devoid of social consciousness and responsibility identifies art as an experiment of imagination" (*Kino*, no.12, 1980). There is exemplified here an impatience, to say the least, for young filmmakers looking for esthetic style. It might seem strange to criticize artists for focusing on experiment and imagination, but the social critics among filmmakers and commentators were concerned that contributions be made to the social situation during this period when it was possible. Esthetic digressions and diversions were often chastised. From a distance, it seems almost like a form of socialist realism in reverse, albeit unofficial of course and less pernicious. The social situation was in fact strained and there were tensions felt on all sides.

August 1980

Just then events were transpiring in the cities of Gdansk, Szczecin, and Gdynia whose effects would be felt throughout all of Poland and which would be followed with avid interest all over the world. A strike occurred in the shipyards of Gdansk which spread to other cities and then all over Poland. There were attempts to reach an agreement with the government which were for a period unsuccessful. Mounting tension led finally to the agreement signed in Gdansk between the workers and the government. The accord agreed that the workers requests would be met, the most important being the creation of independent, self-governing workers' unions. There were also provisions for fundamental reforms of many social institutions and practices, including censorship. "Solidarity" was born.

It is particularly significant that the last stage of negotiations between workers' leaders and representatives of the government took place in front of cameras held by documentarists, something rare if not unprecedented anywhere. It was brought about by the efforts of the Polish Filmmakers Association, and resulted in a famous documentary, *Workers 80* (*Robotnicy 80*)

[1980], assembled by Andrzej Chodakowski and Andrzej Zajączkowski, a unique historical work which managed to capture not simply the very words and gestures exchanged but the strange and unusual atmosphere of those peculiar events.

At the Annual Forum

The agreement was signed ten days before the Gdansk Film Festival, the annual survey of films. On the opening night of the festival, *Workers 80* was screened for the first time and seen by its living protagonists. At the annual forum the president of the Filmmakers Association, Andrzej Wajda, read a report from the executive committee entitled, "Some Thoughts on the Duty of Our Profession to Our Country and Our Epoch." The main subject was cinema but the statement was broader than that in import and placed the cinema of moral concern in a wider context: "The impossibility of having a healthy society without having solid, commonly accepted, moral criteria is a problem that cannot be ignored. Just as pictured in many films, contemporary Polish society is imbued with a number of moral styles of which few can deserve to be called moral. . . . What is said at meetings is different from what is said in the family circle or among friends. What is read in the newspaper is not what the man on the street knows and talks about." This led inevitably to points made regarding artistic freedom. "For many years it has been suggested to us that the idea of freedom of thought, conscience, and beliefs is an invention of small groups of intellectuals who misunderstand the essential historical process. The opinion has been promoted that workers and indeed society are satisfied with intellectual pabulum as provided by television, the simplistic press, and popular culture for children. Yet it was the workers who launched this fight for freedom of discussion, for freedom of expression of differing ideas to serve the good of the country." Focusing on the film industry, the report concluded, "In today's world, cinema is the unique place where an equality of cultural opportunity becomes real every day, where discourse about Poland and the contemporary world takes place. No other medium can substitute, including television. It is up to us if and how a new consciousness for Poland will be born in the cinema theaters."

Recovered Films

1981 saw the release of a number of films heretofore left on the shelves after their production. Marcel Łozinski's film *How Are We to Live?*, made in 1978, was finally released, and a discerning discussion of this unusual film and its social meaning was made possible.

Krzysztof Kieślowski's *Peace*, made for television, was finally shown. Coincidentally, it was about the management of a factory that manipulates its employees, never understanding what it is they want or need. In their mutual grievance they unite and strike. Made in 1976 it was especially appropriate in 1980.

After fourteen years, Skolimowski's *Hands Up!* was finally released. The director decided first to update it. He reedited and shot some contemporary sequences in London and in Lebanon which were meant to broaden the perspective of the film. But the new elements seemed extraneous and ineffective. The added scenes were meant to give a new perspective to the themes of narrow-mindedness and philistinism and had direct reference to the artist himself, illustrating the plight of a director whose film has been taken out of his control. They had no relationship with the characters of the story. It did not emerge an integrated movie; but the sequences made years before showing the young characters' psychological and political adventures before they became smug conformists remain original and powerful.

It was the hurried production of Andrzej Wajda's *Man of Iron* (*Człowiek z żelaza*) [1980], that was, however, the most important event of the film year. This was a sequel to *Man of Marble*, bringing that story up to the then current events in Gdansk. It set a new thematic standard indicating that few subjects remained taboo in filmmaking—at least for a small while.

During such an emotionally vibrant time it was natural for Polish retrospection to return to the traumas of the Stalinist era. After *Nightmares*, Wojciech Marczewski made *Shivers* (*Dreszcze*) [1981], from his own script. It was a story about coming of age, set in the Stalinist fifties. The boy's father is a political prisoner. The mother watches helplessly as the boy is slowly turned into an activist in a state-run Young Pioneer camp. The boy's maturation is modulated by the ideological pressure put upon him. The indoctrination prevails to the point that he is ready to reject his own father. Strong in its political statement, subtle in its psychological development, *Shivers* is one of the more interesting films from the months of Solidarity.

Feliks Falk, in 1981, carried out a project he had had in mind for some years, *There Was Jazz* (*Był jazz*), about a group of musicians who play the jazz music prohibited during the Stalinist years. They work, love, hate, study, and face police repression, but jazz remains their most important preoccupation, because jazz during those depressive years was something more than music. It was an expression of dissent, an escape from gloomy reality.

Jerzy Domaradzki made a film that was to be released five years later, in 1986, again using the fifties as a subject, one of the best of those that did. *The Big Race* (*Wielki bieg*) [1981] is about a long-distance track race, manipulated under cover of sport to be principally a propaganda event. The winners are not necessarily to be the best runners but those who "deserve" to win, nor does the protagonist run for athletic success but to be able to present to the president, who will congratulate the winner, a letter asking for the release of his jailed father. Even in that he is cheated. In a locker room he hears the ovation accorded the fake winner and the president's congratulation. This world depicted by the director is not a caricature. It is a world of bent rules, lies, broken characters, inevitable corruption.

The Last of the Trend

In 1981 the economic crisis was deepening rather than improving. Life was becoming more difficult daily in even the simplest ways. Strikes continued to spread. The agreement of August 31, 1980, offered no relief economically to the country and the spirit of confrontation grew as economic conditions worsened. Film production, too, felt the squeeze. During the summer and fall filmmakers were hastily finishing their current projects. There was very much a sense of trying to get things done while there was still time. Tomasz Zygadło turned over to Janusz Zaorski a script of his own which he had been planning to make. *Child's Play* (*Dziecinne zabawy*) [1981] was about a group of architects fighting demoralization and bureaucracy, not only for the success of their own projects but also for the intrinsic good their projects would bring to people. It was typical of the films of the moral concern movement: journalistic, with clear conflict, and a moral problem. After the August 1980 events Zaorski changed the ending. The conflict within his film sets off a crisis and a strike occurs at a construction site. The architects join the strike. There appears to be an expression here of hope for general solidarity and, through that, social harmony under principles of moral decency. It is quite possible to say, even with the kindest intentions, that the cinema of moral concern sometimes practiced a kind of schematism slightly comparable to what had been practiced in the fifties for other ends and purposes.

In spite of haste and uncertainty, Agnieszka Holland and Krzysztof Kieślowski made their most mature works in 1981. Holland's *A Woman Alone* (*Kobieta Samotna*) did not end up quite as it started. Originally it was conceived when a literary magazine published the diary of a hairdresser, a single mother living with her child in very tough circumstances, who watches every day the glamorous life of her customers. In the screenplay, co-written with Maciej Karpinski, little remained of the original story except the woman living in wretched conditions, abandoned by an alcoholic mate. In this version she is a mail clerk. She lives a life of ugliness, mediocrity, and desperation. In this gloomy world of hers a man appears with whom she becomes heavily involved. Together they dream about a better life somewhere far from the place they live. She decides to steal money she handles that is supposed to be paid to poor pensioners. She and her man buy a shabby used car and quickly leave. For her the escape comes to an end in the first motel along the way. The man chokes her to death with a pillow. There is something reminiscent of Dostoevsky here, and filmically of Bunuel, the dark byways of human misery, relentless destiny, environment as trap. This is not the two-dimensional world of good versus bad as presented so often. Holland's movie shows complex, profound personal and moral anguish. Like *The Big Race* it was made in unit "X."

In "*Tor*," which together with "X" led the trend, Kieślowski produced a film from his own screenplay entitled *Coincidence*. This movie was Kieślowski's most intellectually ambitious piece to this point. It is based on three versions of a banal event, namely, catching a train. First, what would happen if the man catches his train? Second, what happens if he misses it? Third, what would his life have been like if he had never undertaken the journey at all? In each case we deal with the same person, the same traits, the same psychological make-up. In one version, he becomes a revolutionary dissident; in another, an establishment activist; in the third, no one of any consequence at all. Neither *Coincidence* nor *A Woman Alone* were ready in time to be judged during the 1981 Gdansk Film Festival.

In spite of growing production difficulties, some new ventures did get off the ground. Ryszard Bugajski, after months of delay, got script approval for *Interrogation* (*Przesłuchanie*) [1982], a film with some acutely sensitive elements, chief among them a searching and intimate portrayal of a member of the security police. It was a story about the early fifties, involving the treatment of a woman against whom false and distorted accusations are made. The setting is a prison run by the security police, and the depiction spares nothing, portraying grim and horrifying tortures and cruel conditions. The main role is played by Krystyna Janda who had already identified herself with daring films, having played in *Rough Treatment* and *Man of Iron*. Her performance in *Interrogation* is beyond extraordinary; it has to be classed among the greatest acting accomplishments in cinema history. With a strong script, sharp and forceful direction by Bugajski, and Janda's acting, this is perhaps the best of the films that took the 1950s as a subject.

The authorities have refused to distribute *Interrogation*, and except by members of the film community it is not known in Poland, but copies of the film and video tapes have circulated in the West. The Circle Distribution Organization of Washington, D.C., has attempted to arrange for the purchase of distribution rights but, to the time of this writing, has been without success.

Janusz Zaorski got around to making a film that had been tentative for a while, the story taken from a novel by Kazimierz Brandys, *Mother of Kings* (*Matka Królów*). The novel was written in 1957. Zaorski's script faithfully captured the spirit of the book about a working-class family, a mother and her sons, and how history affected their lives. It reflects perfectly the point of view of the left-oriented intelligentsia of the time, condemning the Stalinist period but hopeful for the future.

Tadeusz Chmielewski, master of comedy, who broke out of that genre with *In the Still of the Night,* made another serious film from Stefan Żeromski's classical novel, *Faithful River (Wierna rzeka).* Written in 1912 the novel takes place during the brutally suppressed uprising of 1863 against Czarist Russia. Although begun in 1981, because of various delays and procrastinations the last footage was not shot until February 1983, when a snowfall finally made the shooting of certain scenes propitious. But the delays were probably due as much to a difficult production situation in 1982 and to official foot dragging. A story in which Russian troops mistreat Poles is still highly sensitive, even if the troops were Czarist.

On the night of December 12, going into the morning of December 13, a "state of war" was proclaimed in Poland. This was, in fact, a declaration of martial law, but since there were no legitimate provisions for declaring martial law, the term "state of war" was invoked. Political and social life froze in that cold repressive December. A curfew was declared. There was a mass arrest of Solidarity activists. Phone links were cut, domestic travel was restricted. Public places, including theaters and cinemas, were closed. For the moment, film production stopped.

Within weeks some efforts were made to begin activity, and slowly things began, in fact, to start up again in the film industry. First the movie houses were opened to show children's films, then other films. But many films that had already been widely circulated and that had been made some time ago were proscribed: *Man of Iron, Man of Marble, How Are We to Live?*

Shivers was yanked until 1984, *There Was Jazz* until 1985, *The Big Race* until 1986. *Coincidence* and *Mother of Kings* were released in 1987, followed by *A Woman Alone* and *Faithful River. Interrogation* has not been released at the time of this writing.

1. Andrzej Munk's *Eroica:* a wry look at heroism and its variations

2. *Ashes and Diamonds* by Andrzej Wajda: the film that changed the industry by Poland's greatest director

3. *Ashes and Diamonds:* a nationalist partisan (Zbigniew Cybulski) dies in the rubble of history

4. *Bad Luck* by Andrzej Munk: comic *Bildungsroman* of a born loser

5. *The Night Train* by Jerzy Kawalerowicz: a psychological excursion by a versatile director

6. Andrzej Munk's *The Passenger:* a profound examination of the truth of re-membrance finished for Munk after his untimely death

7. Andrzej Wajda's *Everything for Sale:* the director's somewhat autobiographical response to the sudden death of actor Zbigniew Cybulski

8. *Salt of the Black Earth* by Kazimierz Kutz: industrial strikes in Silesia in the 1930s, part of a working-class saga

9. *The Game* by Jerzy Kawalerowicz

10. Wajda's *Landscape after Battle:* the strangeness of life and choice in a liberated prison camp

11. *Family Life* by Krzysztof Zanussi: the failure of close relationships

12. Wajda's *Man of Marble:* a film about history that made history

13. Jerzy Radziwiłłowicz as Birkut in *Man of Marble*

14. *The Gorgon Affair* by Janusz Majewski: a reconstruction of a famous murder case

15. Feliks Falk's *Top Dog:* a portrayal of cynicism and manipulation

16. *Camera Buff* by Krzysztof Kieślowski: a crisis of honesty in art

17. *Death of the President* by Jerzy Kawalerowicz: accuracy and drama in the presentation of a crucial moment in history

18. *Death of the President*

19. *Nightmares* by Wojciech Marczewski: a moody period piece of the awakening of young senses

20. Krzysztof Zanussi's *Spiral:* a woman (Maja Komorowska) becomes involved with a dying man

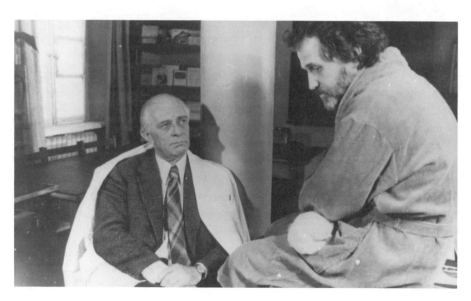

21. *Spiral:* an existentialist drama in which a man (Jan Nowicki) faces death

22. Andrzej Wajda's *The Maids of Wilko:* lyrical, melancholy, and delicate

23. *The Moth* by Tomasz Zygadło: a night host of a radio talk show assumes the problems of his public

24. Zanussi's *Constant Factor:* a man searches for a stable personal and philosophical point of reference

25. Wajda's *Man of Iron:* a sequel to *Man of Marble* set in the time of the forming of Solidarity

26. *The Year of the Quiet Sun* by Krzysztof Zanussi with Scott Wilson and Maja Komorowska

27. *The Year of the Quiet Sun:* a woman reassembles her life and her emotions after World War II

VI

Jerzy Kawalerowicz:
The Search for a Style

It would seem, with quick and superficial evaluation, that the films of Jerzy Kawalerowicz do not fit into the patterns described as characteristic of Polish film work. He has rarely touched upon the great problems of national existence and history (*Death of a President* is an exception); he did not involve himself in retrospective bitterness; he did not treat with dramas in which contemporary man searched for an accepted place in his own society. Those Polish subjects were not his. Rather, he dealt with universal and diversified themes, while going through a number of stylistic metamorphoses. He worked with formats that were naturalistic and some that were almost abstractionist. He practiced psychological realism but was not shy about trying to depict the world of imagination. His tone could be matter-of-fact or moralistic. He gathered renown in Europe from the fifties through the seventies, even though he was an esthetic chameleon.

In fact, this is a characterization he would admit to. "I have no artistic creed. I would not suggest restrictions nor impose them upon myself. The films I make are a result of the present moment, the existing conditions of my life, artistic experiences, and passions. I would not, therefore, make any attempt to say what kind of films I might make in the future. The way I think today is quite different from the way I thought yesterday" (quoted by Janicki, Stanisław, *Polscy twórcy filmowi o sobie*, Warsaw, 1966; our translation). When a French critic tried to identify the director's stylistic debts, Kawalerowicz replied: "I do not think it possible to find in my work the influence of any school or director. I am rather anarchical in my art, which I view in various ways at any given time. I like to move from one subject to another, from one style to another" (Belmans, Jacques, "Jerzy Kawalerowicz ou le realisme interieur," in *Etudes Cinematographiques*, Paris, 1967; our translation). Such remarks are not overly and completely convincing since influences are inevitable. Perhaps they reflect the director's fear of being misunderstood by being too restrictively categorized. Yet it is true that he has been consistently inconsistent, and he has indeed carried out an eclectic (or anarchistic) program during a career in which he has created films of beauty and maturity. How has this come about?

Kawalerowicz was born on January 19, 1922, in Gwozdziec in southeastern Poland, a section since annexed by the Soviet Union. He survived the war working at different jobs, and at that time took up painting. After the war, he studied at the Academy of Fine Arts and then at the new Film Institute, which was later to transfer to Lodz. Buczkowski took him on as an assistant in the making of the first postwar Polish film, *Forbidden Songs*. He also helped make Jakubowska's *Last Stage* as well as Kański's *Devil's Gorge*.

His next step was to enter a competition announced at the famous (infamous?) meeting at Wisła, which was held principally to install socialist realism as official cinema doctrine. With his friend Kazimierz Sumerski, Kawalerowicz wrote a screenplay entitled *Community* which was accepted, and he was allowed to make it into a film in 1952. It was hardly an auspicious beginning. The script conformed to all the rules of socialist realism and was therefore inflexible, schematic, and not credible.

Community

In a village, a group of farmers, gathered together into a cooperative, want to build a new grain mill in order to get out from under the control and exploitation of a rich miller. He, supported by the affluent farmers (Kulaks), does everything to stop them. Class struggle ensues. There are the Kulaks on the one side and the peasants associated with the cooperative on the other. In between are those with moderate farms who will be won over by the new, progressive, communally-minded forces. There is even a romantic subplot which is subjected to the logic of class struggle. That the film is not intrinsically worthless except as a historical curiosity is due to the fact that the crew spent several months on location in a remote village and captured there an atmosphere of authenticity, a record of human faces, customs, and a sense of place that can still be felt today when viewing the film.

Community was roundly criticized, even by those sympathetic with socialist realism, and it won no audience popularity at all. If contemporary film historians go back to it, it is largely because of who Kawalerowicz is and the director he became. His potential importance was made apparent in his very next project.

A special literary event of the early 1950s was the publication by Igor Newerly of his novel *Souvenir of Cellulose (Pamiątka z celulozy)* [1952]. Its subject was social concerns and events of the early 1930s as these developed in the town of Włocławek and the creation there of workers' consciousness. It fit the doctrinaire tenor of the times but was redeemed by a rich text, a good story, and the clear writing talent of the author, which lifted it above the mediocre literature of the period. Together with Newerly, Kawalerowicz did a film adaptation which, because of its volume, was cut into two sections in order to make a two-part movie. Certainly Kawalerowicz was anxious to do something better than *Community*, and he felt that "the characters in Newerly's book are not schematic; they are real people, who think, act, are differentiated and clearly drawn, and who offer the reader a live and artistic experience" (quoted in *Trybuna Robotnicza*, no. 96, 1954; our translation).

Cellulose diptych

The first part of the diptych, *A Night of Remembrance*, *(Celuloza)* [1954], is about the hero coming of age; the second part, *Under the Phrygian Star (Pod gwiazdą frygijską)* [1954], is about his mature life. *A Night of Remembrance* follows the hero, Szczesny, played by Józef Nowak, from the time he leaves his father's farm. The film is retrospectively told in episodes, in the first of which he gets work at the shop of a carpenter and falls in love for the first time with the young wife of his boss. Next he serves in the army, and upon his release becomes a house servant. These things are told to a girl Szczesny has met, Madzia (played by Lucyna Winnicka), who from this point in the story becomes a central character. *Under the Phrygian Star* takes place in Włocławek where Szczesny works in a cellulose factory and becomes a labor activist and a participant in the political struggle. The story climaxes with a big strike. In the meantime, the story of his love for Madzia has also been developed. *A Night of Remembrance* is descriptive. The hero grows and matures and is not overly sensitive to the events that are taking place around him. *Under the Phrygian Star* is much more dramatic, replete with conflicts and political elements. The hero is now a participant rather than a witness to events, and he is a force for action.

The film was a surprise because it was such a sharp contrast with most of the other mediocre, schematic productions of the time. The development of complicated story lines, vivid character portrayals, and respectable intellectual content suggested that here was a young directorial talent suddenly come into full maturity. How was this to be explained? First of all, credit had to be given to the material, Newerly's novel. It provided characters who were psychologically complex, who transcended the usual stereotypical socialistic hero. Second, Kawalerowicz allowed himself range around the periphery of the main plot to explore and record the mores and lifestyle of the working classes in rich texture. Third, Kawalerowicz handled his literary material in what was then an unconventional way. He did not engage in simplification, extracting what would fit a straightforward film plan. Rather, he placed his trust in his literary material to extract from it all that he could irrespective of whether or not he went outside the bounds of conventional filmic practices. Hence the decision to make this into two films instead of one. This surrender to literature, breaking through conventional filmic restrictions by giving priority to the literary material, later helped bring about profound reforms in the cinematic language employed by Polish directors. Fourth, the esthetic of neo-realism gave Kawalerowicz a clarity in his presentation of the relationship between individuals and social mechanisms as well as an effective austerity in his visual compositions. Finally, it is worth mentioning the influence certain Russian film accomplishments had upon him, especially the work done by Kozintsev and Donskoi in the 1930s, which treated with similar social background and gave broad scope to similar subjects.

A Night of Remembrance is a realistic record of people and traditions under austere circumstances, but while the life depicted may be austere, the picture is rich, full of complicated forms and lines, careful lighting with a domination of dark grey lending sadness to a depiction that is in other ways full of life. It fits well the theme of an awkward but intelligent boy gradually maturing and beginning to understand the reality around him. The second part, *Under the Phrygian Star*, is filmically more traditional. The action moves faster. The hero now has in front of him a clear political goal. A love plot warms the movie, and the director adds touches of lyricism and pathos. The project was, indeed, a mature accomplishment. Some of the director's innovations were antecedents of modern forms of film narrative, one Polish critic wrote, especially "when he suddenly passes from an epic rhythm to drama or metaphor, mixing individual genres; or when he treats the world as a reality for the camera to discover rather than as prefabricated material made just for the story" (Jackiewicz, Alexander, "L'Oeuvre de Jerzy Kawalerowicz," *Etudes Cinematographique*, Paris, 1967).

The film was well received by critics and the public, and even the authorities were satisfied because it was an evocation of the class struggle, involved the prewar Communist party, criticized the prewar government, and vaguely expressed faith in revolutionary change. Given all that, the deviation into neo-realist style was overlooked. Kawalerowicz managed to satisfy doctrine while at the same time avoiding all the two-dimensional esthetic qualities which the doctrine usually reflected. This film work rather than the caricatures that had been produced could well have become a model for those who wanted to practice socialist realism, but it was already 1954, and in 1955 that esthetic doctrine would already be under consideration for reform and indeed for rejection. The shrewder critics therefore saw *A Night of Remembrance* and *Under the Phrygian Star* as an evolution away from socialist realism rather than its fulfillment. "Generally, the film got rid of the unbearably vulgar automatism controlling the lives of characters" (Toeplitz, K.T., *Nowa Kultura*, no. 18, 1954; our translation).

Shadow

In 1955 Kawalerowicz set to work on a very tricky project, *The Shadow* (*Cień*), from a screenplay written by Aleksander Ścibor-Rylski, then young and promising, later Poland's most prominent scriptwriter. The story and its form of organization was quite original; the subject itself was exceedingly controversial. It takes place just after the war when the peace of the land is still violated by internecine struggles. At the opening of the tale a man jumps to his death from a moving train. This is the point of reference for three subsequent stories each of which has a mysterious connection with this man. The first story takes place during the war and concerns a guerilla operation. The operation is aborted because of an attack by—we later learn—another guerilla unit, possibly of a different ideological orientation. Men are wounded and killed. The question arises as to whether the attack was a mistake or a provocation. The question is not answered. The second story takes place just after the war when there were active, armed, antigovernment Polish fighting units resisting the left-wing government. The police try to capture the leader of such a group. Two agents infiltrate and make their way to him. One of the two makes a gesture seemingly indicating his sympathy and complicity with the group. Was this a feint? Was this genuine? We never learn because the other throws a grenade. The third story is contemporary with the film, that is, the 1950s, when the police capture a boy wearing a jacket that belonged to the man who at the beginning of the film jumped off the train. The boy tells of having participated in a sabotage action in a coal mine in which the owner of the jacket was killed. There is one element that relates all three tales: In each case the same man, the one killed at the beginning, was determined to be acting against the government.

What we have been following in this cinematic narrative is a kind of shadow of evil action. In a sense, then, *The Shadow* is clearly caught up in the atmosphere and propaganda of the early 1950s, when Poles were warned of the hidden enemy, the spy, the saboteur lurking in every conceivable place.

The style of narration, nonetheless, was new and interesting. After his epic and lyrical diptych, Kawalerowicz was trying his hand at suspense, mystery, the practice of narrative ambiguity. He was successful in building a climate of tension and doubt. The direction was enhanced by the photography of a young cameraman destined to become famous, Jerzy Lipman, whose workmanship gave us lighting effects that enhanced the suspense and create almost unreal clarity of detail. The final product was truly striking with its extraordinary freshness. But because of the subject matter the film came up short in critical appraisal. By the time it appeared on the screen (1956), the idea of the system under threat by spies and saboteurs and such gloomy apparitions of counter-revolution had already been abandoned by the authorities, and also by—needless to say—the audience. Not surprisingly, the film was sharply criticized, but a few critics did notice the innovative form of narrative that, rather than the tendentious content, seems to have been Kawalerowicz's main purpose in making the film.

Thus, it seems that while the theme of *The Shadow* lagged behind the evolution of political thinking in Poland, its form was a bit ahead of its time. *The Shadow* was received better in Western Europe where its innovativeness was appreciated and its content discounted. In France, Francois Debreczeni wrote: "Apart from the story and in contrast to its ideological elements there is a kind of narration along Western lines, comparable to that of Hitchcock or Aldrich, wherein the action, or rather lack of action, functions for its own purposes. . . . Specific shots and entire sequences seem to represent 'purity of vision,' not expressing anything beyond a kind of existence. . . . The meaning of the film emerges from two things: clarity of picture which comes from composition within the frames, and the element of anxiety which is exuded by the visual composition" ("Le tournant d'une ouevre: L'Ombre," *Etudes Cinematographique*, Paris, 1957; our translation).

After his successful two-part epic and his experiment in suspense, Kawalerowicz's creative restlessness turned in still a different direction, in this case a psychological story that takes place within the four walls of a Warsaw apartment, *The Real End of the Great War* (*Prawdziwy Koniec Wielkiej Wojny*) [1957]. Incidentally, this was the time when the directors of the Polish School were engaging in earnest the themes of Polish destiny, a trend which did not at this time involve Kawalerowicz.

The Real End of the Great War

The literary basis for the new film was a story by Jerzy Zawieyski, a Catholic moralist, who together with the director prepared the screenplay. It is about a girl named Roza, played in the film by Lucyna Winnicka, who was in *A Night of Remembrance*, and who was now married to the director. She is, in the film, the wife of Juliusz (Roland Głowacki), a death camp survivor wrecked and alienated by his experience. While he was away, thinking that he had been killed, Roza found another man (Andrzej Szalawski). The three principals now find themselves in an unresolvable situation. The husband is haunted by recurring nightmares, especially one in which a Gestapo sadist forces the prisoners to dance. The wife who once loved him is now full of sympathy for his suffering, but living with him is impossible. Juliusz's crises intensify making Roza's despair increasingly deeper. Finally, and perhaps inevitably, Juliusz attempts suicide.

The filmic narrative is on two planes. The first is after the war, shot in the wife's apartment from which Juliusz's animal-like cries are heard from time to time. The other reflects his terrible hallucinatory visions of the death camp and the insane dance. In presenting the visions the camera has the point of view of the prisoner. The contrast between the present and the nightmare of the past, between the objective reality of the situation and the subjective reality of hideous recollection presents the esthetic problem of the movie.

After the premiere, there was criticism that the project was confounded by the sharp development of the two perspectives which violated unity of narrative and coherence of tone. In an interview, Kawalerowicz responded that "the lack of overall stylistic homogeneity was intended. ... In my opinion, these two planes can make up an organized whole to such an extent that I saw no need to soften the passing from one to the other" (in *Teatr i Film*, September 1957; our translation). In this he seemed to be supported by later experiments by Alain Resnais. Still, the film did not accomplish what it set out to do and was never considered a dramatic success.

One reason may be that the characterization of the wife did not contribute to the articulation of the problem. She was simply a witness of her husband's condition rather than a victim of the situation, a participant. Her motivations were not such as to give depth to her role. We cannot tell very well whether she is acting out of love or mercy or both or neither. Her new male friend was no more than a pawn in the story, and even the main character, Juliusz, was too much of an object, a shred of a character rather than a human being. The mistake, then, was in focusing all the attention on the husband, a fragment of a personality, rather than on Roza, whose situation suggested true dramatic potential. In this Kawalerowicz would have served himself better to have adhered more closely to Zawieyski's original story. Moreover, such a female character was one of the director's ongoing dramatic interests, one he was to return to in *Night Train* and other films. He was, himself, open to acknowledging his esthetic mistake. While demurring that "because of the purely visual appeal of Juliusz's theme and vision, his character becomes much more significant," Kawalerowicz admits that "the main character should have been Roza rather than Juliusz" (*Teatr i Film*, September 1957; our translation).

The Real End of the Great War was never appreciated as the director would have liked, but the theme it introduced was significant: the shadow of war and the trauma that lingers, the subject of wounds that never heal. This was to be important in the making of such works as Konwicki's *Halloween* and *Salto*, Has's *How to Be Loved* and *The Code*, and in a way Wajda's *Landscape after Battle*.

Night Train

Kawalerowicz next decided to do a movie based on a script by Jerzy Lutowski (b. 1923), a project that did not inspire expectations of success among his colleagues who, at the time, were caught up in momentous questions of Polish destiny. *Night Train* [1959] offered simply a setting of a man and a woman sharing a train compartment during a one-night journey under circumstances that provided a bit of melodrama. This seemed, at the time, like small beer, but after all was said and done, *Night Train* became a European classic, one of the most remarkable films of the 1950s. It was typical of Kawalerowicz to take his own special artistic path. The story of *Night Train* imposed upon him severe restrictions regarding space, character development, and dramatic events, restrictions that demanded of the artist a certain virtuosity, like writing a concerto for the left hand.

On a late train leaving a city for a sea resort we see a diverse group of people: an old lawyer with a young wife, a priest leading a group of older women on a pilgrimage, a war-traumatized insomniac, a railway man flirting with the conductress. In one of the compartments a woman (Lucyna Winnicka) and a man (Leon Niemczyk) find themselves placed together by mistake. They are both somber and seemingly dissatisfied with one another's company. Both seem to be fleeing something. It turns out that he is a surgeon who is escaping a recent experience in which his patient died during an operation. She is escaping her marriage. Also on the train is a man she has rejected, who tries to make contact with her. They are involved in an unclear game, and we are never able to determine in any certain way what is transpiring, either with these people or with characters and episodic events in the other compartments. Relationships are barely suggested; things begin but never come to any determinable end. At dawn the monotony of the trip is broken when the train is stopped by police looking for a fugitive murderer. When they find him the passengers and the police engage in a chase, soon over, after which everything returns to normal. When the train reaches the sea resort, the passengers all go their own ways with their own problems.

The discontinuity may suggest metaphor, but its nature is not obvious. Rather, the fragmented events are like those that can be gleaned from a simple journey, except for the police search for a murderer. The personality types, which are barely sketched, are quite stereotypical. Relationships shown are superficial. The depiction of the journey brings us nothing new; nothing is revealed. Even the main characters have not managed to explain anything.

Nevertheless, this fragile, unclear, dramatically anemic story comes off the screen as a breathtaking filmic spectacle full of many meanings. That is what makes it unique, extraordinary. Through setting, rhythm, pace, lighting, physicality, in short with his mise-en-scène Kawalerowicz placed himself among the great directors of Europe. A great deal of the credit goes to Jan Laskowski, cinematographer, whose shifting camera and focus make it seem as if the picture is about to burst through the narrow interiors of compartments and aisles. He employs a regular counterpoint, the flashing landscape behind the window against the static reality of the interior, which in turn intensifies the rhythm determined by the compartment doors opening and closing at metronomic intervals, by the faces appearing and disappearing, by the passing stations. All of this is interrupted during the sequence in which the police and passengers chase the murderer. At that point space is different as well as tempo while the pursuing passengers become participants of a different reality. Soon, however, the train and the film resume the regular rhythm which continues until an empty beach appears behind the windows.

The beginning of the movie offered an atmosphere of expectation, change, adventure, something extraordinary, yet the journey brings disappointment and frustration. The young wife of the aging lawyer fails to attract the attention she needs. The insomniac does not sleep. Nothing happens between the woman and man happenstance placed together in a compartment. Even the murder chase, the event that should have lifted everything to a different plane, is a disappointment. The fugitive is a hunted animal and those who chase him return to the train feeling somewhat ashamed of themselves. Everything returns to smothering normality. All of this leads to an interpretation wherein the train journey is the journey of life, of fate, in which the goals are unclear, the trip not definitive. Now and then there is a spark of human action or reaction, then the empty beach which is the picture of the end. "No other film has been so adept at creating the impression of nihilism. This film journey brings no resolution . . . except the diffusion of self and the coming of emptiness" (Fink, Guido, "Il treno della notte," *Cinema nuovo*, IX, no. 145, 1960; our translation).

To be sure, *Night Train* is a mother lode for clever interpretations simply because it is a mature artistic work of great subtlety. Almost all readings of the film have been pessimistic, but even here there are versions and versions. While it is clear that "love is not easy and life is not gay, yet everything that suggests a waste of talent, opportunity, and virtue has here its own cold and perturbing charm. Maybe the film expresses a fragile hope by posing the question: what if we had not wasted all this?" (Amengual, Barthelemy, "Une dialectique de l'objectivite et de l'interiorite," *Etudes Cinematographiques*, Paris, 1967; our translation).

When the film opened in Poland, most critics, still under the spell of what they saw as greater national themes, dismissed it. It was said to be banal, empty, and pretentious. Only a few noticed that there was something quite new in its subtle themes and form, something masterful.

In his next movie, *Mother Joan of the Angels* (*Matka Joanna od Aniołow*) [1961], Kawalerowicz gave ample evidence that he was truly a master, a man in command of directorial talent as well as intellectual substance. His new subject gave him an opportunity to show his range as well as his technique. The material evolved in an interesting way. A prioress of the

Order of Ursulan nuns in Loudun, France, in the eighteenth century, was possessed by the devil, together with all the sisters of her convent. Their chaplain, one Father Grandier, was burnt at the stake. The phenomenon was confronted and addressed by a special priest exorcist. Mother Joanne, herself, prepared a written record of the entire event, a record that became repeatedly a literary subject from that day to this.

Mother Joan of the Angels

Jarosław Iwaszkiewicz wrote a story based on this material during the German occupation, when the nightmare of evil must have been much on his mind. He gave it the title "Mother Joan of the Angels." This version involved some changes: the action was placed in eastern Poland; the chaplain's name was changed to Garniec and that of the exorcist to Suryn; only the last part of the original story was used, beginning after the execution of the chaplain and the arrival of the exorcist. With the writer Tadeusz Konwicki, Kawalerowicz worked out a script in which all specific reference to time, place, and event were omitted in the interest of endowing the film with universality, although at the outset they thought to emphasize the Polish background of Iwaszkiewicz's story.

Action begins on a barren, pale, almost lunar landscape, a burnt stake-pole in the foreground. There is a primitive inn and some grim characters, including a nobleman, servants, and a nun illegitimately absent from the convent, and beside the inn a pig-sty inhabited by black pigs. On the hill stands the convent, looming, inaccessible, strange, filling us with foreboding. There, the nuns, like weird white birds, rise together with Mother Joan (Lucyna Winnicka) in a frenzied dance. The exorcist, pious Father Suryn (Mieczysław Voit), young and strict, arrives to assume his awful responsibilities. At first a cold antipathy exists between them, but during the endless prayers of exorcism an unclear but seemingly shameful and sinful connection develops between them. We do not know whether this is some understanding, sympathy, or perhaps passion, but it leads to the murder of two servants by Father Suryn. Does he do this to exchange his own soul for that of Mother Joan by taking on such terrible guilt and sure damnation? Is it a displaced act of vengeance against the human condition so vulnerable to abomination? There is no clear answer, although the psychological tension and pain is palpable and manifest.

This is due in no small measure to the austere and terrifying visualization the director creates with the help of cameraman Jerzy Wojcik and art director Roman Mann. Space is treated geometrically, the horizontal lines of the barren landscape, the convent grounds, and the galleries are all played off against the vertical lines of church architecture. Contrasts of black and white dominate, especially the white figures of the nuns placed against dark walls

and backgrounds. Frames are tightly composed, often in half close-ups with
the characters in the center and the camera moving mostly horizontally, occasionally vertically, never diagonally. Kawalerowicz himself felt that the subject imposed the visual form, which in turn was reinforced by the sound
track, with the singing of the nuns echoed strangely in the galleries, the deep
clear tones of the chimes, and the sudden silences. When, for example, Father Suryn commits murder, we see a swinging silent bell. Altogether there
is a grim simplicity of form that italicizes the madness, the demons, the murder. One might almost say that a classicist form is used to express gothic
content, the combination yielding a film of complex esthetic maturity.

Just as the form reflects sophistication so does the content. It would be
difficult to limit the meaning of the film to the idea that the priest drew the demons to himself with his crime in order to rescue Mother Joan, although that
seems to be part of a larger whole according to Kawalerowicz: "I wanted the
film to be about the nature of man, the nature that resists imposed restrictions and dogmas. The most important thing is the feeling we call love.
Mother Joan is, after all, a story of love between a priest and a nun" (Janicki,
Stanisław, *Polscy twórcy filmowi o sobie* [Warsaw, 1964]; our translation).
There is nothing that would surprise us in this; that much is self-evident in the
film. But it is essential to state it in order to understand what it is that seeks
to break through the network of norms, orders, and prohibitions within which
these people lived, what it is that is so strong as to prefer destruction to
safety.

In general, Polish critics interpreted the struggle in the film along more social, less lyrical, lines. It was seen as a drama of rebellion against dogma, a
theme with contemporary relevance from a political point of view. Ironically,
the Catholic community saw much the same thing but from a religious point
of view, and found antireligious elements, so much so that the movie was
black-listed. Such an interpretation is no longer entertained.

Europe received the film with enthusiasm. It was, in 1961, a chief entry
at the Cannes Film Festival and took one of the highest awards there.
Subsequently it has played on the screens of dozens of countries around the
world.

The Pharaoh

Kawalerowicz's next work, *The Pharaoh* (*Faraon*) [1966], fit the trend of
the middle 1960s toward superproduction. Screen spectaculars in Poland,
as we have pointed out elsewhere in this book, included an intellectual element not usually associated with such films in the United States. At that time,
for example, Wajda made his epic *Ashes*, which created some of the sharp-
est artistic polemics of the decade. In *The Pharaoh*, Kawalerowicz indulged
in an esthetic speculation concerning power.

The starting point was a popular Polish classic of the same title written in 1897 by Bolesław Prus (1845–1912). One might expect a novel that was the basis of a film spectacle to be full of large events, chases, romances. This is not such a work, but rather one that contains psychological, moral, and philosophical problems. It has no historical standing, so to speak, since we know relatively little about the world that existed nine centuries before the Christian era. We do not even know if Rameses XIII ever existed. But in a different way, the subject of the novel and the film is quite real, the mechanism of power and the morality of politics. When Prus wrote his book he had in mind not so much some hypothetical Egyptian of ancient times as a Pole of the nineteenth century, a citizen of a nation that was still stateless who meditates on the function of a state, the sacrifices it requires, and the ideology it represents, developing all the doubts, questions, ironies, and grim humor that such reasoning can yield.

Working again with Konwicki, Kawalerowicz adapted the novel, cutting and eliminating much of the background material which was pure invention on the part of Prus and selecting several from among a kaleidoscope of characters who served best to develop the main conflict. That was represented by a clash between two people, a young, naive, but likable ruler and an old, experienced politician in the persona of a priest named Herhor. It involved two generations and two temperaments, and also a look at the strategic requirements of politics as against morality clearly conceived.

The production took months. Shooting was done in Kazakhstan, in the Valley of the Kings in Egypt, and at the Lodz studio. With his cinematographers (Jerzy Wójcik, Wiesław Zdort) and art directors (Jerzy Skrzepiński, Wojciech Krzystofiak), Kawalerowicz had to start from scratch to create images of an unknown world and give them visual coherence. It was not only a problem of architecture, interiors, and costumes, but also of developing styles for personal body motion, behavior, forms of address, all the details that must go into a credible stylistic whole.

And indeed style received the greatest stress, even at the expense of some of the usual conventions of the screen spectacular. Kawalerowicz was so self-confident as to omit the obligatory battle scenes. Only one takes place, and it is in the background. As if to provoke artistic fate, he even had the nerve to make a kissless flic. "We have not found in the iconography of the epoch any evidence supporting the idea that the kiss was a form of erotic encounter," the director pointed out during a press conference at Cannes. The point was to construct a different world, unlike anything modern with respect to appearance, gestures, ritualized reactions. Instead of production values, grand events, and crowds of extras, the emphasis was on creation through style.

The story that is told in this fashion involves young Rameses XIII (Jerzy

Zelnik) newly placed upon the throne. He reigns but has no power. It has remained in the hands of the priests, especially the high priest Herhor (Piotr Pawłowski). The priests have experience and political ability, while Rameses has only his youth and good intentions. He believes that the people expect and deserve more from authority than continuity, but he does not know how to translate his ideas into political action. A strategic contest develops between Rameses and the priests in which their cunning ability at intrigue brings about his defeat and death, proving that victory goes to those with superior experience and knowledge.

The final scenes of the movie make the point eloquently. A crowd is set to attack the temple. The priests are so able to manipulate events (the power of politics) that they arrange for the attack to start at a time of their own choosing. The attack occurs at the moment when, according to their calculations, an eclipse of the sun is to begin (the power of knowledge). The terrified crowd falls back. The people are convinced that truly the heavens are on the side of the priests and one must not challenge the gods.

The cinematic narration of the tale is slow and majestic, ballet-like, the characters using hieratic, ritual gestures, conventionalized like the celebration of a mass. In the background there is always the monotonous and eternal desert. Everything is fully lit by the bright sun. There is no shade, no escape. In some ways this abstract landscape is reminiscent of *Mother Joan of the Angels*, performing stylistic rather than dramatic functions. This visuality combines with a precise orchestration of sounds—songs sung in the temple, the wind whistling, the sand moving, human footsteps—to present a controlled and beautiful esthetic production, which had at the same time extra-esthetic significance.

Although Prus delineated the victory of experience and political skill over nobility of purpose, and the film showed this, Kawalerowicz wanted the arguments of both sides to form a balance. In the end, the logic of the story and the visual realization compel the audience to sympathize with the naive, young ruler. We understand that morality does not win out, but we are charmed by a message of protest against the cynical machinations of politics. Audience and critics both received *The Pharaoh* as an acknowledgment of the moral victory of the young ruler and by extension an acknowledgment of the superiority of youthful romanticism, the heroic attitude, and noble defeat to a soiled state of affairs. Thus the director brings himself into direct connection with the theme of the "Polish School," appreciation of romantic effort even in the pathos of defeat.

The Pharaoh was screened at Cannes during the same festival as *Ashes*. The international critics, particularly the French, were positive. Whereas the story of the Polish legions of the nineteenth century, depicted in *Ashes*, was not overly meaningful for them, the majestic calligraphy of *The Pharaoh* impressed them. Both films shared the same fate when it came to international distribution. Purchased by a German releasing firm, *The Pharaoh* was shortened to the point of being distorted and was not seen commercially outside Poland it its original form. The firm subsequently went bankrupt, and the rights were frozen for years.

After *The Pharaoh* and *Mother Joan of the Angels*, both of which were rigorous esthetic tasks, Kawalerowicz must have been ready for some relief, something less disciplined in style and structure. In any case, *The Game* (*Gra*) [1968] was such a project. The premise was his own; the script was prepared with Andrzej Baniusz, a well-known writer of song lyrics. It was about a psychological game between a middle-aged man and a woman, in which the metaphorical cards to be played are love, eroticism, attachment, and fear of old age. The notion of using the idea of a game as a film subject had long interested the director. *Night Train* could be seen as such a film, and in *Chance Meeting on the Ocean* (*Spotkanie na atlantyku*) [1980] he would return to the idea again. So he had an idea to play with and a desire to work, free of the formal restrictions his last two projects had imposed upon him. "It is quite possible," he said before beginning, "that it will be a film exploring the border of what is true and what is not . . . in the relationship between a man and a woman. . . . I am searching for a form for that subject. I am trying to make a contemporary film in which I can mix all narrative conventions, in which realism overlaps with surrealism, a film in which the only coherence is the point of view" (*Ekran*, no. 23, 1968; our translation).

The Game

The story is straightforward enough. A mature man (Gustaw Holoubek), highly placed in society, is married to a younger woman (Lucyna Winnicka), an architect, upon whom the narrative focuses. After twelve years together they have reached a crisis point. She wants independence, but at the same time she fears loneliness. He wants to preserve appearances although their relationship is burnt out. They both have lovers. The rules of the game are broken when, at a hunting party, she is beset by an irrational fear and flees to take shelter with strangers. Subsequently they try a reconciliation, but it is plainly impossible. This story line is interrupted from time to time with patches from documentaries and scientific films on new things happening in the world, things unrelated to love-jealousy-hate, the main drift. The ancient game is seen as played out in a certain changing environment. We are, after all is said and done, forced to ask ourselves what Kawalerowicz's intentions were in this design. Is it that love and its complications are outdated in a fast-changing modern world, or the opposite, that they are always present no matter how the world changes? It never becomes clear. In that respect the film fails.

But like all this director's films, *The Game* is visually interesting, with a steady rhythm and with esthetic manipulation that is somewhat effective. This goes a little way toward rescuing an unconvincing story, stereotypical psychology, and uneven acting.

The next film, *Magdalena* [1970], was even less successful. It came out of Kawalerowicz's stay in Italy during the years 1969–1970. Joseph Fryd, a small-scale producer, wanted to make a movie with Kawalerowicz as director about a story of love between a priest and a woman, a conflict between religious vocation and human emotions. Clearly this was an echo of *Mother Joan of the Angels*, which was still popular in Europe, and therefore its subject matter and its artistic reception were appealing. For *Magdalena* Kawalerowicz wanted to be more expansively experimental. Perhaps being in the country of Fellini and Antonioni at the end of an extraordinarily creative decade was having too much influence on the Polish director. His desire to reject elementary principles like chronological clarity, defined characters, and so on, led him into conflict with the producer. His efforts resulted in a hybrid film in which those elements that were supposed to be experimental appeared instead to be elementary faults in narrative, characterization, and construction. The finished product was not well received in Italy nor anywhere else. Both the producer and the director were deeply disappointed.

Kawalerowicz returned to Poland and gave up filmmaking for several years. In 1968 he had been obliged to relinquish his position as head of the "KADR" film unit which had been his since 1955, but he returned to head it after the reorganization of 1972. He also dedicated a great deal of effort to the Polish Filmmakers' Association of which he was the chairman.

Death of a President

In 1976, after a long pause, he began a new project involving new subject matter and another digression in form and style. For Kawalerowicz it was almost as if change was bound, sooner or later, to give him what he wanted as an artist. This time he became overtly political and precisely historical. *Death of a President* (*Śmierć Prezydenta*) [1977] was a remarkable early example of what we would call today docudrama, but one in which the elements of tension, suspense, and story are not in the least diminished by its precision. In a certain sense the theme of power and morality descends from *The Pharaoh*. In this instance it is restricted not only by style but also by facts.

Death of a President presents a historical episode from the first years of the independent Republic of Poland, established in 1918. This fledgling democracy had reached a point of crisis in 1922, and the National Assembly resolved it by electing to the presidency one Gabriel Narutowicz, not at all a professional politician, but a professor of engineering and science in Zurich, Switzerland. The election was a surprise to the nation and to Narutowicz himself, a man without political ambitions. Put forward somewhat diffidently by centrists, he received surprising help from the left and was put into the majority because of support from the minorities (Jews, Germans, and Ukrainians). Diehard Polish rightist-nationalists were scandalized and infuriated, and began agitation against the new government. Seven days after the election and three days after inauguration as president, Gabriel Narutowicz was shot by an artist who was a fanatic nationalist at the opening of an art exhibition.

From that incident, Bolesław Michałek and Kawalerowicz wrote a screenplay, capturing the texture of events from documents and the statements of witnesses. Scrupulously observing the order of events during the six days from election to assassination, they delineate a complicated political situation while establishing a credible portrait of Narutowicz as a man and as a liberal. All of this is bracketed by an explication of the motivation of the murderer. At first they had considered parallel plots, following the lives of Narutowicz and his killer, physically brought into each other's presence for only seconds, but this was thought to seem too artificial. Moreover, relatively little is known about the artist-assassin. The most important document relating to him is the text of his defense speech, a speech he delivered at his trial. In it, he spelled out his motivation, admitted guilt, and asked for the most severe punishment, namely the death penalty, which in due course he received. His was an illuminating statement of political fanaticism mixed with an overwhelming sense of his duty. It was incorporated into the screenplay.

At the very beginning of the movie, the murderer appears sharply contrasted against a black background, the effect being to suggest the self-isolation of the fanatic. He is delivering his rationale, his explanation. It is clear to the viewers that it is a defense speech, yet the story has not properly begun on the screen, and for the audience the crime has not yet been committed. *Death of a President* then unfolds as a reconstruction of the events leading to the assassination which necessitated this defense. Narutowicz (Zdzisław Mrożewski) is asked to return to Poland from his professorship in Switzerland to assume a position in the government. The political situation is complex, bogged down, and unexpectedly he is put forward in the National Assembly as a presidential candidate. Considering himself not so much a politician as a scientist of liberal persuasion, he initially demurs but accepts the nomination, convinced in any case that he will not be the final choice. As a result of intricate political maneuvering on the part of several factions, he is ultimately elected. The ultra-nationalists are confounded. Attempts are made to make it impossible for him to take office; there are street demonstrations, public violence, threats. Having decided upon assuming his responsibility, Narutowicz is firm. Crosscutting from street scenes to private meetings to cabinet sessions to the National Assembly builds tension and heightens the pace of the narrative. After the assumption of office there is momentary calm, and the pace slackens until the art show and the three fatal shots from the assassin.

The portrayal of the president is plain, objective, yielding nothing to sentimentalism. Yet as the character develops he becomes three-dimensional, even likable and quite admirable, which sets up the viewers for the shock of the revolver shots. The shock is enhanced because the scene is plain, placid, ordinary in contrast to the violent scenes that depicted the few days before the inauguration. In the funeral sequence that follows, the screen reflects emotions that have not so much to do with the short and insignificant presidency of Narutowicz as with the currents of Polish history and national destiny. There is a shot of Józef Piłsudski, founding father of the new state, playing solitaire as the cortège passes.

It is worth mentioning that Piłsudski was portrayed for the first time since World War II in this film. Heretofore, it was not permissible to deal with him in literature or drama, notwithstanding the fact that he was and is probably the single most significant figure in twentieth century Polish history. The character appears only two or three times and then very, very briefly, but the acting, make-up, and the director's talent bring this off in such a way that the shadow of Piłsudski hovers over all the action.

The Polish audience responded to *Death of a President* as something more than the depiction of a historical event. Of special note to the younger viewers was the depiction of democratic process broadly conceived—the role of the majority in the light of and maybe even composed of minorities, freedom of speech, aggressive opposition, the legislature as a viable entity capable of making profound decisions, the way a multi-party system functions, and the like. In that the president was assassinated partly because he was supported by minorities, the film evokes the ideals of tolerance. For everyone it was an indictment of the ultra-nationalism which played such a role in the prewar years, and which was revived in some surprising ways in postwar history.

Kawalerowicz's films seem to evolve from one another: *Death of a President* from *The Pharaoh, Magdalena* from *Mother Joan of the Angels*, and the director's next film has points of reference to *Night Train. A Chance Meeting on the Ocean* [1980] came out of an idea the director had after a conversation with a person whom he could not recall having met before. In fact, both parties maintained that they had never met before, yet both were bothered by that conclusion. The longer the conversation lasted the more unbearable the feeling became. The idea was developed into a premise that folded itself into another favorite idea, one that had already been carried out in *Night Train*, that of an enclosed space within which people cannot avoid one another and must enter into relationships however undesired.

The screenplay working these ideas out was written in collaboration again with Bolesław Michałek, a precise script laying out the situation of two people aboard an ocean liner. It was a delicate playing off of uncertainties, vague relationships, and rivalry among two men and a small group of people peripherally involved. A doctor (Ignacy Gogolewski) returns from America with his wife (Teresa Budzisz-Krzyżanowska). He has a heart condition and must avoid excitement. On the ship there is a man who appears to have the doctor under close observation. Anxious to know why, he starts to observe in return. In this way a strange connection develops between the two. The man appears to behave in a way suggesting that he may bear an old grievance, perhaps intending to avenge something the doctor did long ago, something he cannot recall. The uncertainty generates fear for the doctor. During the journey the ship crosses paths with a yacht being sailed across the Atlantic by a solitary old man. The captain of the liner, to entertain the passengers, improvises a conversation with the solo traveler. Questions are asked and answered. The doctor asks, "Do you feel free?" The sailor answers, "Only that man is free who manages to overcome fear." The doctor dies. It turns out that the man who had been watching him had somehow sensed the doctor's fear and guilt and had been playing a game. In fact, they had never met before. Other revelations follow. In its fashion the journey on the ship analyzes and reassembles the lives of the travelers.

The production was simple. Kawalerowicz did not want to work in a studio, not even for such typical studio scenes as those taking place in passengers' cabins. Shooting was done quickly with few preparations. *A Chance Meeting on the Ocean* was shot in four weeks on the ocean liner *Batory* during one round trip from Gdynia to Montreal and back. Conditions for filming were less than ideal: no large spaces, no rehearsal time, and worst of all no control over the filmed material. The director was able to see the rushes only after the return and after all the filming had been concluded.

This had its consequences. The subject, which was supposed to have been developed like a delicate spider web of small crises, was not well articulated. Characters never reached clarity and so the main conflict was only partly visible on the surface. The reception accorded the film was no better than it deserved. At the same time, Poland could already feel the windshift of approaching crisis, and the screens were dominated by films with a strong social preoccupation. This was the time of the cinema of moral concern. *A Chance Meeting on the Ocean*, imperfectly put together from vagaries and psychological understatement, interested nobody.

Austeria

This was not at all the case with *Austeria* [1981], which has gotten a great deal of attention in and out of Poland. Kawalerowicz based it on an excellent novel of the same title written by Julian Stryjkowski (b. 1905), an old time Communist who returned to the memories of his childhood for his material and probably also to the folklore of his parents and friends. In the novel, Stryjkowski evoked brilliantly the life of Jews living in eastern Galicia before World War I. The story is centered around a Jewish inn, a place that focused the microcosm of a world that has since vanished. A diversity of characters, a multitude of subplots, and an originality of expression make the novel a treasure trove of East European Jewish civilization, blending culture, ethnography, spirituality, tragedy, comedy, faith, and skepticism.

Kawalerowicz came from the same region. He recalled that the population of his little town was 60 percent Jewish. The project was, for him, a trip into his own earliest memories. When he first attempted to bring it to fruition in the 1970s, having prepared a screenplay with Konwicki, the proposal was rejected. The subject of Jews in the territory of what is now the Soviet Union was avoided. Boundary legitimacy is always a sensitive issue, as is the treatment and mistreatment of Jews. The novel was available, true, but a film of large scope by a popular film director was another question. (There is something interesting implied here regarding the power of cinema.) In the winter of 1980–81, during a very liberal period, Kawalerowicz was given permission to make *Austeria*.

The screenplay was a large and somewhat metaphysical mural, at the center of which stood the character of Tag the innkeeper, but in a film as rich as *Austeria*, script is only a framework. The director spent a great deal of time and effort systematically accumulating Jewish cultural facts, songs, music, and mores, partly with the help of the Yiddish Theater in Warsaw. He searched earnestly for human faces that would authenticate the milieu. In an interview, Kawalerowicz reported on his progress at one point: "I am sitting and selecting human faces because I have to create an entirely different world. It can be created only from human faces, nothing else." He summed up the whole of his vision for the film in this way: "Writing the script with Stryjkowski and Konwicki, I fantasized a film about an extinct world, a community now dead, its culture, customs, habits, religion . . ." (*Kino*, no. 10, 1981).

The story itself takes place at the outbreak of World War I in Galicia, at the time part of the Austrian Empire, hard up against the border of Czarist Russia. Through this region the troops of both powers marched, and some of the first blood of the war was spilled here. Tag's inn, "Austeria," is where various people find themselves sheltered as hostilities break out: some small local merchants, craftsmen, a baroness, an officer, a group of orthodox Jews and a rabbi who pray and sing. The innkeeper, Tag (Franciszek Pieczka), is the character who links all those who have gathered to wait. The night of fearful visions seems interminable. At daybreak, the Jews want to celebrate their survival with a cleansing bath in a pond. They enter with the joyful salutation, "What a joy it is to be a Jew!" But, ironically, that heralds their end, as the pond turns red with their blood, ominously portending what will happen forty years later during the holocaust.

The depiction is stately, careful, sometimes like a ballet, enriched with elaborate detail. Kawalerowicz wrought a beautiful pageant replete with ethnic texture. In one respect he went across the grain of the novel. In the book, Tag looms larger. He is the repository of the book's philosophical and spiritual sense. The old Jew is at one and the same time a believer and a skeptic, a wise reckoner who can communicate universally: with orthodox Jews, with mystics, Austrians, Cossacks, fanatics. Kawalerowicz emphasized more the colorful richness, the particularity of this community, making Tag more of a witness and chorus and less of a mover of actions. The concept of spectacle, in every good meaning of the term, prevailed over a dramatic exposition of character. But because of that emphasis, the film has something in it of the discovery of a lost world of tradition, culture, and faith.

VII

Andrzej Munk:
The Perspective of a Skeptic

Andrzej Munk (1921–1961) came to full maturity during World War II and the German occupation. His aspirations and outlook crystallized during the first few postwar years. His intellectual sense of direction was predictable, which is to say his maturity grew logically out of his childhood and youth. Munk came from the Cracow intelligentsia, a special environment dominated by common sense, rationalism, and a certain skepticism to ideological and patriotic dogmas and excesses. Indeed, he was intellectually mischievous, ironic, wry, analytical.

Perhaps it was because of his temperament that he originally set out to become a cameraman and documentarist. He seemed not to be interested in the movie camera as an instrument for creating compositions. To him it was more an instrument by which to learn, examine, and analyze fact and reality, particularly social reality. The national myths, which Polish artists either praised or denounced (they were never indifferent!), were at first not within the range of Munk's interest. Only later did he offer his skeptical and ambiguous appraisal of the Polish historical myths.

At Lodz he was cameraman on two films before his independent debut as a documentarist took place in 1950. This was at the peak of the push for socialist realism, and his first films were affected by that esthetic doctrine: *It Started in Spain* (*Zaczęło się w Hiszpanii*) [1950]; *Science Closer to Art* (*Nauka bliżej życia*) [1951]; *Direction: Nowa Huta* (*Kierunek Nowa Huta*) [1951]; *"Fairy Tale" Visits Ursus* (*"Bajka" w Ursusie*) [1952]; and *Peasant Diaries* (*Pamiętniki chłopów*) [1953]. During those years documentary films were affected by socialist realism much the same way as feature films were affected —even more, since this was still the pretelevision period, and documentaries were the principal vehicles for propaganda and agitation. It was of course necessary to project victory of socialism over capitalism, the "new order" over the "old order," the exaltation of the working class, and so forth. A peculiar esthetic approach accompanied this purposiveness. Editing was to reflect points by making sharp contrasts. Overample verbal commentary was to be provided to insure proper clarity of message.

Munk attempted to avoid the artistic pitfalls of such an approach or to go around them. He tried an original idea with *Peasant Diaries(Pamiętniki chłopów)* [1953]. In the thirties some sociologists had collected statements from a number of peasants about what they saw as their situation. Munk sought out some of these people and confronted them with what they had said. Not surprisingly, they now had different things to say. Mostly the new interviews suggested that they felt better about their fate. No doubt, there was a great deal of truth in these statements, making the propaganda palatable. In any case, Munk managed to bring some freshness and variation to the rules he was pretty much required to follow.

Railwayman's Pledge

Munk's most important documentary, it is generally agreed, is *A Railwayman's Pledge (Kolejarskie słowo)* [1953]. It is a depiction of the journey of one train from a harbor to a coal mine, a report on the efforts of the many people who without fanfare or great notice make possible the normal functioning of transportation, a commonplace documentary subject. Munk was careful not to load the film with obtrusive commentary and also did not make insistent references to the effectiveness of the new social system. As should be, the film spoke for itself with its simplicity, even austerity, its keen observation, and in the use of real people as actors in playing out some parts within the documentary. (Using ordinary people instead of actors became characteristic of Munk, even while making feature films.) While it was a modest success as a documentary in absolute terms, it is worth noting as an example not only of Munk's basic filmmaking skills but also of his cleverness in avoiding and detouring the exigencies of heavy doctrine.

The Stars Must Shine

Munk's first feature film was *The Stars Must Shine (Gwiazdy muszą płonać)* [1954], although oddly, not everyone at the time knew it was a "feature film." The term was becoming ambiguous in relation to his films. He and Witold Lesiewicz (b. 1922), another documentarist, decided to cooperate on a project. Not contented with the idea of doing reportage, they each wrote a full-length screenplay that they intended to combine. Lesiewicz's story is sentimental but with a clever twist: an old miner who works far down in a coal mine is about to retire. His old horse, who is blind from having spent his life in the depths of the mine pulling carts loaded with coal, is going to be retired at the same time as his master. Finally, at the end of his days he will go to the surface to feel the sun which he cannot see and to breathe a different air.

The part written by Munk is about a coal mine in which the reserves are depleted. There must be a search to find new seams in formerly abandoned mines. On one level this concerns the stock socialist realist theme of increasing production, but really it turns into a nostalgic narrative of an expedition into a world full of remnants and souvenirs of other times, a film about generations of miners who spent so much of their lives far below the surface of the earth.

The finished product, made by two documentarists, had a number of documentary elements, but finally it is a staged feature film using as actors the miners themselves. These amateurs were not at all a disadvantage. Through editing, Munk captured that which was most genuine, most effective. This authenticity, enhanced by the gloomy setting in the mines, established a mood of simple nobility under awful circumstances. Something heroic was evoked and this evocation added grace to the believable people and the skillful dramaturgy. In short, it was a successful feature, or documentary for that matter, an accomplishment to remark upon just as the esthetic precepts were changing and restraints and constraints beginning to dissipate. At about the same time, during the winter of 1954–55, Andrzej Wajda was beginning work on *Generation*.

Munk next made a small piece entitled *Sunday Morning* (*Niedzielny poranek*) [1955], subtitled "Scherzo." It too was a mix of fiction and nonfiction in the form of a lyrical, lighthearted view of a city as watched through the windows of a bus. Full of warmth, it is hard to say what is plain observation and what has been staged by the director. Witty, light commentary made *Sunday Morning* a pleasant trifle. While the film is devoid of any great significance, it and Munk were beginning to get attention, and he took prizes for it at Edinburgh and Mannheim.

Blue Cross

During the same year Munk made a much more serious film, *Blue Cross* (*Błękitny krzyż*) [1955]. It was about something that took place in the Tatra Mountains in the winter of 1945. A group of local mountaineers accomplished an incredible feat. From an underground hospital in still-occupied Slovakia, they brought some sick and wounded partisans through German lines and across mountain ranges to Zakopane, a Polish mountain resort.

Munk's initial goal was to make a documentary, a journalistic report, but his intentions took a turn. He wrote a screenplay with an outline of action, formulated characters, including suggestions of psychological motivation, even a subplot love story. Was this to be Munk's first unambiguous feature film? Not quite.

As in *The Stars Must Shine*, he decided to use people who had actually participated in the occurrence or whose families were involved, engaging mountain guides from local families and only one professional actor, Wojciech Siemion. The film was shot at its true location. In every way, Munk tried to stay as close to the facts as he could. The result was, once again, an interesting hybrid film, either documentary or feature or both—or neither, which was the point made by the critics who received *Blue Cross* without enthusiasm.

The main point to consider, however, is not genre but quality. How successful was it in creating emotional response, projecting dramatic force? The film was only partly effective, marred by some narrative inconsistency and naive staging. Another serious flaw was the disproportion between the faces and gestures of the mountaineers compared to the elaborate acting of the one professional in the cast. The behavioral patterns of the mountain men take away from the credibility of the professional actor, while he on the other hand calls attention to the acting deficiencies of these simple people. The film is only of historical interest. He tells of something that took place, filming it very skillfully in its splendid mountain setting, but not extricating from the events their implicit drama or creating clear and intriguing characters. He quoted the past but did not recreate it.

What of the experiment in mixing genres? Was Munk deliberately trying to break molds? Was this a conscious esthetic experiment in response to the new and fluid situation in the film industry? Or was the form largely dictated by the fact that Munk worked at the Warsaw documentary studio? Certainly he was aware of the fact that he was pushing against the edges of the documentary form, but maybe only because he had a hankering to make a feature film. *Blue Cross* was not a pioneer film or a new form, certainly not a Polish equivalent of the first neo-realist Italian productions as was postulated by some critics. Nonetheless, Munk would push further in the direction of feature work, as in his next film, *Man on the Track* [1956].

Man on the Track

For this film, the writer Jerzy Stefan Stawiński had a straightforward idea: the body of an old railroad man is found on the tracks. Was it murder, suicide, or accident? Maybe even sabotage? From this he did a script and presented it to the cinema administration. Stawiński was told that the idea was most unusual and irregular. He was informed that in the Polish Peoples Republic old railwaymen did not, as a rule, perish under trains. In any case, he was told it was not a fit subject for a film.

Munk read the script and immediately took an active interest. Stawiński recollects: "Munk found the key to my story, three reports of the event often contradicting one another, filed by three people in the case. On the basis of these reports the audience was to draw its own conclusion. Inspired by Munk's suggestions I set to work. A month later the committee of the Central Office of Cinematography accepted our screenplay, at the same time warning us not to bend anything out of shape. It turns out that Munk shaped his material so carefully the villain was not the station master, the committee's candidate for bad guy, but the system in which the railwaymen worked. This was a deft political twist" (*Andrzej Munk*, a collection of essays about him, [Warsaw, 1964]). Munk began shooting in April 1956. The premiere took place at the beginning of 1957. These dates are important for understanding the political context within which the film found itself.

As the movie starts, a spirited discussion is taking place in a railroad station office concerning the death of Orzechowski, an old engine driver whose body was found on the tracks. Participating are his co-workers, supervisors, and the authorities. Who was this man? What was he up to? The first version is that of the stationmaster, Orzechowski's boss. As a man of these "new times," his picture of Orzechowski is negative and prejudiced. Orzechowski was, after all, a product of capitalist times, an old man who felt threatened by the young and the new order of things. On the verge of forced retirement he was looking for revenge, perhaps had sabotage in mind. Orzechowski's young helper offered his version, which is quite different, more intricate psychologically, an ambiguous picture of the old man. According to him, the man was a professional but now felt alienated, lacked confidence. For this reason he did not participate in labor competition. Perhaps he saw his retirement as a result of a conspiracy among the younger men and his own supervisors. The third version, that of a lineman, seems most damning for Orzechowski. But Munk shows on the screen something other than what the words of the lineman present. By direction and editing he makes it look as if the old man died trying to prevent a railway catastrophe. The viewing audience learns this, but those gathered in the film to discuss the case have no inkling. The last version is a recapitulation by the representative of the authorities. It is, as far as it can be, a coherent reconstruction. When the man finishes his version there is a long silence. One of the participants, moving restlessly about the room, goes to the window and opens it violently saying, "It is stifling here." This phrase entered the colloquial language as an expression that typified, in its understated way, life during the Stalinist era.

The screenplay of *Man on the Track* was an act of courage in the fall of 1955. It challenged basic doctrine. The old railwayman, product of capitalist times, appears as the best and noblest character to be considered in the story, while the younger products of the "new times," as well as the station master representing a kind of authority, appear shortsighted. However, by the time the film was actually shown in January 1957, just a few months after the October 1956 events, it was not a political sensation. So fast had the atmosphere changed! One critic even complained that it seemed like a late echo of socialist realism! Munk himself admitted the loss of some effect. "We meant our film to start a certain discussion which at the time of the premiere proved to be outdated. This was a reason for optimism" (quoted by S. Janicki, in *Andrzej Munk*, [Warsaw, 1964].

Man on the Track may have been out of phase as far as political timing is concerned, but that does not cancel its value at all. It was instrumental in questioning socialist realism by challenging it in one of the most sensitive areas, the workplace, the locus of production. The positive socialist realist message here was inverted: In the struggle of the "new" with the "old," the new (socialist) way did not necessarily compare favorably. The implications and consequences were extensive. First, *Man on the Track* proved to the industry and the audience that it was possible to make a film about labor problems. There were so many film failures due to socialist realism, no one would have believed it feasible to be forthright and candid. It was a very sensitive area. The result of *Man on the Track* was that other films would now be made on the theme. Second, the story was told in such a way as to challenge the notion of an objective report. Munk's technique of comparing different versions reflected the need for truthful search and pluralistic orientation, something that made dogmatists quite uncomfortable. Reality was perhaps not an objective entity. "This concept of narrative, in which the author's point of view was not imposed on the viewer, was meant to respect reality (as André Bazin understood it), on the one hand; and on the other hand to include the viewer in the active process of its interpretation" (Nurczynska-Fidelska, Eweline, *Andrzej Munk* [Cracow, 1985]; our translation). This process of search for reality was reflected in Munk's use of a relevant photographic style. "The camera wandering around the set continuously revealing different perspectives of people, objects, landscapes, and interiors, allowed the director to remain beyond the story, leaving it to the viewer" Jackiewicz, Aleksander, in *Andrzej Munk*, a collection of essays about him, [Warsaw, 1964].

Obviously Munk was not the first director to play with reality by using different versions of the same event or of the same story. There had been Welles's *Citizen Kane* and Kurosawa's *Rashomon*. Munk surely knew these films and it is not unlikely that he was influenced. In any case, in the Polish environment the formula proved seminal. It introduced ideas about objectivism, cognitive skepticism, and it forced intellectual reflection. It set aside not only the worn-out models of socialist realism, but challenged as well the cinema of sentiment, emotion, and national myth. Munk offered Poland and this quarter of Europe a new formula.

Man on the Track met with an enthusiastic reception from the critics who noticed at once its innovative form and who also recognized the message announcing political changes that made it possible to have something other than a homogeneous view of social reality. In other socialist countries the film was received without enthusiasm. Presented at the festival in Karlove Vary in 1957, it did not gain any significant award although it was the most important film there. But it succeeded in stirring up a discussion among the Czech critics, even though it would be some years yet before the atmosphere there would be such as to appreciate it as an example perhaps to learn from.

This propensity of Munk to explore both the perception and the meaning of events, a task in accord with his skeptical philosophical viewpoint, led him to make films that were inevitably compared with those of Wajda. Was Wajda's *Canal* critical or apologetic concerning the events depicted? Were they heroic even in their futility? Stawiński's script for *Canal* stressed the futility. Certainly as an active participant in the events depicted he had a right to his viewpoint. But Wajda's romantic directorial style and outlook gave the production heroic and affirmative meaning, not completely but mostly so. It is an open question as to whether or not Munk saw himself as part of a debate on the question of heroism and its role in Polish destiny, but his viewpoint contrasted with Wajda's, inviting the notion of dialogue of philosophy and styles between Wajda and Munk.

Eroica

This was encouraged by the fact that Munk used the writing of this same Stawiński, whom Wajda had worked with on *Canal* and whom Munk had worked with in *Man on the Track*, to write *Eroica* (since the theme of heroism was in the air). The title was borrowed from Beethoven and the three separate stories from which the film was to be composed were given musical story titles.

The first piece of the film, "The Nun," subtitled "Con bravura," is about a woman courier in the underground who is trying to get to Hungary disguised as a nun. She fails and dies. Neither Munk nor Stawiński were satisfied with this portion. It was not a bad story, but—as they saw it—less important than the other two. As a result, Munk excised the story from the film, and Stawiński omitted it from his published fictional version. In 1972 the whole version, as a curiosity including "The Nun," was presented on television as part of a special historical program.

The film as originally released began with the second tale, "The Hungarians: Scherzo alla polacca." During the Warsaw Uprising of 1944, an ordinary man called Dzidziuś finds himself in the center of the city when the uprising starts. His wife has remained in their elegant house outside town. The man, a cynical but rather nice operator, uninvolved in any patriotic cause, joins one of the fighting units without enthusiasm. When subjected to military drill he decides that it makes no sense at all and manages to escape through two lines, Polish and German, to reach his house, where he finds his delectable wife in a flirtation with a Hungarian officer attached to the German army with his artillery team. At this time, the Hungarians were reluctant allies of the Germans and were trying to figure a way out of the war, which the Germans were in any case, in the process of losing. The officer offers Dzidziuś an important mission, to go back again through the lines and carry the Polish leadership a message: the Hungarian detachment will join the uprising and contribute their weapons if the Poles will recognize them as allies when the Red Army arrives. Dzidziuś, quite annoyed but somewhat duty bound, has to make two more trips through the lines as a sort of courier carrying messages which appear to be absurd. The insurgent army leaders had no contact with the approaching Red Army and were apprehensive concerning their own fate. When Dzidziuś returns with a Polish emissary it is soon apparent that nothing will come of these talks. Dzidziuś is relieved to believe that the nightmare is over. Yet when the emissary returns to the city where the hopeless fight continues, Dzidziuś inexplicably follows him.

The atmosphere of the narration of this story is comic. Dzidziuś is himself a comic type, a recognizable Warsaw character figure: funny, likable, cynical, a small-time operator, a drinker—as if composed by a Polish Damon Runyon. His adventures are farcical. His unorthodox role as negotiator during such critical circumstances lends incongruity to events. His trip through the lines with a bottle of Vodka becomes broad comedy when he discards the bottle and hears a metallic clunk. The bottle had hit a passing German tank. What a wry comparison to the actual and deadly use of Molotov cocktails during the uprising! In comparison to *Canal*, for example, here are no dark and gloomy sewers; here are fields on the outskirts, ownerless chickens wandering, children playing at war games! The tone created is cheerful and comic, but also scornful and challenging. Only in the queer ending, when the street-wise con man decides to return—who knows why?—to the battle is there anything pathetic, and possibly slightly heroic. Even this Munk presents only half-seriously, maintaining his mask of skepticism.

The second story of *Eroica*, "The Escape: Ostinato Lugubre," is placed in a POW camp, where officers of the uprising were sent after it collapsed in October 1944. There they meet Polish POWs from the 1939 campaign who have been in the camp for five years. They are tired, neurotic, argumentative. The Warsaw insurrectionists also have their traumas, but what keeps all of them together is the example of a certain courageous officer, the only one in the camp who managed to escape and who must, they think, even now be fighting the Germans somewhere. This lieutenant Zawistowski (Tadeusz Łomnicki) is a symbol of courage and a legend for the POWs. It turns out that Zawistowski is hiding in the attic of the same barracks in a water tank. The few who know about it feed him secretly, not wanting to ruin the legend for the rest of the prisoners. When he dies of exhaustion, those who knew about him get the Germans to get rid of the water tank. So the legend survived.

Told slowly and calmly this tale has a completely different tone from "Scherzo alla pollaca," as the musical term does indeed suggest. This one is "Ostinato lugubre." The hiding and the death are not funny, albeit grotesque.

The tone of visualization and dramatization is serious, reflective, with each scene carefully planned.

This esthetic mix in *Eroica* may be startling when experienced, but despite the difference in rhythms and tones, both parts of *Eroica* are dominated by a realistic approach. The characters in both stories are developed credibly, without any heroic magnification and without caricature. The events are kept within probability in spite of the irony implicit in both plots and their premises. In addition to the realism, what truly and permanently combines and gives coherence to the two parts is not so much the style as the outlook, the philosophical and historical evaluation. That special intellectual quality is what puts *Eroica* among the outstanding cultural events following October 1956.

It is worth considering again the very special topic of heroism and its thematic implications in Polish culture. Why was the subject so sensitive and painful? First take into consideration the particular history of Poland, its many defenses against invasions, the loss of its statehood for 150 years during a period marked by numerous patriotic insurrections, the retrieval of its independence. Next, factor in the defeat it suffered in 1939, only to be followed by renewed resistance and struggle. Consider that nationalism, patriotism, and heroic suffering played roles in all these epochs. Then remember that the valiant struggle of the Home Army, the largest resistance group, was presented falsely, libeled, and those who took part in that struggle were even victimized during the Stalinist period, and it is no wonder that many people waited for some satisfaction to their sensibilities, waited for compensation, as it were. Some justice came finally. Politicians made gestures of appreciation, mostly reluctantly, more to bring reconciliation than to give credit.

It fell to the artists to portray glory or to criticize the sway it had upon Poles. For that reason, as indicated in the chapter on Wajda, when *Canal*, a threnody to the Warsaw insurrectionists, appeared it was received as a tribute to heroes. *Eroica*, released eleven months after *Canal*, caricatured heroism. Where *Canal* offered romanticism, *Eroica* offered skepticism. This skepticism, sometimes called realism, was and had been the other side of the heroic coin. Romanticism praised the heroic fight, regardless of success; the realistic approach praised a positivistic attitude of adjustment. This positivism had once been known as "organic work" and denoted meliorism.

There was obviously a contradiction here, but each attitude was also a complement to the other. Positivism and organic work seemed to be the dominant attitude just after 1945, which is not surprising since the material and economic circumstances were such as to stress accommodation to political circumstances and improvement of physical conditions. But in 1956, after the riots in Poznan, the dialectic was reborn as a debate. Wajda and Munk reminded the nation of both attitudes, the romantic and the positivist.

Canal, by recalling the uprising reproduced a sense of historical sacrifice. *Eroica*, while admitting to a certain heroic impulse, a kind of consciousness of heroism, allows it little credit for common sense. The films are not pure opposites; they carry ambiguities and complexities. They carry on the debate of the Polish dilemma not so much by presenting polarities as by presenting complementary versions. To make a point, they represent the yin and yang of the Polish dilemma.

In 1958 Munk allowed himself more exercise in following his musical instincts. He made a film based on an idea by the composer Andrzej Markowski called *A Walk in the Old Town*, a portrayal of a girl, a student of music, who walks along the narrow streets of Warsaw's Old Town registering everything with her preternatural hearing: street noises, laughter, a cobbler's hammer, an organ being tuned, airplanes overhead, the scratching of a broom. What might be cacophony is composed into a special concert of actuality, an arranged piece of contemporary music. A perfect assembly of sound and photography, *A Walk in the Old Town* was a success at many European festivals concerned with documentaries and film experiments.

Bad Luck

Entering the current of discussions that occurred in 1959 and concerned "the Polish School," "Polish destiny," and the meaning of history, Munk had the help again of Jerzy S. Stawiński, who was making another dissection of Polish myths. His story "The Six Incarnations of Jan Piszczyk" was about a typical loser carried along on the tides of modern times, never coming up on the winning end of things. It is somewhat reminiscent of the first part of *Eroica*. The model was Voltaire's character Candide, a simple man baffled by life and history and unable to find a solid place for himself. Munk's filmic version, *Bad Luck* (more accurately *Cockeyed Luck*, Zezowate szczęście) [1960], consists of several long sequences from the life and times of the hero, Jan Piszczyk, played by the famous actor Bogumil Kobiela, himself a tragic victim of life's twists. The sequences are from the 1930s, 1940s, and 1950s. In the early episodes the hero is a valiant and enthusiastic boy scout who loves the military drill, plays the bugle, participates fully, and for all this experiences his first defeat. This sequence is told farcically and in the convention of the silent movies.

Later on in his student life Piszczyk becomes involved in anti-Semitic demonstrations at the university. Because of his prominent nose he is himself taken for a Jew, so as compensation he enrolls as a member of a progovernment youth group and becomes a fiery nationalist. This also ends badly when he botches a political demonstration and earns contempt.

When the war breaks out, his great time of testing is at hand and he dreams of becoming a hero. During the turmoil he searches for his military unit, but when he reaches his barracks he finds them empty. He hurries into his uniform, gazes at himself in the mirror, and sees in the mirror a German soldier behind him. In the prison camp he postures as a heroic officer cadet in the 1939 campaign. That too doesn't work for long. He is unmasked as a parvenu civilian, an impostor, and not a hero. More shame for Piszczyk, who is then detailed to work in a German armaments factory where he earnestly carries huge shells about but is so clumsy the Germans decide it is safest to release him and send him home. The factory scenes may owe something to Chaplin's *Modern Times*.

In occupied Warsaw, our hero pretends to be an officer cadet who has escaped from a POW camp, thereby earning involvement in the underground and the flirtatious attention of an old girlfriend who admires his heroic pose. Again the situation disintegrates because he is recognized as a man who has never been active in the army and has never, in fact, escaped from any prison camp.

Finding himself in Crakow after the war, he opens a kind of detective office for private investigations. Given the political situation in Poland during those years this is automatically funny, and of course he ends up getting arrested. Finally, in the 1950s he works as a bureaucrat in some large unidentifiable in stitution as a most loyal and eager servant. Naturally there is a catastrophe. At the end we learn that the film was in the form of a long confession, a retrospective narrative, made to a man who turns out to be the warden of a prison. Piszczyk begs the warden to leave him behind bars, protected from the currents of history.

The tone of *Bad Luck* is often farcical and sometimes bitterly realistic, a mixture of various conventions from silent movies to socialist realism. The mix is not wholly a successful one and is exacerbated by an erratic rhythm. Sometimes the pace of narrative is very quick; sometimes it drags. Unlike *Eroica*, it does not possess a common denominator of style. Nor does it help that the same premise is repeated over and over, albeit the results are often funny. Even the acting of Bogumil Kobiela is not all that it should be, with all due respect to an outstanding comedian. His character as he created him is so long on caricature that he tends to become a bit monotonous. In Kobiela's interpretation, Piszczyk was not a pathetic and comic victim of history as completely as he should have been. Instead, he was merely an awkward simpleton.

Nonetheless, *Bad Luck* was an important film, not so much esthetically as polemically—it contributed to the great debate about history and patriotism. What was its meaning? Consider again the comparison with the character Candide. Candide was simple, unsophisticated, and likable withal, not a mere caricature. He was not at fault because the world he lived in was absurd. In that fashion, Voltaire indicted his epoch, his world, his society. *Bad Luck* also includes social criticism and a wry view of history, a history so changeable that a man like Piszczyk cannot adjust. Mostly, however, the film is a lampoon of a man who is an officious conformist, whose bad luck is caused by his fickle zealousness, his truckling to the times, his stupidity, his entanglement in national legends and myths, in short, his emotional instability.

In this sense the message of *Bad Luck* comes close to being the most critical view of "the Polish character," a view parallel to that of Witold Gombrowicz, a prominent twentieth-century Polish writer, in his novel *Ferdydurke* (1937) and later in his memoirs and the dramatic pieces he wrote in exile. It is an uncompromisingly bitter analysis: Poles, their culture, their thinking, their politics are jejune and undeveloped, tangled up in myth and legend like the world as thought of by adolescents. This imagined world, according to Gombrowicz, makes it impossible for Poles to evaluate reality properly. This is pretty much what *Bad Luck* was communicating in its popular, comic, somewhat awkward way. The character of Piszczyk has something in it of the provincial Polish would-be patriot, always defeated, starting anew, and turned upside down again. In this sense, *Bad Luck* by Munk and Stawiński was an important addition to the ongoing polemics.

It is no surprise that *Bad Luck* aroused some controversy when it opened in April 1960. While the public received it enthusiastically, the critics differed and quarreled with it and among themselves. Individual opinions themselves were ambiguous and ambivalent, for example, Andrzej Kijowski's: "I saw a film that was at once praiseworthy and wrongheaded. Quite simply, it is impossible to create a character who can function as a hero of our tragic history and be at the same time a scoundrel who ridicules that history. ("Polska szkoła masochizmu," in *Przegląd Kulturalny*, no. 17, 1960). It is all part of the old argument outlined elsewhere in this book, one that involved, among others, Gombrowicz, Konwicki, Miłosz, and Wajda, as well as Stawiński and Munk. A succinct passage in one of the volumes of *Historia Filmu Polskiego* (*The History of Polish Film*, Jerzy Toeplitz, ed., vol. 4 [Warsaw, 1980]) summarizes it thus: "The story of the hero of *Bad Luck* and his mishaps, played against a real historical background . . . is an attempt—not always well-aimed or intellectually accurate—to explain that, in Poland, special circumstances and historical disasters require a commitment of one's self and one's attitude, and require the making of value-laden decisions. Piszczyk is unable to make real choices . . . and he lacks identity and character" (our translation).

The Passenger

In 1959 Munk happened to hear on the radio a story written by Zofia Posmysz-Piasecka entitled "The Passenger." This was the beginning of a project. The story captured Munk's imagination. In it the action takes place on board an Atlantic steamer. A middle-aged German couple, Liza and Walter, are going from Hamburg to a port in the United States. She notices in the crowd a certain woman, and this engenders anxiety. Little by little as Liza discusses things with her husband, we learn more and more about her past. She was, it turns out, a supervisor at Auschwitz. The woman she noticed reminded her of one of the victims she had met at the camp. The secrets that surround her past, her sense of guilt and uncertainty, her desire to excuse herself—all of these build up a conflict within herself and between herself and her husband, a "good German." There is a personal crisis, yet there is never a determination whether or not the passenger was the person from Auschwitz.

Munk asked Zofia Posmysz-Piasecka to write a television script from which he made a television drama in October 1960. The basic story had been expanded, new characters introduced, and the husband-wife conflict sharpened. While revealing that Liza's past has a moral dimension, there is also the consideration that it might endanger Walter's career. In the television versions Auschwitz memories and images were only verbalized, never visualized. The story focused on Germans of the postwar world, using memories of Auschwitz as a trigger for the psychology of the drama.

This was changed in Munk's film version, made in collaboration with the same author. In the film, the past is the focus as Auschwitz is visualized, and the relationship between Liza and the passenger, Marta, is precisely defined and extended, with scenes on board the ship serving as narrative framework. Munk began shooting in 1961 with cameraman Krzysztof Winiewicz and documentary director Andrzej Brzozowski. The retrospective part concerning the prison camp was addressed first, with the result that this portion seemed to take control of the whole story. The relationship between Liza and her victim, Marta, took on greater weight and ambiguity, morally and psychologically. The shipboard contemporary scenes suffered. Munk shot only several thousand feet focusing on that part and did not seem satisfied at all. It seemed certain that the narrative frame was going to be changed, but it was not certain how.

On September 20, 1961, having finished shooting the prison-camp sequences, Munk was driving back from Lodz to Warsaw and was killed in a head-on collision with a truck. He left an unfinished film and an unclear screenplay. In 1963, after several attempts to reconstruct the material, Munk's friends and colleagues, Andrzej Brzozowski, director Witold Lesiewicz, and the writer Wiktor Woroszylski figured out what to do with the project. The decision was not to add anything new, but to limit the work to editing the Auschwitz flashback and framing the shipboard sequences as narrative frame. They added a narrative commentary by Woroszylski that explains the film and its unfinished nature. In short, they were to let the public see the film as it was made, leaving its ultimate meaning up in the air. In that form, the film was released on September 20, 1963, and created a stir. It was deemed important enough to be presented at the festivals at Cannes and Venice. There is no way to speculate profitably concerning what the film might have become. We have only what we have, the assembled aborted version.

The film begins descriptively and somewhat chaotically with Liza's memories evoked by her meeting with Marta. Liza is played by Aleksandra Śląska, Marta by Anna Ciepielewska. It is a brief picturization, almost symbolic of the horror: the selection lines, naked prisoners, SS soldiers with dogs, a prisoner's body hanging on the electrified wires. Later there is another flashback, a more articulated retrospection of as much of the story as Liza is able to tell her husband. It includes only what to her is permissible, conceivable, and self-justifying. Finally in the third flashback, which is a filmic internal monologue, we obtain the full picture of the strange relationship between Liza and Marta cast against the background of the death camp.

The peculiar story of the two women emerges in this fashion—the story of a captor and her victim and a search for some motivation to their behavior. Despite her job, Liza wants to help Marta in some way, maybe even save her. At first Marta accepts the help and through it manages to prolong survival. At the same time she feels there is something ambivalent about the help offered her by one whose function is to be a tormentor, and suspects Liza is searching for some kind of forgiveness, some sort of moral alibi for her position. For Marta, Liza is part of a heinous system and deserves no alibi. A struggle commences when Liza understands that Marta does not want to accept her help, help tendered in spite of Liza's official function. An unexpected occurrence brings the final irony: Marta, the victim, feels free, while Liza, the tormentor, is even more deeply caught up as a captive of the system.

Two things are especially worth noting. First there is Munk's cool, even cold, sternness in his creation of the background. There seems to be no affection, no sympathy even, as he depicts the appearance of the camp, the daily routine, the suffering. It is a calculated coldness that by its very nature horrifies more than a portrayal in which the director's sympathies are apparent. His approach resembles the dispassionate prose of Tadeusz Borowski (discussed in relation to Wajda's *Landscape after Battle*) and the ironic distance of Arnost Lustig's concentration camp stories. The second thing to notice, and it is not unrelated to the first point, is that Munk has created an ambivalent rather than a clear picture from the moral point of view. This is quite unlike most death camp portrayals, and again its effect is not to excuse anything but to go deeper into what happened, in this case between these two people. It is a search for the motivations governing human behavior. The drama does not unfold as a conflict between a psychopathic tormentor and a martyr, but as a psychological phenomenon that may occur, does occur, between people, irrespective of the expected. In this film, Auschwitz was shown not as mass madness, animalism, collective paranoia, but as a place where things happened between individual people. Munk's accomplishment glosses over none of the horror and, at the same time, gives depth to individuals caught therein.

Its originality and profundity, the quality of its mise-en-scène, and—yes—the shadow of the director's untimely death, made *The Passenger* a work unique in the history of Polish cinema, and indeed all cinema. Munk the rationalist, Munk the sceptic, showed in this film a deeper quality than heretofore—which is not to diminish *Eroica* or *Man on the Track*. Even while his style remained cool and objective, he seemed desperately to want to discover the mystery of human suffering and human values under extreme tension.

VIII

Andrzej Wajda:
The Essential Pole

The Polish film director who is best known outside his own country is curiously the one who is most especially and particularly "Polish," whose work is most deeply and broadly related to the history and literature of Poland or directly involved in contemporary and topical social and political issues. With special exceptions, Wajda does not strain to capture universal themes so much as he strains to play upon those that relate to the nation's consciousness.

Wajda hears at once the echoes of his country's history and the sounds of its life. He listens for the tones, harmonious or dissonant, and thus captures his special cinematic music. His identity as a Pole has only from time to time permitted him to detach himself enough to make something like a calm meditation on human existence.

Certainly Wajda's life helped determine his special personality. He was born on March 6, 1926, in a small town called Suwalki in the northeast of Poland, where his father, a professional soldier, was stationed. After one hundred and fifty years of foreign occupation of Poland ended in 1918, Polish patriotism had special energy, nowhere more apparent than in the army. "God and Country" was the ubiquitous motto. The army thought of itself as the guardian of this sentiment. In such an atmosphere of commitment we find part of the genesis of Wajda's sensibility. Another part of it, the heroic and romantic part, is adumbrated by other memories: "I was brought up in a cavalry barracks, and I can remember watching gun carriages drawn by three pairs of horses come hurtling toward me at a gallop" (*Kino*, no. 1, 1968; our translation). Patriotism, its glories and dedications, left a mark on the work of this great director.

When World War II broke out in September 1939, Wajda was thirteen years old. His father was killed during the war and his mother made her way to Radom with her sons. There, south of Warsaw, young Andrzej worked as a manual laborer, went to school, and participated in underground activities of the Home Army. Significantly he also took up drawing and painting, and even involved himself in the restoration of some church art. Located as he was in Radom, he missed the epic event so many of his friends knew at first hand, an event he would nonetheless pay attention to in his filmmaking, namely the Warsaw Uprising of 1944.

After the war he became a student at the Academy of Fine Arts in Crakow. It is an open question as to whether he doubted his own ability as a painter, but he left the academy in 1949. He took away with him a painter's eye, which influenced the way he composed pictures on the screen and mastered so well the visuality of cinema. From the academy he transferred to the newly opened film school in Lodz. There he made several documentary pieces and some feature studies, which brought him to the attention of Aleksander Ford, who chose him as his assistant in the making of *Five Boys from Barska Street*. Ford also made it possible for this young talented man, with little experience, to make his own independent, full-length film in 1954 and 1955.

A Generation (1955)

A Generation was based on the novel by Bohdan Czeszko whose experiences during the occupation were similar in ways to Wajda's own. The story, in fact, concerns the experiences of boys growing up at the time the Germans controlled and ran the country. One might have thought that Wajda intended yet another film on what was a frequently used theme. The background of the story is a working-class neighborhood in Warsaw; the focus is on two boys growing up under these conditions (acted by Tadeusz Janczar and Tadeusz Łomnicki). One of them quickly joins the underground, the other only after some hesitation. The latter dies tragically trying to bring help to the Jewish ghetto at the time of the ghetto uprising. Woven into the plot is the story of an activist girl (played by Urszula Modrzyńska) who is also killed. On the surface this resembles many other films, the more so because Czeszko's novel largely followed the political formula of the early fifties.

But *A Generation* turned out to be not only the beginning of a great career, it was also—in spite of its formulaic basis—to be a turning point in the history of Polish postwar cinema. Roman Polański, who played a minor role in the film, recalled it this way: "For us it was a film of tremendous importance. All of Polish cinema was beginning with it. It was a marvellous experience . . . the whole crew was very young. Wajda was very young and sincere. We worked night and day. Wajda believed in what he was doing. This was something utterly new in Poland (it was still the time of Stalinism). That film was different, young" (from an interview with Bolesław Michałek, quoted in Trinon, Hadelin, *Andrzej Wajda* [Paris, 1964]; our translation). What was it that set this film apart?

To begin with, the characters were understated, certainly not statuesque as was fashionable in the early fifties. Wajda is known to have observed that if there was anything heroic about the characters they must have been unaware of it. Motivation was somehow differently treated. In a departure from what was usually being done, an internal dilemma was created resulting in a suicide, something not at all in keeping with socialist realism where ambivalence was unacceptable. But the movie did more than challenge the rickety standards of an absurd doctrine.

A chemistry occurred in the making of *A Generation* that went to the heart of filmmaking. Perhaps part of the reason was that all the makers were of approximately the same age—from the writer (Czeszko), to the director of photography (Jerzy Lipman), to the composer of music (Andrzej Markowski), to the actors. They were young and enthusiastic, entering the studio without the reactions and prejudices of the older generation. They had evolved new viewpoints, were fond of realism and neo-realism, and explored the medium searching for a reflection of their own experience.

A Generation, in its particular simplicity, owed something to neo-realism. The staging and settings avoided old habits. Every possible advantage was taken of rain, cloudy days, atmosphere that would contribute to a new sense of reality on the screen. To avoid the studio effect, studio work was treated merely as auxiliary help. Likewise, in order to avoid artificiality, the dialogue was kept free of hackneyed slogans and tendentious phrasing. And, finally, the acting was marked by natural and moving performances on the part of almost every actor. Something came into being in *A Generation* that, outside of Italy, had not yet been realized anywhere in Europe.

Superimposed upon the film and its neo-realistic character was the particular style of Andrzej Wajda. That included a striving for maximum dramatic effect in every scene, every confrontation among the characters. It also included the visual intensity that was characteristic of his work all through the years, displaying his painterly artist's eye. And in the film there appeared, here and there, some symbols. That symbolism would become more dense over the years. Some of these characteristics would evolve so markedly that eventually the terms "expressionistic" and "baroque" would be used in connection with Wajda's work.

The reception of the film on the part of the cultural authorities was far from positive. Wajda remembered that he was charged with choosing an environment "resembling a lumpen-proletariat rather than the true healthy Polish working class" (interview in *Positif* (Paris), no. 21, 1957; our translation). He was also berated for using too much violence and brutality. Nonetheless, the film was released and the premiere took place on January 25, 1955.

The critics were positive but their approval likewise was not enthusiastic; in fact, there was a mixed reaction. Some were perturbed by remnants of socialist realism in the story—this was just the period during which that formulaic approach was under challenge. On the other hand, critics who were more officially oriented reproached Wajda for his use of neo-realism, a style that did not enjoy official approval. From a later perspective, the review that best summarized what this film accomplished was written by Antoni Boh-dziewicz, a director himself as well as a professor at the Lodz school and one of Wajda's mentors, who, incidentally, seldom wrote reviews. In this case, Bohdziewicz wrote: "Real life has been seen upon the screen in place of stale pap" (*Lodz Literacka*, II/III, 1955; our translation).

Canal

Wajda's next project was in collaboration with the writer Jerzy S. Stawiński, a man who exerted an inordinate influence on Polish cinema in the late fifties. Stawiński had been an officer in the Home Army. One of his experiences consisted of taking his unit from a southern district of Warsaw to the center of the city during the uprising by going through the sewers, or—as they are called in Polish—canals. He described this in a story that was later changed into the screenplay *Canal* (*Kanał*) [1957]. It had obviously seemed like a fitting vehicle for Wajda. It was full of threat, despair, daring, and fear, no doubt appealing to Wajda's sense of drama. The underground world of sewers held a suggestion of Dante's Inferno, lending symbolic consciousness that stood in visual counterpoint to the fighting scenes on the surface. There was also the theme that would continue to attract this director—the national experience, in this case exemplified by the legend-making Warsaw Uprising of 1944 during which character was determined and the fate of the nation formulated. It was 1956 and Wajda easily received approval to make the film Stalinism had swept aside. The time was propitious to address the subject of the uprising boldly and honestly, a subject previously either ignored or condemned.

Canal is the story of one unit of insurgents that receives orders to withdraw from its position and move out through the sewers. It is divided into three subplots connected with three separate groups. None of them succeeds in reaching their destination. One couple makes it to a barred exit to the river, trapped within view of the lovely river landscape. A second group is caught by the Germans. The third group—which includes the commander—disintegrates along the way. The officer makes it to the surface, but upon discovery that he has been betrayed by a cowardly sergeant and has lost track of his unit, he shoots the sergeant and returns to the sewers alone.

The story posed a challenge to the dramatic skill of the still young and relatively inexperienced director. In preproduction notes Wajda wrote: "The picture must swell in time with the action of the story and so the whole of the first part . . . ought to be made as documentary-like as possible: long takes, traveling shots, long shots, no close-ups. Part two: the images intensify, flickering lights from flames, close-ups, highlight the church with the charred statues, the wounded. The Dantesque descent into the sewers. Part three: the sewers. The descent and first part normal, then especially in the close-up scenes, a disturbing depth of focus (double exposure). The emergence from the sewers thoroughly jolting and an uncanny establishing shot" (*Teatr i Film*, no. 1, vol. II, 1957; our translation). Thus the esthetic key was established at the start, a progression from plain realism to a visual symbolism, from details of the war to a game with fate.

With his second film, Wajda demonstrated the depth and breadth of his talent. Given the constraints and restraints of a small, as yet undeveloped, politically influenced film industry, his accomplishment was truly notable. The film was visually rich, skillfully composed, incisive, and expressive. Its substance touched very sensitive areas. By dialogue, by character exposition, by the climate of despair, loss, and suffering, Wajda demonstrated that the uprising brought little but pain and death to the young. On the other hand, in the mise-en-scène, in the way of presenting the fate of participants, in the romantic tone of narration, in the heroic nature of their commitments and gestures, Wajda implies admiration and approval of this historic event, and that set the tone for *Canal*.

The film at first did not evoke enthusiasm on the part of the public. Doubts and condemnations could be heard among the generation now middle-aged which had known well and survived the uprising. Some of these criticisms came from people who, like Wajda, praised the uprising, but who did not like the director's approach to this hallowed event. It must be remembered that this was the first film to deal with the subject, the first expression concerning a national drama, concerning an episode previously distorted or ignored. The public, on the whole, seemed to be waiting for a story that would glorify sincere, if pathetic, effort, that would canonize patriotism in pure and cleansing sunlight. Wajda's drama of despair was sunk in the mud and filth of sewers. Patriots did not want to see the heroism of the time immersed in a sewer. Even among critics, few understood that they were dealing with an outstanding film, a film breaking many precedents and setting new ones.

Several weeks after the Polish premiere, April 20, 1957, *Canal* was presented at the Cannes festival, where it carried off one of the highest awards. The name of Andrzej Wajda appeared for the first time on the international cinema scene. French critic Ado Kyrou wrote: "Wajda is an artist of important matters, and artist of tomorrow. . . . He is probably the only young European director, who—in the contemporary world of senile art, intellectual laziness, and superficial psychology—can afford a violent and passionate tone resembling that of Bunuel" (*Positif* (Paris), 25/26, 1957).

Ashes and Diamonds

Clearly Wajda was making his mark, and with his next film he would establish himself as a major international cinematic figure. *Ashes and Diamonds* (1958) was based on a novel by the same title published in 1947, written by one of Poland's foremost postwar authors, Jerzy Andrzejewski (1909–1982). Andrzejewski's work is characterized by moral search and a spare style. In the story of *Ashes and Diamonds*, a young man from the anti-Communist underground army undertakes an assassination mission against a Communist party official. The novel illustrated the political complexity of the times and seemed to call out for national reconciliation. Upon publication it was received enthusiastically by the authorities, but their approval dissipated in the early fifties when the subject proved too controversial for the primitive ideology of that time. Certainly, making a film of it did not seem at all viable. But in 1957 Wajda and Andrzejewski made an adaptation in which the time span was condensed, certain characters eliminated, and some new scenes added. It was accepted for production and made, becoming perhaps the most important film to be produced in Poland up to that time and earning recognition as one of the finest films made in any country in that decade.

The story takes place in May 1945, in a provincial town. German occupation has only just ended; something new is to begin the shape of which is still not known. Maciek Chełmicki (played by Zbigniew Cybulski), a soldier in an anti-Communist resistance organization receives his orders to kill the Communist official Szczuka (Wacław Zastrzyżyński), who has just arrived to organize civilian government. The initial attempt is a tragic botch. An innocent man is killed. The rest of the action takes place almost entirely in a small hotel in which both assassin and target are staying. Maciek's will to murder falters. The war against the Germans is, after all, over. Maciek has a quick but intense encounter with a barmaid who, like him, is lost in the turn of events from occupation and war to peace and whatever is to follow. This short but bright affair gives Maciek more reason to hesitate. He makes a decision influenced both by his own sense of soldierly duty and by his collaborator and immediate superior. He kills Szczuka late at night and in the morning is himself shot by a military patrol, just as an official independence celebration is coming to an end in the hotel.

In the foreground there is a story, then, of love and murder, but there is a larger subject in the background, the drama of Poland finding itself after the lost years of the war. People come out of the oppression of the occupation not knowing what awaits them now. The old rules were to fight the enemy. New directions had to be found to suit a situation of perplexing political ambivalence. There is no status quo to refer to; all has changed since prewar times: the political system, moral hierarchies, patriotic principles, social and economic systems. *Ashes and Diamonds* was a story about the problem faced by the Poles the day after Hitler's defeat, the choices they were faced with, the difficulties of communicating under raw, new political conditions.

The story is structured in a way that reminds us a little of Greek tragedy. It begins one afternoon and ends the following morning. As much as one can do so cinematically, while remaining faithful to the medium, Wajda observes the unities of place and action as well as time. Events follow one another relentlessly and seem inevitable. Each shot, scene, and sequence that tells the story is dense, intensive, full of contrasts, full of meaning. Drinking with his friend and superior in one scene, Maciek recollects dead brothers-in-arms. On the bar are glasses of vodka. One after another he lights them with a match and makes them into votive flames, naming the comrades. A trivial scene becomes symbolic; the vodka glasses are votive candles like those that burn in Polish cemeteries on All-Saints Day; the fire burns like patriotism in the heart; drunken speech turns into inspired elegy. In the scene in which Maciek coolly carries out his assassination, the victim staggers forward into his arms, and they stand in embrace for a second or two, like father and son (in fact, Szczuka was looking for his son in a subplot). Is there in this something suggestive of national parricide as well? The point, in general, is that Wajda has poured depth of content into each visual effect within a dramaturgical frame that is simple yet forceful.

While the form is quite direct and simple, complexity and ambivalence are everywhere reflected. Both main characters, assassin as well as target, are victims. The Communist has returned to learn that his son has become a member of the opposition underground, like the assassin who stalks him. The son has just been arrested by the security service, which he would have verified one way or another if he had not been assassinated first. Maciek, in contrast to the old man who is himself a weary veteran of the good fight (in his case the Spanish Civil War), represents youth and its idealism contaminated by death, brutal innocence. He is a tall figure in dark glasses who hunches himself from time to time as if protecting himself from thoughts. He carries within him the mystery of his generation, people who have matured too fast in a bloody struggle. It is hardly surprising that this figure, as magnificently interpreted by Zbigniew Cybulski, became a legend for the young of the fifties and sixties. Cybulski himself became almost legendary, partly because of his own tragic life and early death (which was dramatized by Wajda in his film *Everything for Sale* [*Wszystko na sprzedaż*], [1970]).

In addition to the visual substance and the dramatic force and complexity, Wajda added to the richness of *Ashes and Diamonds* by allusions and references to Polish literature and culture, particularly from the romantic era. The title itself is borrowed from a poem by Cyprian Norwid:

> Will only ashes remain and the tumult
> Of the storm in the abyss? Or will there be
> Beneath the ashes a starry diamond . . . .

It is poetic reference to the tragedies of Polish history. There are also references to the dramatic work of Juliusz Słowacki (1809–1849).

The final scene in which Maciek is dying alone as we watch a macabre Polonaise grand march is an ironic allusion to *The Wedding* by Stanisław Wyspiański (1869–1907), which Wajda would later make into a film. It is clear that Wajda quite deliberately meant to evoke the tradition of Polish romantic culture, its literature and drama. It all conspires to present once again the grand theme of the nation as martyr and its people as victims of destiny. It explains much to cite Wajda himself: "A romantic artist was not somebody who fulfilled himself in the fabric of his art—in poetry, painting, or sculpture. The romantic artist had to transcend himself. . . . He had to be more than a maker; he had to be the conscience of the nation, a prophet, a social institution . . ." (*Kino*, no. 1, 1968; our translation).

Both critics and public received the film with something more than approval. It was received with nothing less than reverence. Only the official reception and that of the "official" critics was cold. These claimed that the movie justified the anti-Communist assassin. While it is true that the figure of Maciek is attractive and even sympathetic, it is simply false to find that the film anywhere justifies his mission. Still, it was nothing less than amazing to think that a film would be allowed in which the most attractive figure was an anti-Communist partisan. It is no surprise that the authorities at first did not want the film shown abroad. Simply by chance the film was presented at the Venice festival, not as part of the main events, but peripherally. That was enough to make it into an artistic event of importance. Soon it was recognized as the most important postwar Polish film, and even the most important Polish film ever made. Eventually this was acknowledged by the administration.

Lotna

Mention is made from time to time of Wajda's "war trilogy." As a matter of fact there were four films that make a group. *Lotna (Lotna)* [1959] must be added to *A Generation, Canal,* and *Ashes and Diamonds*. It is less known than the others and justifiably so, but characteristic of this *auteur* in every way. The idea was taken from Wojciech Żukrowski's (b. 1916) story of the same title, written in 1946. In the film the time is set as September 1939. A cavalry unit carries on a lonely and desperate fight against the Nazi juggernaut. There is a beautiful mare named Lotna, envy of all the uhlans (cavalrymen). The plot is simple: the commanding officer dies and the horse is taken over by the next in line, and that repeats itself several times. Is it Lotna that brings bad luck? At the end of the campaign with all its disasters, a sergeant kills the now handicapped mare, and all the other soldiers go their separate ways.

Consider how Polish and how Wajdaesque the film is. At the center there is a white horse, a cavalry horse like the ones he admired as a child. There are uhlans, cavalry charges, lances, sabers, a desperate squadron of men facing German power. Of course what is portrayed is a military anachronism, but one that reflects at the same time a nostalgia for a lost world of glory, heroic gestures however useless.

Unfortunately, Żukrowski's story, though brilliant and shrewd, was brief and did not include enough in it for a full-length feature film. Working with the author, Wajda tried to develop a tale, but ultimately the finished product came about by improvisation. The story of the horse was moving and attractive; the picture of defeat texturally rich; still the movie remained somehow empty, hollow. The characters were two-dimensional and their relationships remained undefined. So the result was that the drama of campaign and defeat was expressed more through the mass background scenes than through the portrayal of individuals.

Wajda felt he had to fill the void with what had always been his special technique, the creation of a clear, vibrant, and even violent picture. Thus he employed a surfeit of visual devices that combined precision and realism with anomalous absurdity and fantasy, something bordering on surrealism. In this Polish autumn landscape appear strange pictorial fragments: a fish dying under the knife of a cook, twisted bodies lying in the fields, a burning stuffed eagle (the eagle is a symbol of Poland), a snow-white handkerchief wiping the blood from a saber (white and red are Polish national colors), red berries caught in a trooper's stirrups like drops of blood. Such ornamentation and symbolism were not enough to fill the dramatic void.

The critics were merciless with *Lotna*, perhaps treating it worse than it deserved. The artistic weaknesses mentioned were pointed out, but the fiercest attack was to come a couple of years later when it was charged that he ridiculed the Polish army of 1939 by showing the cavalry charging against tanks. This was categorically false. It is probably historically accurate that no such thing ever occurred, but the story belongs to folklore and not to recorded history. Wajda did take such a desperate charge from the realm of lore and tried to make out of it a sort of visual opera, but the legend itself conjured up for Wajda a wonderful picture of the desperate heroism of Poles. Actually, even he thought of it as an esthetic failure, but it remains his most personal project, the only film in his career that he says he would like to make again.

These first four pieces, *A Generation*, *Canal*, *Ashes and Diamonds*, and *Lotna*, gave Wajda fame and reputation far beyond Poland. They also established him as an *auteur* by showing his individual approach, his style, his viewpoint. A central element of that viewpoint was his view of the relationship between the artist and society. For Wajda, the task of the artist is not to entertain, threaten, or cajole, but rather to carry out a settlement of accounts on behalf of his nation, its aspirations, disappointments, in short its history.

Wajda did not generally present conflicts that were between one person and another. Certainly dramatic conflicts were developed in his films, but they were not the center of attention, the *raison d'être* of his work. Even saying that he pictured the tension between man and society falls short of adequate description. For Wajda, the subject that mattered was what was happening between a man and history, between an individual Pole and the irreversible course of events to which one is subjected. In each of the films so far, with the exception of *A Generation* which was still partly distorted by socialist realism, the individual does not accept the verdict of seemingly ineluctable history. Wajda's hero (in some cases heroine) objects to determined verdicts, struggles, fights, if necessary to the point of self-destruction—or to call it something else, heroic sacrifice.

Innocent Sorcerers

By 1960 the public and Wadja felt the need of relief from so much focus and concentration on war and occupation. He found a partial answer to the problem in a script written for him by Jerzy Andrzejewski, author of *Ashes and Diamonds*, and Jerzy Skolimowski, a young director, actor, and writer. The script, *Innocent Sorcerers* (*Niewinni czarnodzieje*) [1960], was clever. These two consummate talents created a story of an all-night psychological game between a young man and woman, who hide constantly behind their own words, expressions, poses, because they seem unable to be honest about their central desire, sex. The story was written with subtle proficiency and the acting did full justice to the screenplay. Moreover, it established a contrast with Wajda's previous work and turned thematic direction. These characters were quite different from those he had created before. The young man (played by Tadeusz Łomnicki) was a sports doctor not a beleaguered soldier, an enthusiast of jazz not patriotic songs. He and the girl (played by Krystyna Stypułkowska) have no greater goal than fulfilling their love fantasy.

In a sense it could be said that Wajda was paying his dues to the younger generation and made the film somewhat half-heartedly. The center of the film, the attitude that prevents the couple from honest exchange and communication, could have been developed more and its depth and significance enhanced. There is also a problem in accepting the relevance of the couple, their worth, so to speak. Why do we care if they are honest with themselves or not? The result of the weaknesses in *Innocent Sorcerers* makes the film a weak link in the chain of Wajda's works. It is worth observing, nonetheless, the change that Wajda made in his approach to this movie. His usual richness, violence and intensity were displaced by cold, coy analysis. The nation was not at issue, only two people. Wajda was used to making cinematic symphony; this was pictorial chamber music.

The critics were dissatisfied, and ultimately Wajda himself was also. At one point he thought his success had been diminished because at the outset he knew too little about this young generation, which led him to the mistake of barely touching the surfaces of its personal concerns. In the context of his other works, *Innocent Sorcerers* is not at all a successful film. It is possible that the critics and the director himself were too demanding. In an environment not overwhelmed by history and nationhood, the film would have been considered beautiful and valuable. (One thinks of Bergman's lighter movies.) But this leeway was not accorded in Poland to a man who had undertaken Wajda's momentous esthetic obligations.

Love at Twenty

Contemporary youth was the subject again when Wajda was invited to do one of the five parts of a portmanteau film, made by five directors from five different countries. The film was *Love at Twenty* (*L'amour a vingt ans*) [1962], produced by Pierre Roustang. The general idea was to make film depicting the character of youth in the modern world as exemplified in different countries. François Truffaut made the French segment, Marcel Ophuls the German, Shintaro Ishihara the Japanese, and Wajda the Polish. Wajda took the occasion to fashion a contrast between two generations, those who remembered the war and those who didn't, and if he was diffident toward the young in *Innocent Sorcerers* he was hostile in *Love at Twenty*. With writer Jerzy Stawiński he devised a simple plot ploy. In the Warsaw zoo a child has somehow gotten into the polar bear's pit. There are many young people about, but none of them seems to know what to do, except one who snaps pictures. A middle-aged, bland meter-reader (Zbigniew Cybulski) pushes through, climbs coolly over the barrier and retrieves the child. Fascinated by such calm courage a young girl (Barbara Kwiatkowska-Lass) invites him to her party. There the novelty of his heroism wears thin even though it comes out that he had been a hero before, in the resistance. He drinks a good deal and becomes comic to a younger generation that knows nothing of old heroism or this newest heroic gesture. They are vapid, frivolous, callous. He is all that is left of the fiery-eyed heroes of *Lotna* or those who inched through the sewers in steely determination. *Love at Twenty* was wonderfully incisive and delivered much in a very short space.

Samson

In the meantime, before *Love at Twenty* and following the somewhat disappointing reception of *Innocent Sorcerers*, Wajda had returned to working in operatic proportions with tested themes. *Samson* (*Samson*) [1961] is the story of the life of a young Jew, Jakub Gold, from the prewar period through the war years and his haunted survival, through his conversion to a counterfighter, to his end. The plot is meant to be loosely, very loosely, connected to the biblical tale of Samson and Delilah. There are motifs that suggest such a connection, like the cutting of hair, but the principal parallel is in the final commitment to shake the pillars of the world if that is the only way to fight back.

As a university student before the war he is attacked by anti-Semites and injures one of them in a fight. He is sent to prison but is released at the time of the invasion. He finds himself hiding first in the ghetto and later among the Gentiles. Each hiding place is only another punctuation in time and space of his hunted and haunted existence. By happenstance he meets up with a former fellow prisoner, now an underground leader in the Communist resistance. Through his help and in his new situation he turns his life around and seems to take hold of it just before he is killed in a Nazi attack.

The story is based on a novel of the same title by Kazimierz Brandys (b. 1916), published in 1947. An otherwise excellent writer, Brandys was quite influenced during the early fifties by socialist realism, and the novel reflected that so heavily that the screenplay based on it was not free of its influence. In this film, as in the book, the forces of history are all defined ideologically. On the one side there are fascism, nationalism, racism; on the other there is communism. Episodes, characters, types, opinions, and attitudes are depicted elaborating such a simplistic dialectical interpretation. This constitutes the weak frame of the film.

The strength of the film is in its depiction of Jakub Gold's aloneness, his despair, his fear, a depiction so skillfully visualized that the feeling of being hunted becomes almost palpable. There are sharp, clear dramatic and visual contrasts, a brooding play of light and dark, an occasional strangeness that borders on the surrealistic.

The reception was hostile, perhaps more so than for any other of Wajda's films. Part of this may have been in reaction to the schematism of Brandys that remained in the film script and final product. Much of it was directed against Wajda's rendition of the plight of the Jew in prewar and even wartime Poland. He was charged with inaccuracy, but the charges were too angry to make it seem that the fuss was about exactness. That was never a valid point. Looking at it today, what we have is a portrayal of helplessness and despair that can still evoke terror while watching Samson.

Siberian Lady MacBeth

For some time, even antedating the Samson project, Wajda was interested in making a film from a story by the Russian writer Nikolai Leskov, "Lady MacBeth of Mtsensk." When Avala Film of Belgrade, Yugoslavia, became interested in the project, Wajda responded with alacrity. The adaptation was done by a Yugoslav, Sveta Lukić. The lead role was played by Olivera Marković, an extraordinary actress.

The story of *Siberian Lady MacBeth* (*Sybirski Lady Makbet*) [1962] takes place in a Russian village where Katerina (Marković), an imperious and voracious woman, betrays her absent husband. When his father obstructs her affair, she poisons him without hesitation. Upon her husband's return she instructs her lover to kill him and bury him secretly. When she and her lover attempt to suffocate a cousin, they are caught and banished to Siberia. In the forced march with other deportees, the lover's eyes and attentions turn to another woman and his treatment of Katerina changes. Her response is to cause the drowning of the woman and to jump into the icy Volga herself. In the foreground is this irrepressible, unscrupulous, immorally powerful, beautiful woman caught up in a strange passion. Wajda up to this time had not brought out the dramatic contours of a woman so prominently. He was to do that with regularity from this point forward, but he would not (perhaps could not) ever exceed the baroque delineation of Katerina.

Atmospherically the movie was austere, with no elaborate attempt to capture the Russian landscape. In fact, it was mostly shot inside as if it were being acted out on an Elizabethan stage. This was an appropriate touch in that the tensions, the dramatic pulse of the story, was quite Shakespearean. It is curious to observe that Leskov borrowed from Shakespeare, and Wajda in borrowing from Leskov gave it back to Shakespeare.

The film has been little appreciated; in fact, it is seldom discussed. When released it created little stir in either Yugoslavia or Poland and is almost never revived. It remains mostly in archives as an example of Wajda's evolution as a cinematic artist. His earlier successes were, it seems, in large part due to their political and historical strength. His explorations into the fundamentals of the human condition, his more psychological explorations, were not what was expected of Wajda and, perhaps because of the strength of expectations, were ignored undeservedly.

Ashes

That was hardly the case with *Ashes* (*Popioły*) [1965], which was not universally acclaimed but which received a great deal of attention. It was based on a novel by Stefan Żeromski (1864–1925) who wrote intensively and extensively of the great national and social themes. He was a novelist of refined romantic style and earned a lasting popularity. *Ashes* (1904) was an elaborate fictional mural set in the first decades of the nineteenth century. The Poles had lost their independence and statehood and were seeking some means of coming out from under the thrall of Prussia, Russia, and Austria. They entrusted their hopes largely to Napoleon and fought with his armies on all fronts until his final defeat. The novel has several stories in it, the most important revolving around a Polish nobleman named Rafał Olbromski. It is a story told of war and love, hope and defeat, loftiness and triviality, styled with flamboyant metaphors and elevated emotion. On one level the book concerns the formation of a new Polish identity, one relevant to the partition of the country. Thus it is about the topic of "the Polish character," a topic quite central to Wajda's vision, also a topic that remained a permanent part of Polish consciousness and was continually redefined in response to the spontaneous patriotism that led to the uprisings of 1830, 1848, 1863, and 1905, and episodes of dissent in 1956, 1960, 1968, 1976, and 1980.

It was clearly the kind of book to attract Wajda in spite of the problems it presented to a film maker. In size and scope it was huge. Adaptation would be difficult. Wajda tried it the hard way. He decided to be faithful to the novel, which means he chose not to select one theme or story or character to fol-low, but rather to make the whole thing in miniature, chapter by chapter. It was a risky approach undertaken together with screenwriter Aleksander Ścibor-Rylski. The production commitment was also bold. The movie took 666 days to make, 116 actors, thousands of extras, 1700 uniforms, 900 muskets.

After a tremendous effort, the four-hour production was ready. In defer-ence to Żeromski, Wajda wanted to include the whole legacy of the novel and the epoch of which it treated. He added his own touches—his love of strong contrasts, rich metaphors, symbolism, elevated emotional visualization, terri-fying effects. The main role was played by Daniel Olbrychski, his first major role. (From this point on Olbrychski would be Wadja's favorite leading char-acter.)

Esthetically the project was perhaps too ambitious. It did not turn out to be the director's magnum opus. The multiplicity of plots weakened the story line of each. The plethora of characters weakened individual characteriza-tions. The number of historical and mythical references vitiated the central meaning. It was ultimately evaluated as an unusual, rich, baroque work of cinematic art, with an overabundance of content. But esthetic considerations receded when the film opened in favor of a broad debate about the Polish character and the way it was handled in Wajda's version. Żeromski's novel had been critical; Wajda was perhaps even more uncompromising than Żeromski. Actually the debate this film touched off went beyond both Żerom-ski and Wajda and took on life of its own . . . again. The imponderables were posed. Who are "we" (the Poles): Is Poland a nation of irrational fanatics, of immature political movements led by people who lack common sense? Wajda's critics claimed he painted just such a picture. Basically it was the same debate between romantic nonconformism and political realism so fa-miliar to generations of participants. Ashes served as a signal for its renewal. In this case, Wajda was criticized as a slanderer of heroism, a man who de-rided a noble chapter in Poland's tragic saga. The director, who usually was seen as an upholder of the patriotic and tragic gesture, was attacked for demeaning it. His answer was to call attention to the project not the broader debate: "I am not interested in literature of national consensus, in the litera- ture of reconciliation. I am interested in Żeromski, full of bitterness and con- tradictions ... " (*Polityka*, no. 38, 1965).

Ashes met with a mixed reception at Cannes. It was sufficiently admired so that attempts were made to gain suitable international distribution for it. The rights were sold to a West German firm that tried to enhance the commercial attractiveness by making wholly unauthorized cuts, but it never did reach broad distribution in any form. Actually, the West German company went bankrupt, and the rights to *Ashes* were frozen for a number of years.

The Gates of Paradise

After *Ashes* a chapter of the director's career transpired about which he is to this day reluctant to speak. He made a film called *The Gates of Paradise* (*Bramy raju*) [1967], which has never been shown commercially, for which Wajda is grateful. *The Gates of Paradise* was written by Jerzy Andrzejewski as a screenplay and later incorporated into a novel. It is about an occurrence in the year 1213, during one of the crusades. A shepherd, Jacques de Cloy, has a revelation that instructs him that the grave of Christ can only be redeemed from the heathens by those not contaminated by sin, by the innocent. This was the beginning of the children's crusade. Andrzejewski's text gave this a twist. One night the children make a confession to their spiritual mentor. It turns out that each of the supposedly innocent children is contaminated by sin: passion, vanity, hate, envy, greed. The production was made by Avala Film of Yugoslavia in coproduction with a British company under unfortu- nate circumstances for Wajda. According to his recollection, "I had no con- tact with the actors and, what is more, I knew next to nothing about working with children. There was a sort of barrier between me and the crew and in the end, I found myself desperately doing my best not to hold things up." More- over, he recollects, "I followed the script too blindly. The idea of a picture of children trying to do adult work in setting the world right simply failed to come across" (private papers; our translation). While it was shown at some festivals, it was never distributed. Some prints seem to be around in various hands. They are most likely of a reedited version that Wajda rejects.

Everything for Sale

In the winter of 1966-67, Wajda was contemplating a film around the char- acter of Zbigniew Cybulski, the actor whose role in *Ashes and Diamonds* helped make him into a pop legend similar to the American phenomenon that surrounded James Dean. On January 8, 1967, the director received the news that Cybulski, running to catch a train, had fallen under its wheels and been killed. This was a cultural shock for the nation and a personal one for

Wajda. The personal void he felt led him to an esthetic decision on the film he had been thinking about. Since Cybulski was no longer with us, let the film be about that. That was the special genesis of *Everything for Sale* (*Wszystko na sprzedaż*) [1967].

This time Wajda himself did the screenplay. He had never done that before, although he had in various ways cowritten his films. His decision to be sole author makes this project that much more a personal one. The composition is peculiar. There is no unity of action, and of course the main character (Cybulski) does not appear on the screen. The film can be considered in two parts. In the first half there is a search for the actor who has not appeared on set during the shooting of a film as he was supposed to. The search element becomes loaded with anxiety. In the second half, when it has been learned that the actor was lost in a banal accident, we study the drama of the director's response. How can the film be made now that the actor, who is at the same time the subject of the film, is gone? Wajda then reconstructs his own emotional and professional experience. The roles in the film include that of the director (played by Andrzej Łapicki), the director's wife (Beata Tyszkiewicz, who actually was Wajda's wife at the time), and a whole crowd of mutual colleagues and friends who played themselves.

Within that framework various related themes and subjects are loosely composed into a pattern. First, there is the story of the actor, his legend, his originality and uniqueness, the feelings he inspires among his friends as well as among millions of movie watchers. Second, there is a thematic play on death and its aftermath. What is left of a man and his legend? How can his place be filled? How and for how long can a director be faithful to the memory of the man, even in making his story into a film, when present life demands practical solutions? New films are waiting to be made by new people. Third, there is the theme of transformation which is important to the second half of the film, life into art, truth into illusion, actual experiences into performed and recreated experiences. Such transformation must be carried out without embarrassment or diffidence. Intimate feelings need to be made into a language for the cinema. Hence the title—*Everything for Sale*: all our experiences, feelings, reflections, anxieties, are put up for sale in our art.

For a director to make a movie so self-consciously about himself is an unusual thing. Few have done so, and usually only the greatest have tried it. It is a filmic version of authors writing indirectly about their process. One thinks of Thomas Mann, André Gide, John Fowles, John Barth. In such books, the struggle of the writer with the literary matter and with himself becomes the subject. Truffaut, Bergman, and Fellini have done this sort of thing in films. At the time of the making of *Everything for Sale* only Fellini had tried it in his film *8 1/2*. Wajda knew the film well, but there is no close comparison that can be drawn between the two. In his work, Fellini dramatized the *auteur's* frustration, organisms of film production in their many dimensions, and the break-up of contemporary civilization. Wajda, on the other hand, stressed the moral barriers one faced, the difficulties of overcoming trauma and embarrassment in order to express personal truth about himself and those who are close to him and his work.

There is nothing in it about the Polish cause. For this reason and for its own intrinsic specialness it is quite different from anything he had done before. It does not examine man's confrontation with history. It does link with his past work by involving the theme of generations, which both Wajda and Cybulski had explored together before. Stylistically it was a new departure. The texture is different. Scenes that dramatize the production of the film overlap with scenes of the film being produced, interspersed with documentary footage (Cybulski's funeral) and real comments and observations made by Cybulski's friends and some fans. The assembly has the feeling of haphazard nonchalance in contrast to Wajda's usual impression of careful construction. If most of Wajda's previous work was in the nature of assertion, *Everything for Sale* could be characterized as a ragged sort of conversation about death and other retrospective things, a rumination about the commonality of fiction and fact, life and illusion, the cries of the heart, the past and the present.

It is a record, not a conclusion about anything. It is a plaint about loss of someone dear and how such a void is filled, because filled it will be. Beyond this the important thing is to discover how to tell about such things honestly. It is an extraordinary experiment in filmmaking and also a remarkable achievement. One of the most interesting European films of the 1960s, it nonetheless met with very limited success because of its unusual texture and its novel introspection. It is still little-known outside Poland.

Roly-Poly

As he approached the decade of the seventies, Wajda felt some need for reinvigoration, change of pace, new ideas. He was aware, perhaps sometimes uncomfortably aware, of a new generation close behind him with a quite different sense of the art of cinema. Perhaps for that reason he accepted an offer to make a thirty-minute television film titled *Roly-Poly* (*Przekładaniec*) [1968]. It was based on a story by Stanislaw Lem, a famous science fiction writer, and was about an issue of contemporary interest, heart transplants. The discussion about the subject was both medical and moral. What does transplantation have to do with personal identity? Can one remain himself with someone else's heart beating inside? Lem's story was wry, meant to be comical. It takes place some time in the near future when a daring race-car driver succeeds in being alive in an entirely new body, having exchanged one part after another in a series of accidents. The change, however, is not merely physical; his personality is transformed along the way. With his inclination for sharp contrasts, Wajda changed the story into heavier satire than it had been, almost into farce. The critics considered the piece to be an artistic trifle with little impact. But the idea of making something funny stayed with Wajda for a while.

Hunting Flies

He decided to make *Hunting Flies* (*Polowanie na muchy*) [1968], from a story by Janusz Głowacki, his last try at comedy. The story is itself about a writer whom an ambitious woman wants to make famous. He leaves his wife and squalidly submits to the mean manipulation of his lover. The fact is he has no talent, so she can't make him famous. He returns to his wife who, in the meantime, has been transformed into a domineering, imperious woman like his lover. Now *she* wants to drive her husband to success of some kind. As background for the film, we have a polished picture of the intellectual and artistic world of Warsaw, which was just at this time an object of criticism and some contempt. The background gave sharp edges to the theme which had appeal for the director, who saw in it something of the myth of Pygmalion and Galatea reversed, that is, the woman was the transformer. It is worth recalling that Wajda had touched a related motif in *Siberian Lady MacBeth*, and was to return again to the theme of the strong and effective woman.

Hunting Flies remains the director's least important work. The main male character, played by Zygmunt Malanowicz, lacks interest and charm, even comic charm. The female, played by Małgorzata Braunek, is done almost to caricature. In fact, the entire film was done in a style much too broad. It would have greatly benefited from a lighter touch. In the creation of comedy those qualities that were ordinarily Wajda's strength—intensity, clarity of conflict, dramatic encounter—functioned to disadvantage. *Hunting Flies* was presented at Cannes in 1969 without arousing much interest. Something different was expected of the maker of *Canal* and *Ashes and Diamonds*, a reaction that also manifested itself somewhat in Poland, although it did gain some popularity with the box-office audience.

Landscape after Battle

Having had his change of pace and tone, Wajda returned to high seriousness, the great Polish problems, and the atmosphere of despair. He started work on *Landscape after Battle* (*Krajobraz po bitwie*) [1970]. The genesis as usual was literary, in this case from the work of Tadeusz Borowski, a most extraordinary writer, a man who survived his boyhood in Auschwitz, and later wrote of it with great effectiveness, portraying not only the degradation and cruelty of the oppressors but of the victims as well. With the detachment of an entomologist, Borowski presents the behavior of weak people in extreme situations, not shying even from a description of cannibalism. There is no sentimental humanism in Borowski's stories. His cold irony is nicely captured in the title of one of his best known stories, "This Way to the Gas Chambers, Ladies and Gentlemen!" It was Borowski who coined the expression for a syndrome he noted in his generation, "contaminated by death." Himself one of the arch-sufferers of this syndrome, he committed suicide in 1951.

The screenplay for *Landscape after Battle* is based on Borowski's "The Battle at Grunwald," in which the scene is set in an American displaced-persons camp in Germany in 1945. There, having survived the death camp, the hero goes through a psychological crisis. The movie begins with an event that actually comes from another of Borowski's stories, "Silence." After the liberation of a death camp, the survivors literally stomp into the earth a man who had served as a foreman over them. This is followed by the story of a young intellectual, played by Daniel Olbrychski, and what happens to him. While for the rest of the nationalities the end of the war meant the end of a nightmare, the end of deep problems, for the Poles a dilemma was created, a question arose: Should they return to a new and somewhat alien authority, or should they go into exile, burning their bridges behind them? The hero, a poet, is not quite like the others in the camp, the potential exiles and emigrés. It hardly seems that their destiny can be related to his. The problem for him is sharpened when he meets a girl who has just escaped from Poland. Incidents conspire to a crisis when a spectacle produced by the emigrés to commemorate the battle of Grunwald (1410, in which the Poles defeated the Teutonic Knights) abruptly turns into a fight involving everyone. The girl is shot accidentally. Finally, the poet decides to return to Poland in spite of the uncertainty facing him there.

Landscape after Battle is complex and ambiguous in its presentation of the hero and the other inmates of the camp. The community of "old Poles" is depicted with visual and dramatic sarcasm laid on to such an extent that the depiction borders on caricature. The hero is presented as disappointed, angry, even quietly, internally aggressive against everything and everybody. Then there is the introduction of the regenerative power of love. Shattered by events, hardened, callous, he begins to feel, live, suffer in a more human way when he meets the girl who has fled Poland. Her death cuts short this emotional revival in him. Wajda has introduced this theme of regenerative love before. In *Ashes and Diamonds*, the hero meets a girl who gives him a new will to live and change just hours before he is gunned down. Love, however, is a subtheme.

The main theme is still "the Polish character." In one way the film depicts an out-of-date and trashy kind of patriotism, a call to be loyal to the "old" Poland, whatever that was. Wajda is not sympathetic in his treatment. On the other hand, the hero's arguments for a return to Poland in spite of doubts and negative feelings are unclear even if sincere. Why return? Out of spite? For one's convictions? Out of despair? Is there any positive direction? *Landscape after Battle* is a reflection of all the perplexity of the Polish dilemma played out against a grim, lost, almost surreal backdrop. Wajda's curious positioning of himself just this side of patriotism with a full view of skepticism is essentially the same as the stance he took in *Canal* and *Lotna* where he played out the Polish dilemma question using different plots and backdrops.

In retrospect, the film appears to be mainly a documentation of the sensibility of restless and changing times. It experienced a critical reaction similar to that accorded *Ashes* five years earlier. It was attacked for giving a negative picture of Poles as hysterical, unbalanced, sometimes just stupid. Some claimed it to be a slander. The defense of the film is best summed up in the comment of Melchior Wańkowicz, once just such an emigré as the film lacerates: "There is a scab that must be removed from an old wound. . . . You must dig your nails into it and tear it away, like Wajda does" (*Kultura*, no. 40, 1970).

The Birch-Wood

Quite different in tone and esthetic was Wajda's next project, *The Birch-Wood* (*Brzezina*) [1970]. Television turned to him to make another piece. He suggested a short story by Jarosław Iwaszkiewicz (1894–1980), at first thinking very modestly about the scope of the work. It turned out, however, that he decided to make a full-length film from the story, a film that would reflect the director in a new dimension. The author of the piece, Iwaszkiewicz, was one of Poland's foremost twentieth-century writers—novelist, short story writer, poet. His subjects were universal: love, loneliness, death, sin, the human condition. In contrast to so many other Polish writers, he seldom, perhaps never, placed man into his work as a historical figure, always as himself, simply. The story, "Birch-Wood," written in 1932, reflected well the talent, sensitivity, and subtlety of the author. It was so well knit, it required practically no script at all. Wajda made the film directly from the story.

The tale is one of two brothers, played by Daniel Olbrychski and Olgierd Łukaszewicz, one of them a coarse man who chooses to live in the forest with his daughter after the death of his wife, the other a pianist suffering from consumption who comes to his brother's house in the forest to get well or to die. It is a story of love, death, and change. In the full flower of spring the film ends with a second cross beside the wife's, that of the artist brother. The pianist had found temporary escape from death only in the arms of a country girl. With fine subtlety, Wajda draws out the theme of Eros and Thanatos, the life-urge and the death-urge. The story moves on a succession of small tensions, sudden and quickly suppressed crises, all very true to the original story that inspired it.

Equally inspiring to Wajda, who we must remember is a painter, was the art nouveau work of Jacek Malczewski who seemed to be obsessed with the theme of Eros and Thanatos. One of Malczewski's paintings of Thanatos is central to the film in two ways: It hangs in the living room during the film, lending domination by virtue of its subject matter, but more importantly modulating the visuality of the entire picture because Wajda borrowed the colors and tones of the painting and worked with them throughout the film, which is a melange of yellows, greens, violets, all of a rather cadaverous hue. The stylistics make death a component of much of the film, but this is brilliantly set off by the naturalistic play of muscles, in the human shapes, in the poses of figures towering over surroundings, a clear sense of the vigor and vitality that stands in opposition to deathly pallor.

These attempts were new. When earlier he had sought for relief from his usual national and historical themes, he turned to comedy, unsuccessfully. In *The Birch-Wood* he discovered a new dramatical and visual way for himself which he was to follow again in *The Young Maids of Wilko*, *The Conductor*, and *Chronicles of Love*.

The film was extremely well received in all of Europe, especially so in France. Through *The Birch-Wood*, Wajda who had so far been a name familiar to intellectuals and film buffs became quite broadly known. Indeed, from this time on, a close connection developed between France and Wajda. When not in Warsaw he is to be found in Paris. He would go on later to make films in coproduction with French producers. A phenomenon was once noted that indicates the reception accorded his films. On one particular day in the early 1980s, more films of Wajda's were showing on Paris screens than the films of any other director, not excluding French directors.

Pilate and Others

At the beginning of the seventies, Wajda was taken with the notion of making a movie presenting the Passion of Christ in a contemporary environment. Perhaps the dreamy idealism, the communes, the wandering and searching for salvation on the part of the young gave rise to the idea. Mikhail Bulgakov's novel, *The Master and Margarita* gave him a more precise direction. The novels of Bulgakov (1891–1940) were rediscovered in the sixties. This particular novel takes place in the Moscow of the twenties in an environment of artists, writers, activists, devils, and angels. It is a rare combination of fantasy, irony, and lyricism. One side story in the novel, not centrally connected to the main line, involved a Roman governor and a certain Joshua whose life depends on him. The story is told not from the point of view of Joshua, who is of course Jesus, but from the point of view of Pilate. Wajda took this as the departure point for his film which was produced by a West German television network (Zweites Deutsches Fernsehen). Wajda gave it the title *Pilate and Others (Pilat i inni)* [1972].

The evangelical story is not relevant here. Following Bulgakov, Wajda focuses on Pilate's choice and decision. A Jewish prophet named Joshua (Wojciech Pszoniak) is brought before Pilate (Jan Kreczmar) together with other characters: Afranius (Andrzej Łapicki), chief-of-police; Caiaphas (Vladek Sheybal), a Jewish official; Judas (Jerzy Zelik); and Matthew (Daniel Olbrychski). How is this case to be adjudicated? Pilate faces up to a relevant and timely problem, the conflict between practical necessity and conscience, between responsibility and the desire to remain uninvolved. There is no attempt to vindicate Pilate or to be reductionist with the biblical story. What Wajda was doing was attempting to translate the story to the times.

The idea of doing it as a costume film was rejected. Instead of filming at a location that might resemble Palestine, the locations chosen were in contemporary Germany. Some of the characters were dressed in costume, the rest in modern clothes. Joshua's interrogation by Pilate takes place in the stadium at Nuremberg; the ring around Frankfurt-am-Main becomes the Via Dolorosa; the crucifixion occurs on a giant rubbish dump next to the Autobahn in Wiesbaden. It was a transparent reminder that such things could occur today in a world riddled with indifference.

The artistic and dramatic risks here were great. At first taste, the strange mix of historical reference and modern framing, the old words and the modern gestures, seems unconvincing. The film seems in fact somewhat incoherent, unclear, lost in a maze of artistry. After fifteen minutes or so a willing suspension of disbelief takes place because the mise-en-scène and the photographic style are simple, matter of fact, almost like television reportage. Then we discover we are backstage in a sort of theater where crew are talking to a cast dressed in their costumes. The set decorations clash with the real landscape. This turns into a new interpretation of the situation, a new reality almost, within which the drama of Pilate and Jesus takes place.

The premiere of the film on television was treated as an event. It was shown first on Good Friday, March 29, 1972. Unfortunately it has never been shown in movie theaters on a commercial basis. When this was tried in France, a distributor ran into many obstacles. Thanks to Wajda, one or two copies of the film were made available for art-theater showings in Warsaw.

The Wedding (1972)

It is not in the least surprising that a project as experimental as *Pilate and Others* should be followed by Wajda's direct address to the most famous of all Polish experimental plays, Stanisław Wyspiański's *The Wedding (Wesele)*, a classic of dramatic literature that had long fascinated him. Wyspiański

(1869–1907) was a legendary figure from the fin de siècle, a poet, dramatist, painter, stained glass artist, and graphic designer. He was, not to put too fine a point on it, quite simply a genius. He electrified staid and dignified Crakow and drew others to it and to the region around it just with his presence. His *The Wedding* was a verse play quite misunderstood at first but later recognized as a prophetic masterpiece. Because of its rich symbolism, it is even today a subject of continual reinterpretation. It contains, as well as its dense symbolism, rich allusions to folklore, and a rich and deep texture that is quintessentially Polish.

The actual origin of the play was the inspiration Wyspiański received from the wedding of a country girl and a Crakow poet in a village near Crakow in 1900. The playwright saw in this affair a statement of equality and national unity. In this play, Wyspiański brings a number of fascinating characters to this strange country wedding: a journalist, a rabbi, a poet, peasants, country wives, and others. He introduces personae who are interjections into the drama of a most imaginative kind, including a spectral visit to the journalist by the ghost of the famous fifteenth-century court jester, Stańczyk, an ironist whose ideology seems related to the realism of Crakow conservatives. The poet, in turn, is visited by a Black Knight, epitome of Poland's past might and glory; the peasant by Szela, a desperado who led a massacre of Polish gentry in 1848, who may stand as a contradiction to the national ideal of solidarity. An important debate is held concerning the nation, its weakness and its might, and the way to liberate Poland from foreign domination. The drama ends curiously when the wedding guests, all of whom are waiting for a special sign which is to be delivered by a young peasant—it is a peacock feather which he loses—culminate the action with a weird somnambulistic dance to the rhythm of a melody played by a kind of straw scarecrow.

There are, of course, innumerable interpretations. Among the more reliable are these: the play is a reflection of the quandary of the Crakow intelligentsia around 1900 who desired national unity on the one hand, but who did not trust the peasants on the other. Even more often the play is seen as a vision of Poland and the Polish personality rendered satirically and even bitterly. Society is weighted by inertia, incapable of action, its mission lost and vague.

In any case, it is a beautiful and rich play, linguistically brilliant and perfectly structured. The Polish writer and critic Tadeusz Boy-Żeleński aptly described it this way: "It is a drama which succeeds in blending every tone: gravity, nobility, elan, pungent acerbity, sarcasm, the friction of a mystery being fulfilled. It is a play in which paradoxes, sayings, and deep truths, which were later adopted into the everyday language, shine like diamonds" (*Pisma*, Warsaw, 1956–1975).

Was such a thing amenable to being transformed into the world of film?

Can a movie bear the artificiality of rhymed verses? Will it not be muffled overmuch by being limited to two country rooms? Wajda wanted to and did remain faithful to the play, introducing slight changes only. With the help of writer Andrzej Kijowski he added some opening scenes simply to introduce the characters and place the action in 1900. For the rest he accelerated the rhythm of the work more than could have been done on stage, and he added visual elements for the screen which are close to the style and contents of Wyspiański's own paintings. In addition, there was a bit more movement, agitation, and alcoholic mist than the play usually reflects. As the action develops, the atmosphere becomes heavier, the expectation for some special thing to happen becomes agitating, unbearable until it is dissolved in the dance of the final scene. Wajda also points up elements to make them more prominent. He heightens the disillusionment of the peasantry with the intelligentsia, which with all its talking and theoretical discussion is unable to solve anything.

Wajda certainly meant to emphasize the split between the intellectual elite and the masses, a split that still exists in Poland (at least as much as everywhere else). It is extraordinary that the intelligentsia remains so locked up in nineteenth-century Romanticism and all the related and attendant controversies, which, although often possessing an amazing relevance to contemporary dilemmas, belong nevertheless to their own age.

The main consideration with respect to *The Wedding* is its perfection with regard to structure, to dramatic action, to progressive tension, to conflict, in short to cinematic drama. Wajda has created an esthetic reality upon which judgment must be based. *The Wedding* is cinema of archetype and cinema of drama at their best.

Land of Promise (1974)

After *The Wedding* there was a brief pause in Wajda's directorial career because of his duties as artistic manager of unit "X" and the vigor with which he worked promoting productions for all the personnel of the company. He wanted to make it into an entity that would attract young talent, which it did, and foreign talent, which proved to be unfeasible.

In 1973 he turned to a screenplay that he had prepared himself some years ago, a project based on an epic novel by the Nobel winning writer Władystaw Reymont (1868–1925), *The Promised Land*. Its subject was the milieu of Lodz in the 1860s when industrial development came with a vengeance. Under the occupation of the three powers (Germany, Austria, and Prussia) Poland had remained, up to the second half of the nineteenth century, almost exclusively an agricultural country. Circumstances were propitious for the evolution of Lodz into a major textile center, producing goods primarily for the Russian market. Lodz belonged to Russia at the time. Economic promise was sufficiently great to attract many entrepreneurs, small and large, from a number of countries to the growing city. Most of the new businessmen were from Germany and Russia, a large proportion of them Jews. With growth and ethnic diversity, Lodz became a genuine city.

Reymont described the whole process of change and development with accuracy as well as imagination, modulated of course with his own point of view. He saw Lodz as a challenge to the Polish intelligentsia which was still mired in the country-nobility tradition and scorned the industrial revolution. A supporter of Polish Positivism, which praised economic and technological development, Reymont set out to warn the Polish traditionalists that they must either contribute and participate in the process or they would vanish as an influence. He made the main character of the novel a Polish nobleman turned businessman. Reymont portrays him as virtuous and effective, while he tarnishes the character of the other new capitalists, Germans, Russians, and Jews. Was this arrant and prejudiced nationalism? Probably so, expressed in order to turn the minds of the Polish intelligentsia to the new world of capitalism.

It was certainly more the literary quality of the novel than its contents that attracted Wajda. Reymont was a rich, realistic writer whose novels were in the tradition of Zola. His characters were colorful, vivid, and true to life, while his plots were skillfully complex. This was quite to Wajda's taste and offered him rich opportunities for visualization. There was another reason for his interest in *The Promised Land*. In 1974 there were still some factories in Lodz that had been operating since before the turn of the century, as well as the mansions of the industrial magnates, preserved with all the splendor and bad taste of the period. In fact, one of those mansions now belongs to the Lodz film school. It was, therefore, possible to make a big historical movie, totally realistic, without the problem of building expensive new sets. The film was indeed shot in the existing buildings. With the use of two crews it was done quickly and efficiently. The finished product has a screening time of 179 minutes. It was premiered on February 21, 1975.

The main personae are three young businessmen; a Pole named Karol (Daniel Olbrychski), a German named Max (Andrzej Seweryn), and a Jew named Moryc (Wojciech Pszoniak), who together decide to start a factory. The film deals with their separate and joint interests. They do manage to open the factory and eventually end up destroying it. Apart from that subject there is also the depiction of life in a country house, a picture of a world that was dying out.

The movie is spectacular, and yet at the same time it obeys all the rules of film narration and remains teeming, vivid, boisterous. Generally Wajda had been more capricious in his narrative technique, looking for effects other than narrative correctness. In *Land of Promise*, everything is quite according to the usual esthetic regulations: the characters are clear as are the changing relationships among them; each of them has a particular goal; and the story develops step by step from the beginning to the finale. This does not, however, detract at all from the violent, colorful originality of the piece. It is not at all a simple costume work with a touch of history. The vividness of the portrayals, the sharp and clear clashes, the unexpected crises are somewhat breathtaking, for all the regularity of the narrative structure. In addition, the authentic environment of factories and mansions was brilliantly photographed by Witold Sobociński and Edward Kłosiński. Everything was there to make it attractive to millions. In fact it was a box-office success, and it was nominated for an Oscar.

But something happened that no one expected, least of all Wajda. After showings in Scandinavia and the United States in 1976, *Land of Promise* was charged with containing anti-Semitism by virtue of its negative portrayal of the Jews in Lodz. Wajda was quite simply shocked and appalled. There are elements in the novel by Reymont that can be considered suggestively anti-Semitic, but Wajda had gone to some lengths to change these around in the film version. He makes the personality and character of Moryc, the Jew, the most likeable of the three main roles. In the final scenes, it is the Polish nobleman who is portrayed as perfidious and despicable. To be sure, each ethnic representation in the film comes in for some negative treatment—the film is after all about the negative aspects of laissez faire development. But since there are Jewish characters among the rest of those who are satirized, the argument was advanced that that kind of portrayal, a negative depiction of characters who are Jewish, constitutes, ipso facto, anti-Semitism. The real conflict in the film has nothing to do with nationalities; it has to do with capital and labor. All this was obscured by the allegations. Wajda, whose record of integrity in matters of human rights and any kind of discrimination, whose conduct during and after the political crisis of 1968 with its distinct elements of anti-Semitism, should have made him the least likely to be the subject of such charges, was not given credibility. To this day, against any sensible interpretation of the reality of the thing, the film is thought to be anti-Semitic in Scandinavia and the United States. Interestingly, this is not at all the case in France or Italy, where perhaps Zolaesque realism, with all its candor and completeness, is better understood. In any case, Reymont's book caused a certain injustice to occur to Wajda, even while it provided him with a rich literary artifact from which to start a film.

The Shadow Line
Another turn-of-the-century Polish author—rather, an English author who was a Pole—Joseph Conrad (Teodor Józef Konrad Korzeniowski), provided the literary inspiration for Wajda's next project. Conrad (1857–1924), whose

English style has amazed and intrigued critics and readers for generations was always felt, by Poles, to possess a vision, a way of seeing the world, that was basically Polish. In verification of this, anyone who has ever read *Under Western Eyes*, has seen a Polish sensibility through the pellucid English prose. This interested Wajda.

He chose as a point of departure an episode late in Conrad's life when, in 1917 during World War I, he received permission to join an English trap-ship searching for German submarines. What was Conrad trying to do? Live out one more sea adventure? Rediscover the characters of his novels? Certainly, it was a good idea for a movie that would seem to have something in it of Conrad's love of adventure, his ideals, his life, in short his literature.

Wajda found a coproducer, Thames Television, and a screenwriter, a Pole living in England, Bolesław Sulik. In the writing of the screenplay it turned out that the event was difficult to dramatize and seemed to have little to do with Conrad's literary works. Another idea occurred, namely to make two parallel stories with points of connection, one from the biographical episode, the other from a Conrad novella, *The Shadow Line*, which was about a young captain just about to begin his career. The coproducers agreed to this and the film was to be shot off the coast of Bulgaria on the Black Sea.

Conrad's literature proved to be extremely resistant to the cinematic medium. His reflectiveness, introspection, psychological and moralistic observation, do not easily translate into the language of dramatic action and character visualization. This is especially true of *The Shadow Line*, a semi-biographical story in which the protagonist is the narrator. Wajda considered adding subplots, but these did not fit the literary character of Conrad's work. Ultimately, Wajda remained totally faithful to the original.

The Shadow Line (*Smuga cienia*) [1976], is about a young officer made captain and brought into responsibility for all the men under his command. At sea he is beset by extraordinary problems with the weather and the psychology of some of the crew. He endures his tests as tests of maturity, as a rite of passage, during which he crosses the shadow line to a different plane of life.

Wajda gave up the notion of running this film in tandem with another based on Conrad's 1917 biographical episode. *The Shadow Line*, as finally made, is linear, static, follows one plot, and has one tone, a marked contrast with the director's previous film, *Land of Promise*. It was not a bad film, but Wajda considered it so and still recalls the helplessness he faced in trying to deal with it. Whenever he struggled with challenging literary material, he was almost invariably successful. This time he was stymied by the crystal prose of Conrad. The film was critically received without enthusiasm and without condemnation. It was shown in a number of countries abroad and on television in England, Germany, and France.

Man of Marble

Wajda himself was to cross a certain kind of shadow line in his very next film similar to the one he crossed with the making of *Ashes and Diamonds*, a line demarking another plane of directorial maturity as well as one of historical assertiveness. In the winter of 1975–76, Wajda attempted to receive authorization to proceed to make a film from a screenplay written fourteen years earlier by Aleksander Ścibor-Rylski. He had tried several times since the script had first been composed and had been summarily rejected by the Ministry of Culture. The story dealt with sensitive things: the 1950s, Stalinism, manipulation, overwhelming ideology, repression. This time, surprisingly, the proposal was accepted with some small changes. Apparently, Stalinism was not such a hot topic anymore. The decision was itself notable and much discussed. The period of "errors and distortions," as it was officially called, was not mentioned in literature, art, or even history.

Ścibor-Rylski's script was based on the texture of genuine events. This is the background: In the early fifties, bricklayers, miners, weavers, and others with a rate of productivity exceeding 500 percent of the norm became part of the propaganda landscape. The so-called "work-emulation" movement, based on the Soviet Stakhanovite phenomenon, was cultivated, and chosen workers were exploited for publicity to inspire or pressure their peers to greater efforts. In real life, the workmates of one such record-breaking bricklayer, angry with the effects his production had on their own piece-work rates, passed him a hot brick causing serious burns. The authorities considered this sabotage of a most serious kind—this was in an atmosphere where simple accidents were treated as sabotage and people were imprisoned for them. There was a social enemy behind the failure to meet any quota.

Around this, Ścibor-Rylski and Wajda wove a story involving one Mateusz Birkut (played by Jerzy Radziwiłowicz), a simple, good-natured bricklayer, perfectly willing to do his best. He becomes the subject of rampant propaganda and is hailed as a national hero. Then comes the turning point; he is passed the hot brick. At this point the plot turns and so does the character of Birkut. He takes the side of a fellow worker who is spuriously accused of sabotage in the incident, and so aggressively does he pursue the defense of his friend that he too finds himself in the dock and is sent to prison. Instantaneously, the huge pictures of him are taken down, the press drops any mention of him, he becomes an unperson. A marble statue of him, a typical work of art of the period, disappears into the basement of a museum. That's the backdrop.

Wajda's intention was to make this film into an experience of discovery for the young in his audience, and rediscovery for those who remembered. The young knew little about Stalinism, the ruthlessness and fear as well as the intensity of ideological pursuit that marked the period. It had all been shrouded through the years and muffled in silence. As a bridge to the young, Wajda centered the discovery of the story-within-a-story in a young documentarist, half investigative reporter, half filmmaker, who is making her diploma film. For Agnieszka (Krystyna Janda), the years in question are a mystery. She lives in contemporary Poland. Only by happenstance, while watching some old newsreels, does she discover that there was a grand marble statue to a person now not at all known. She finds the statue in the museum basement and proceeds to try to find and reconstruct the rest of the story of the man who was its subject.

As she plunges deeper into the story the people and circumstances emerge in rough contours. The more she learns, the more resistance she encounters among those who were originally involved. So we follow two stories at once, the bricklayer's and the filmmaker's, but they are related. One is about the manipulation of reality, the other is about trying to find out what reality is. One is about the repression of human beings, the other is about the repression of the truth. Both are about integrity. It is at that point that Birkut and Agnieszka, who of course never met, meet. They also meet in a way when Agnieszka finds Birkut's son and learns that Birkut is dead. There are suggestions that he might very well have been involved in the workers' riots of 1970 and might have been shot down. (A cemetery scene that makes this explicit was cut out of the film and later included in *Man of Iron*.) This was hard to articulate in 1976, because by then the riots of 1970 were being subjected to the kind of silence the film is about.

Agnieszka does not complete her film, although there is a hopeful hint that she may one day do so. Her project is aborted, ostensibly because it is not complete enough, but possibly because the person whose approval is necessary is himself not willing to risk anything by approving this controversial work. In a gentler way, it is a kind of continuing repression of the truth, another bureaucratic cycle. However, the overriding message is that as long as there are people like Agnieszka, one of Wajda's strong women, there is progress.

The film was made during the spring and summer of 1976, with enthusiasm, given the new territory that was being charted, and with haste, given the nervousness that the project should be completed before someone changed his mind. It was finished in the fall. When it was screened for the authorities, there was consternation, to put it mildly. The film was hot and no one knew what to do with it, bureaucratically. It was ready and had attracted attention in Poland and elsewhere. To shelve it would have been a real embarrassment during a period when the atmosphere was relatively liberal. In the end, it was released, but with very little fuss, and only in one theater on a try-out basis.

It was screened at the Wars Theater in the New Town section. On opening day, February 25, 1977, crowds gathered in the square outside the theater and there was the ozone scent of demonstration in the air, something which had to be headed off. The main thing was to get the crowds thinned out by dispersing them to a number of theaters. So the film was cleared for wider exhibition and *Man of Marble* began a normal run.

In Gdansk, in September 1977, during the annual festival of Polish films, *Man of Marble* was shown, but it was flagrantly excluded from tribute by the official jury in spite of the fact that it was manifestly the most important as well as the most outstanding film of the year. The film journalists at the festival tried to right this wrong by voting it their own award, unofficial though it was. The authorities forbade any official presentation at the closing ceremony. So, following that ceremony, the award was presented to Wajda on the stairs among hundreds of spectators, journalists, and cameramen, a bizarre ceremony! Andrzej Ochalski, a film critic and chairman of the ad hoc jury, presented the director with the award, a brick tied with a red ribbon.

While the screen run of *Man of Marble* was a huge success, there were other problems. It was openly condemned at the highest political forum in the country, the Plenary meeting of the Central Committee of the Party. Even so, it was not banned. What was banned, quietly, was praise for it. Censorship embargoed all articles positively evaluating the film. There was even a limit on negative criticism so that it would not be overly advertised by rebound. Polish audiences are wise enough to know that all-out attack betokens something of surpassing interest. If one were to base one's evaluation on a review of the press of the period, it would seem that the film was a marginal phenomenon of little interest. In reality, it became the center of political discussion in Poland.

Man of Marble is a mural, the kind of composition that Wajda finds himself most comfortable with. It is a complicated picture about two periods and their social and spiritual concerns, and about people subjected to the pressures of history. The concerns of the fifties and the concerns of the seventies overlap and formulate a commentary on one another, even as the gulf between them is dramatized. Poland of the fifties is shown as a country caught up in the harsh demands of reconstruction; Poland of the seventies is portrayed as more developed industrially, materially better off, perhaps able to offer some optimism. Common to both decade representations is the same concern over fundamental values, over the truth.

Birkut is a country boy caught up by the labor currents of a big construction site. He brings with him strength, skill, willingness, and a kind of country honor and truthfulness. Wajda turns him into a proletarian hero. Agnieszka is educated, a girl of the seventies, modern with little direct emotional connection to the past. As she learns about Birkut, she begins to identify with him. Despite her jeans, her feminine aggressiveness, her style, she is basically cast in the same mold as Birkut. They meet across a generation of time, a quarter of a century, bridging the gap in their desire to see lies repudiated.

A related theme of this panoramic mural is the subject of social manipulation. The story of Birkut is a parable of manipulation in its starkest form. His willingness, honesty, and trust are exploited. When he realizes that he has danced like a puppet, it is too late. A roughly parallel thing occurs in the Agnieszka story. Television, for which she is making her film, resists having the past raked up. Not willing to stop her overtly and directly, she is allowed to proceed, the assumption being that she will not find the material she needs. She does and she doesn't. She has the makings of a good story, but because she can't put the dot over the final *i* of the Birkut story, her project is canceled. She has been manipulated by a producer who believes it is his job to mold the mass imagination, to decide what it can be nourished by and what must be considered toxic.

Viewed from the perspective of the story of Poland since World War II and from the story of Wajda's creative life up to 1976, we find a special theme that is so much Wajda's as well as Poland's, man and history, or, if you will, man versus history. When the cavalrymen in *Lotna* charge Panzer tanks with lances, when the soldiers in *Canal* descend into the sewers, when Chełmicki in *Ashes and Diamonds* fires his senseless shot, they are all giving vent to the same protest against oppressive history. They are all making the same gesture of defiance against what may be necessary and inevitable.

Man and history, man against history, these have regularly been used in speaking of Wajda's cinema. What does that mean, exactly? History is, after all, not the same kind of detached and purely physical force as the eruption of a volcano or an earthquake. It is the outcome of a combination of social, political, and economic forces, which for all their intricacies possess a human logic, since humans are involved. It may be that in the aggregate, history becomes a pattern of necessities beyond any individualism, a pattern the sensible individual should yield to or at least take into account in making decisions. What sense is there in any revolt against the patterns and forces involved?

Without a doubt, such behavior cannot be expedient. Neither Birkut nor Agnieszka can gain anything with their defiance. But Wajda's individual in *Man of Marble*, and in his other films where the dilemma is treated, rejects historical necessity because that necessity may indeed be illusory, false, and in any case it is nothing in comparison to the illumination that comes from the existential self. The world is not merely objective; it is also subjective. The world is not only politics; it is also ethics. History seems to seek conformity;

it finds its drama in the gesture of the nonconformist. There is something greater than accommodation; there is honor. Revolt against odds is the answer to historical necessity.

Rough Treatment

After *Man of Marble* Wajda, and indeed unit "X," were subjected to some discrimination. Most of the unit's proposals were rejected, while Wajda, the most popular of Polish directors and one of the most popular people in the country, disappeared for a while from public notice in the media. In such a situation, the idea of a movie about a man who was suddenly the subject of such exclusion was logical. Agnieszka Holland decided to write such a screenplay. Not surprisingly given the atmosphere, the approval for such a film was hardly probable. It turned out that the death of an official from the Ministry of Culture in a plane crash and a new reassessment brought about the approval for making *Rough Treatment* (more accurately, Without Anesthesia, *Bez znieczulenia*) [1978]. The production was efficient and quick.

The movie is a story of a journalist (played by Zbigniew Zapasiewicz, one of the best Polish actors of his generation) who returns from abroad to find that his wife is leaving him and that he is the subject of a bureaucratic freeze-out as the result of a certain outspokenness during an initial television interview. He is subjected to hostility and suspicion; his friends avoid him; his acquaintances cross the street when they see him; his enemies begin their denunciations. When he has pretty much lost on all fronts, including being subjected to slander in the divorce court, a slander more the fault of his wife's lawyer than his wife, he dies by burning to death. We are left to wonder whether it was suicide or accident.

There are two subjects in this film, both of which were relevant at the time. First, there is again the theme of manipulation, or how it is possible to change the image of a man into something negative and to change his situation so that he hardly seems to exist at all. Next, we follow the mechanism that functions to eliminate outstanding personalities, replacing them with talents of mediocrity and conformism. ("It is too good!" This is what one of the officials says of his television interview, praise which is the ironic equivalent of condemnation.) These clearly had something to do with Wajda's personal experience after the making of *Man of Marble* . In addition we are led to wonder why and how a person like this can be suddenly destroyed? Whose fault is it? There is no clear answer because everything happens without a clear reason. We cannot tell why anyone has done what he has done.

In this film, we are presented with a society in which such things can happen without a clear reason because there is no social, moral framework by which to gauge accurately the norms of human behavior. There are no de-

pendable standards of good and evil, of quality and mediocrity. The magnificent of today may tomorrow be on the bottom of the pile. Because there are
no dependable rules of social obligation and moral judgment, cynical manipulation is all the more possible.

The film was made with an unusual simplicity and directness for a director
famous for his baroque style and structural complexity. There are no magnificent scenes, no epic breadth, no search for symbol and metaphor. Everything is matter of fact, as in a television docudrama. Part of the answer to this
variation in style may be in what was happening around Wajda at the time.
The young generation of filmmakers was in the stream of the moral anxiety
movement. As we have pointed out in chapter 5, this trend was gaining more
and more sway in the film community, and it was especially prominent in
Wajda's unit "X." The films of the moral concern direction were all on relevant social themes and issues, directly made, simply composed, and hard-
hitting. Perhaps Wajda was demonstrating that an older director, even one
used to a more decorative and elaborate film language, could work in the
terms of this newer epoch. In any case, whether he set out to do that or not,
he did prove his excellence working in such a plain and journalistic mode.
Rough Treatment takes a rightful place among the best films in the cinema
of moral anxiety.

The Maids of Wilko (1979)

Then, as if to prove his versatility, Wajda took on a completely different
kind of project, non-political, lyrical, delicate, and nostalgic, about the passage of time, memories, love. If Chekhov were a film maker, this is the kind
of film he would make. *The Maids of Wilko* will probably remain Wajda's
most preciously beautiful piece; it is difficult to believe he can surpass its esthetic lyricism. Why does he shift modes so much? His answer has always
been this: "I am first and foremost a filmmaker, not an activist. I make whatever gives me the richest material at a given moment, the best chance of a
good film" (in conversation with F. Turaj). We take that with a grain of salt,
given his highly developed Polish sensibility and his dedication to causes, but
certainly it is partly true; he does have a remarkably sensitive perception of
timing.

There are some cogent reasons for this film being made just when it was.
He was encouraged by his French distributor who was very successful with
The Birch-Wood, another lyrical piece, and wanted to repeat that success.
Another reason, and probably the most important one, was the fact that
Jarosław Iwaszkiewicz, author of the story "The Birch-Wood," was in his
eighties. Between Wajda and Iwaszkiewicz there was a special friendship and,
because of the success of *The Birch-Wood*, some gratitude on the part of

Wajda. He wanted to make a gesture of tribute to the writer while he was still alive, so he chose another Iwaszkiewicz story, "The Maids of Wilko," for a film. The writer died a year after the film was made.

Perhaps Wajda chose this story in particular because of its rich, delicately efficient, portraiture of a number of women. During the course of his career Wajda had become increasingly interested in the delineation and portrayal of female characters. He felt, in fact, that he had slighted this aspect of human drama in the past. The screenplay was done by Zbigniew Kamiński, a director in unit "X," who rendered a faithful reading of the story. Wajda's fascination was with the atmosphere Iwaszkiewicz created, the nostalgia full of understatement. The character development necessarily had to be supported by mood, since given the number of more or less equally important personae, definitive and clear exposition was not possible. Character realization would be by impressionistic technique, reinforced by milieu and visual qualities. Wajda focused, on creating the right atmosphere.

He always insisted that it is not enough to have an idea for a story, a plot that brings characters together and follows their fictional evolution. One must also have a visual idea. In *The Birch-Wood* this was supplied by the painting of Jacek Malczewski, as we have explained. In *The Maids of Wilko* it was contained in the concept of "autumn." This was to be an autumnal film, a film about the way nature withers, of people caught in nature's eternal rhythms wherein the autumn of their lives diminishes, even extinguishes, all that was once new, fresh, vibrant.

The story is set in the early thirties. Wiktor Ruben (Daniel Olbrychski), turning forty, has just lost his closest friend. Sick of heart and body he decides to visit his native countryside and stay with his uncle. He calls in first at the neighboring estate of Wilko, inhabited by five women he had known well in the past. There had been six, but one—who had been in love with Wiktor—was now dead. They are delighted to see him, and it is quickly apparent that to each of them he means something different, represents some different part of their past. Each of these roles is preciously, precisely, and most effectively executed by Krystyna Zachwatowicz, Maja Komorowska, Christine Pascal, Anna Seniuk, and Stanislawa Celińska.

All of them, and Wiktor as well, have changed in their own ways. One has grown bitter; another is preoccupied with her disintegrating marriage; the third is under the heavy hand of a domineering husband; the fourth is overstrung, skittish, restless, and still looking for fulfillment; the youngest is infatuated by this rediscovered old friend of the family. Wiktor's time at Wilko, which he visits daily while staying with his uncle, is spent trying to recapture relationships and understandings that are no longer recoverable, but the past cannot be recreated. Himself scarred, but rescued from the despair that held him in thrall at the beginning of the film, Wiktor bids a thoughtful farewell to

Wilko on a tranquil late autumn afternoon, departing as meaninglessly as he arrived.

Released in 1979, the film met with a unanimously enthusiastic reception from the critics. Those who had supported Wajda's cinema of commitment found in *The Maids of Wilko* evidence of a new reservoir of creativity in the *auteur*, a man who in the course of a single year could turn out such contrasting works, one a bitter social document, the other a literary melancholy evocation, both of them works of the first rank. Those who had violently attacked *Man of Marble* and *Rough Treatment*, the "official" critics, now wrote about the director's masterpiece. If they thought Wajda had abandoned social criticism or were hinting that *The Maids of Wilko* was the kind of film Wajda should concentrate on, they were to be disappointed later when Wajda made *Man of Iron*, his most uncompromising indictment of Polish politics.

The movie played very well outside of Poland also. Wajda's distributor in Paris, Toni Molière, had been correct in encouraging the piece and predicting that it would be a hit. It played especially well in France and quite well in Europe in general. Although it never gained an effective distributor in the United States and has been rarely screened here, it was nominated for an Academy Award (the second nomination for Wajda) as Best Foreign Film.

The Conductor

Wajda's next work, The Conductor (*Dyrygent*) [1980], was unlike either of the preceding two. It was neither political nor atmospheric. It was based on an anecdote about a provincial orchestra that played under a new visiting director each week. Under such a routine, the orchestra would meet with the new director on a Saturday for the first rehearsal and the first problems; conflicts would ripen on Monday; the situation would be aggravated on Tuesday; a crisis would develop on Wednesday; disaster loomed on Thursday; on Friday the concert was held—a great success! Everything started over on Saturday.

Andrzej Kijowski, critic and writer, did a screenplay from this, stretching the plot to include a world-famous conductor who comes to such a town to serve as guest artist. It was a cool intellectual script of great literary merit, but without the kind of central character who could serve as a linch-pin for a drama. Wajda was doubtful. He had always developed lively, rich characters and did not feel comfortable with the plan. In the meantime John Gielgud, the great English actor whose family origins were Polish, the actor to whom Wajda had turned even before the script was ready, unexpectedly agreed to play the role, but could only do so within a limited time.

The production, of necessity, began immediately under uncertain auspices in that the main problems had not yet been resolved. There was essentially no main character in the script, making the conflicts that needed to be developed quite unclear. Wajda therefore started in a most unorthodox way, filming minor background scenes that he knew he would need to include. As the production continued, the main line of the story was developed and the central character emerged with some clarity.

In the story, an orchestra in a small provincial city leads an inglorious, professional existence under its managing director, Adam (Andrzej Seweryn), an energetic man more interested in his career than in music. His wife, Marta (Krystyna Janda), the first violinist, had once met, during a stay in America, a world-famous conductor who had left this same town fifty years ago. It seems he is now living out his last days. She is quite taken by the conductor, who used to know her mother, and because she is immensely impressed with his artistry invites him to the town, assuming that he would probably politely refuse. Unexpectedly, he comes to direct the orchestra in Beethoven's Fifth Symphony, just as he did fifty years ago. For Adam it is an extraordinary chance to gain fame, and help his career. The plot turns because Marta, fascinated by the old maestro, begins to perceive the weakness and mediocrity of her husband. Meanwhile, disappointed with the conditions around him, particularly the manipulation, the conductor decides to leave without conducting. He notices, then, a long line of young people waiting to buy tickets in advance of his concert. On an impulse, he sits at the end of the line of young people, falls asleep, and dies. In a final long conversation between Marta and her husband, the husband's character is completely dissected, his hatred for everyone, his mediocrity, his disdain for music, are all revealed.

Some had assumed that the film would be allegorically political, with the director signifying the regime and the orchestra the nation. In actuality, the film was a thoughtful, delicate examination of art, love, and maturity, and a simultaneous analysis of the destructive force of hatred. It is especially effective in its treatment of old age as a time of harmony, when the anxieties and sick ambitions of youth fall away. A political reading between the lines makes no sense here.

Wajda was not overly pleased with this film, but he may have underrated it, perhaps because of the confusing process of getting it to production. Nonetheless, it was enthusiastically received in Paris, praised generally by the critics, distributed in a number of countries, but somehow made little impact on the Polish film audience. The minds of all Poles, including Wajda, were turning elsewhere in 1980, and Wajda, even while *The Conductor* was being released, had his mind on another project, a highly political one.

Man of Iron (1981)

In the Lenin shipyards in Gdansk in August 1980, a strike broke out that precipitated the greatest political crisis since World War II. It became something of a national strike, albeit loosely structured. The negotiators in Gdansk ended up negotiating for Polish workers universally. "Solidarity" was born as a labor movement, with the Polish state in the role of both government and management. During the strike Wajda went to Gdansk to look into a documentary that was being shot at the negotiations, *Workers, 80* (*Robotnicy, 80*) [1980]. The guards set up by the strikers did not let strangers into the yards for fear of admitting provocateurs. When Wajda introduced himself as "the director of *Man of Marble* ," he was immediately admitted. On the way to the strike committee, a young man said, "You should now make a new film, this time about a man of iron." That suggestion was the beginning of the next film.

Upon his return to Warsaw, Wajda turned to Ścibor-Rylski, writer of *Man of Marble*, and asked for a screenplay for *Man of Iron* (*Człowiek z żelaza*). There was a certain time pressure upon everyone because of the fear that circumstances would quickly change in such a way as to make an outspoken film impossible. Ścibor-Rylski had a first draft in eight days. This is not to say that it was an easy project, far from it! It was, on the one hand, necessary to be absolutely topical with respect to the events transpiring; on the other hand, everything would need to be incorporated into the story and form of *Man of Marble*, a form which made use of two time periods, the fifties and the seventies. One of the key additions was the detailed articulation of Birkut's death during the riots of 1970. There was a complex mix here of epochs, events, and characters, from which a strong man of iron would need to emerge, Birkut's son. The first draft gave general guidance, but work on the script continued without interruption during the entire production of the film.

At the same time there was the problem of getting approval to make the film, a film which would go politically beyond anything that had ever been done. The man who had been Minister of Culture at the time of the making of *Man of Marble*, Józef Tejchma, had been dismissed, one of the reasons being his approval of the film. In a new change of governmental positions, Tejchma was once again appointed to be minister, and the screenplay for *Man of Iron* was placed on his desk. Once more he gave his approval, and once more he was dismissed.

Production started in early spring in the Gdansk shipyards, marked by haste, nervousness, and by doubts concerning the final form of the intricate screenplay. To tie things together, Ścibor-Rylski introduced a new character, a journalist of questionable credentials who was a heavy drinker, a man recruited by the authorities to gather information at the shipyard that would help discredit the strike leaders. Presumably, after the suppression of the strike, it would be useful to publish this kind of damning information. Ultimately, he refuses to cooperate in this perfidy. That subplot was filmed first, and the result was quite convincing. The problem was that this moved some-one else, the journalist, into the center of the story, a man of rubber instead of a man of iron. The script had to be changed again to diminish this strand and to amplify the other part of the story.

On May 8, 1981, the first closed showing of the film, as it then stood, took place. The version was not effective. There were too many time planes (1970, the late seventies, 1980); there was a heavy accumulation of plots, and there was a problem with the ambivalent character of the journalist. Nevertheless, through it all one could sense the power, the relevance, and the reality, that the final version would have. For maximum political impact, as well as for its own sake, the film had to be finished in time to be shown at Cannes, where the program for May 31 reflected in print the question of the day: WAJDA OR NO WAJDA?

The director worked day and night to reshape what he had. Only days be-fore the planned screening in Cannes he received the Ministry of Culture's final approval of the movie. It was shown at Cannes on the last day of the fes-tival and was awarded the highest prize, The Golden Palm. The Polish open-ing was held at the end of July.

In the story of the film, the journalist Winkiel, blackmailed into gathering information for the authorities, looks into the background of the strike leader, Tomczyk. He meets a number of people who tell him things that dovetail into a growing picture. This Tomczyk (Jerzy Radziwiłowicz) is the son of Birkut, who was the man of marble. After the death of Birkut in the riots of 1970, Tomczyk works for a movement of free trade unions. He links up with a girl (Krystyna Janda) who was the television documentarist in *Man of Marble* who never finished the film about Birkut but met Tomczyk in her searches. Their life and fate after the timeframe of *Man of Marble* include loneliness, unemployment, and imprisonment, all of which go into the making of the plot for *Man of Iron*. Eventually there is a victorious strike, which is in prog-ress in the timeframe of *Man of Iron*. Winkiel, in the meantime, loses his cyn-icism as he learns more and more about Tomczyk. He turns his back on the official figure who had suborned him, but by then the workers, who have grown suspicious of him, refuse to accept him as a friend. Rejected by both sides, he leaves the yards after the agreement that represents a victory for the strikers, and just then encounters his former boss, who dismisses the agreement as useless, a meaningless piece of paper. This final scene was to be prophetic, considering what happened a few months later.

Artistically, *Man of Iron* is definitely not one of Wajda's best films. It lacks structural balance, the narrative seems ragged, some episodes are not com-pletely clear, and most important the figure of Tomczyk is too one-dimen-sional. He emerges as a spotless hero with few flaws and uncertainties. There are uneven seams between the staged sequences, the documentary material that was included, and the material related to *Man of Marble* .

However, the film possesses something that few other films do: the viewer gets the impression of being right in the middle of a historical event of great importance. For all its artistic imperfections, there is a power running through the work that makes it a unique document of its kind. Wajda has determinedly returned again and again to the theme of man and history. *Man of Iron* takes a special place, therefore, in this director's canon. In his own words he told what he has been trying to do all along, and had done again in *Man of Iron*. In an address after having received an honorary Doctor of Humane Letters degree at The American University in Washington, D.C., in October 1981, he said: "I have not tried for their own sake to evoke bygone ages, or to create great figures, or recount battles, or reveal staffwork and the cabinet secrets of the powers that be, or for their own sake any of those things which make up what we call history. On the contrary, I have attempted to describe living people and what happened to them and between them, except that these people were always caught up in the currents of history."

As we have discussed, Wajda's heroes resisted the tide of history, which heretofore had always carried them away to destruction. In the case of *Man of Iron*, people seem to have halted the engine, even reversed it. It appears that history's force, which is paradoxically both abstract and brutal, has been overcome. After decades of historical pessimism, we have here an air of optimism, one that was foreshadowed by the resolute, stubborn, and honest posture of Agnieszka at the close of *Man of Marble* . The sequel, *Man of Iron*, goes some distance toward the redemption of the gestures of glory that Wajda built into so many films.

It opened in Poland on July 26, 1981, and quickly proved itself to be the most popular film of all time. The very fact that millions were given a chance to see it was a sign of fundamental new conditions existing in society. But since December 12, 1981, when martial law was declared, *Man of Iron* has not been seen again in Poland.

Danton

Many found reverberations of the events of 1980 and 1981 in Wajda's next film, *Danton* [1983]. Some American critics claimed to discover Lech Wałęsa, the Solidarity leader, in the character of Georges Danton and General Wojciech Jaruželski in the character of Maximilien Robespierre. Trying to find a strong parallel seems like an abuse of the material, but it is clear that there are certain comparisons that naturally occur while watching the film, whether or not they were intentionally inserted. The posture and carriage of Wojciech Pszoniak, who plays Robespierre, seems very much like an imitation of the posture of Jaruželski. This is superficial, to be sure, but it does inspire reading between the lines. Nor is it difficult to find political reference points in the dialogue. Incontrovertibly, the Polish audience looked for and found metaphors, some convincing, some incongruous. But it is equally incontrovertible that the creators of *Danton* wanted to identify the character Danton with the historical Danton and the character Robespierre with the historical Robespierre long before the world knew of Wałęsa and Jarużelski.

In 1975, during the filming of *Land of Promise*, Wajda took the time to direct a play for the legitimate theater, *The Danton Affair*, a play that strongly moved its Warsaw audience. The author of it was Stanisława Przybyszewska (1901–1935), daughter of a more famous, eccentric, modernist writer, Stanisław Przybyszewski (1868–1927). The playwright daughter was completely preoccupied with the French Revolution and obsessed with the figure of Robespierre. Her drama had been staged only once before, during the 1930s and with no success. Wajda's production brought it back onto the playbills and awakened interest in the author.

The next step toward this subject becoming a film was taken when Wajda met the French actor Gerard Depardieu, whom he immediately thought of as the perfect Danton. In 1980 a Polish-French coproduction was arranged with the Gaumont Company and events accelerated. A screenplay based on Przybyszewska's drama was undertaken by the French novelist and scriptwriter Jean-Claude Carrière. Production was to begin in 1981, but it had to be postponed so that Wajda could finish *Man of Iron*. With *Man of Iron* on the screen, production was slated for December 1981 and January 1982. Studio sequences were to be done in Poland, location scenes in France.

Events intervened. On December 12-13, martial law was introduced in Poland, borders were closed, communications cut, curfew was introduced. Of course the studios were closed to activity. It seemed that the project was finished. But in January 1982, one of the first planes to come to Warsaw from Paris carried Margaret Menegoz, the production manager, who suggested moving all activities to Paris. The authorities agreed, a big surprise considering the nature of the times. Several dozen people involved in the movie went to Paris to work and brought with them some set decorations and some other related things. Officially the film remained a coproduction, but now of course the French end of things was considerably more significant. Shooting began in April, even while the script was still being reshaped by Bolesław Michałek and Agnieszka Holland. It was finished in the fall and the French premiere occurred in Paris on January 6, 1983. In Poland it opened on January 28.

The action takes place in the spring of 1794, four years after the storming of the Bastille, when the revolution had reached a point of crisis. There was war, poverty, and dissatisfaction. The government, which is to say the Committee of National Salvation led by Robespierre (Wojciech Pszoniak), wants to keep the revolution moving and proclaims a ruthless campaign against the opposition. The rule of terror commences. Danton (Gerard Depardieu), another chief leader of the revolution, returns to Paris after having removed himself temporarily from political life. As a popular idol he is perceived as a potentially dangerous opponent of the government. In contrast to the powers that rule, he wants to stop the terror, provide bread and peace, and promote normal life. To Robespierre and the committee this meant aborting the revolution. The terror is part of the revolutionary process, the process must proceed, stopping it means stopping the revolution. The film *Danton* thus is the story of the confrontation between the two leaders and between two ideals. Danton is vanquished and goes to the guillotine. Ultimately, Robespierre concludes that, "the revolution went off course." That diversion had enough momentum to destroy him; three months later Robespierre went to the guillotine.

From the beginning Wajda was aware of the main traps the film could fall into. There was the danger that it could become a historical costume entertainment, a typical period piece whose banal plots, decorations, and embellishments could overwhelm its substance. There was also the danger of making it into a dry, purely intellectual and ideological exposition of the political doctrines involved. Wajda wanted balance. He brought this off with classical craft.

First, he imposed on the film a strict dramatic construction. We have two men who not only represent two ways of seeing the world of politics, but who personally are radically different from each other. Robespierre is strict, doctrinaire, a purist, a flinty sufferer. Danton is a trifle the cynic but open to life, very human and likable. In this there were sharp changes from the outlook of Przybyszewska, who saw Robespierre as spotlessly heroic and Danton as a treacherous demagogue. The fact is that, as much as he wanted to work from what the playwright had done, Wajda considered this polarization wrong for the drama he wanted to create for the screen.

Second, the director imposed a concentration of time upon the story. The events actually took place over several weeks, but in the film everything takes three days. The action inevitably consists of a repetition of certain kinds of scenes—meetings, discussions, gatherings of the populus, and tribunals—but this did not keep Wajda from extracting maximum dramatic conflict. That had always been a forte of his.

Finally, Wajda introduced the feeling of threat from the very start of the film and sustained that tension throughout. Threat looms over Danton and his family as well as all his allies, but it also seems to loom over his adversaries. An atmosphere of danger, sometimes very real, sometimes almost abstract, permeates every scene. Fear is the engine of politics here.

Pszoniak, the actor who played Robespierre, played the same role in the 1975 Warsaw theatrical production. He creates here a pellucidly clear ideologue, an unselfish ascetic, so much so that he kindles antipathy. Depardieu (Danton) is robust, loud, bombastic, a man who likes food and drink, women and money. His human verve is his strength. It is quite possible to see the two as allegorical representations of their outlooks and ideologies. That would not be out of line at all since people do tend to live the way they think.

It is not surprising that the humanly flawed character of Danton had much more appeal for the audience than did the character of Robespierre. However, it was a little surprising to Wajda that the role would draw so much sympathy to it (a tribute to the two chief actors, actually) that in the perception of the viewers, the vanquished and doomed Danton is transformed into the victor. Clearly, the film ends up favoring Danton and his philosophy. That is how it was understood in Poland, France, and also in the United States.

In France, *Danton* set off a small political controversy. The Republican and Gaullist opposition identified itself with Danton and linked the ruling Socialists with the doctrinaire Robespierre. The makers of the film (director and writers) insist they had no such intention. It is their position that a sort of Danton-Robespierre dialog exists in each and every political grouping from conservative to Communist. Whatever their intentions, the fact is that the public had fun making more particular interpretations.

Love in Germany

The same French company, Gaumont, that had worked with Wajda on *Danton*, was only too happy to link with him on another project, *Love in Germany (Miłość w Niemczech)* [1984]. It was a project the director had had under consideration since 1981, when he was approached by Artur Brauner, a producer from West Berlin, with the proposition to make a film from the book by the same title by Rolf Hochhut, a book currently popular in Germany. The book is half reportage and half essay, reconstructing certain events that took place in a small German village in 1940. At that time a Polish prisoner of war was hanged for having an affair with a German woman, the proprietor of a grocery. Hochhut took the facts and transformed them into an essay on history, collective psychology, and Nazi paranoia. He enhanced the texture of his work by reproducing documents of the period related to the event which were intrinsically startling. For example, there is one inclusion, in which extraordinarily Germanic directions are laid out in detail for handling such a case: what the court procedure should be like, who the hangman is to be, the hangman's fee (three cigarettes), how the casket is to be paid for, and what to do with it after the body is delivered to an anatomy lab.

It was Bolesław Michałek's task to make a screenplay from the book, one that would extract the story from the essay but keep Hochhut's concerns in view. The story needed to illustrate how a small, peaceful village, inhabited by ostensibly decent, kind people could be stained by such a murder. Along the way Michałek was joined in scripting by Agnieszka Holland.

Love in Germany was shot in the summer of 1983 in Brauner's studio in Berlin and in the actual village where the episode happened.

In the story, a Polish POW named Stanisław, called in the film Stani (Piotr Łysak), has a torrid love affair with his employer—some POWs were assigned to private people as unpaid employees—who is named Pauline (Hanna Schygulla). The affair comes to the attention of the local Gestapo official, who is required to begin the process for treating with such things. This Gestapo man is not a monstrosity of the conventional kind. In fact, he is even ready to spare the young man and release the woman if the Pole agrees to become a member of German society. He is deemed to qualify for membership by an anatomical examination, including having his skull measured by calipers. Racially, he is acceptable. Stani rejects the proposal. He will remain a Pole, a defiant, self-destructive gesture. Now the administrative details are worked out. The Nazi law in this case prescribed that a Pole can only be hung by another Pole, who will receive the three cigarette payment. If that Pole refuses to act as hangman, he in turn is liable to be hung by yet another Pole, etc., etc. One Pole, played by Daniel Olbrychski, does refuse to act as executioner, but eventually Stani is hung and Pauline is sent to a camp.

Love in Germany is realistic in convention. It is told as flashback as we follow a man and a boy who are reconstructing the story. There is an implication that they are the son and grandson of Pauline. During the long flashback narration, the milieu is presented with great attention to detail, reproducing the atmosphere of the village, its everyday activities, its pettiness, its insignificant quarrels. Wajda manages a skillful conjunction of two facets of the same story. One facet is the tale of unbearable and uncontrollable passions, the other is the satirical delineation of an inhuman bureaucracy. As different as the subject matter of these two facets would appear to be at first glance, Wajda manages to bring them together seamlessly, two sides of the same story.

The tale of passion gives us at one and the same time one of the strongest and one of the weakest elements in the movie. Hanna Schygulla, as a woman who has lost emotional and sexual control of herself, is lusciously and devastatingly convincing. It is an unbelievably sensuous performance. It is perhaps the overwhelming total sensuousness of Schygulla that diminishes by contrast the figure and performance of Piotr Łysak. His acting is quite good, but he is simply not believable as a figure who could inspire such total abandonment on the part of a strong and passionate woman.

The facet of the film that depicts the inhuman bureaucracy is made especially effective by the use of ironic understatement. Many films have depicted the monstrosity of Nazism by focusing on brutality, shouting, vicious cruelty, and the like. In this film Nazism is not demonstrated by mass annihilation, nor grand devastation, but rather by a small story from a small village. As nice as the village seems, its inhabitants accept without reservation the paranoid system. This is only in the most indirect way an indictment of Hitler or the structure of the Reich. Through a matter-of-fact description of one marginal event, *Love in Germany* accuses the ordinary and mediocre citizen for being an accomplice to murder.

Probably for this reason the film was not received well in Germany. It was charged with presenting a false picture in detail and in its evocation of atmosphere. Naturally, the accusations implicit in the film would be hard to accept on the part of any community. If the film had been the usual caricature of Nazism, it probably would have been more easily accepted. In presenting the ordinary citizen as a participant in Nazi inhumanity, Wajda was on sensitive ground indeed.

In other countries the film had a fine reception, especially in England and the United States. To this day it has not been shown in Poland. Even at the beginning of the planning, when a coproduction was proposed, the cinema authorities rejected the idea. The claim was that the film might somehow be understood as in some way justifying Nazi crimes. A more believable reason was the antipathy the authorities felt toward Wajda.

Both *Danton* and *Love in Germany* were done abroad at a time when the relationship between Wajda and the cultural and political authorities was bad. Conditions came to a head in 1983 and the regime dissolved unit "X," dismissing Wajda and Bolesław Michałek, his literary director. Wajda also found it necessary to step down as chairman of the Polish Association of Filmmakers in order to diminish the probability that the authorities would dissolve that association as they had done with others. His resignation was carried out with great dignity; it was tendered to the peers who had elected him, not to the administration, and those peers proceeded to elect their own next chairman. Once again his name was little used by the media, and the authorities attempted to make of him an unperson. That is impossible.

In Poland, this most Polish of all directors remains one of the nation's most respected artists and citizens. When a poll was taken in 1985 at a Warsaw theater over a period of time to determine the public's perception of Poland's ten greatest films, three of the ten were by Andrzej Wajda. At the top of the list was *Ashes and Diamonds*.

IX

Krzysztof Zanussi:
The Cinema of Intellectual Inquiry

In the middle 1960s, the rather close-knit film community in Poland distributed the report of an unusually interesting group of artists coming along at the Lodz school. The name heard most frequently was Krzysztof Zanussi, whose diploma film received a good deal of attention. *Death of a Provincial* (*Śmierć Prowincjała*) [1966] was a short feature, not so much a story as a meditation on the last moments before death of the prior of a monastery. Virtually plotless and thin in its characterization of the old monk, it nonetheless captivated its viewers by evoking with special atmosphere a reflection of age, of the evanescence of life, of the meaning of faith and duty.

Zanussi, in fact, was already a rigorous intellectual with a developed interest in film art before he entered the Lodz school. He studied physics at the University of Warsaw and philosophy at the Jagiellonian University in Krakow. As a student he had been active in film clubs and had made a number of 8-mm and 16-mm shorts. These went unnoticed by the professionals because of the clear separation between the industry and amateurs, in spite of the fact that nine of his eleven projects received prizes at competitions. One simply did not gain entry to the industry through the amateur route. Zanussi there- fore took the regular path and, with his two degrees, enrolled at the film school to earn a third. He was atypical.

One popular notion has it, in Poland as elsewhere, that the career of film director is one imbued with great status, a career that combines dedication, renown, and material success. Purportedly, filmmakers are inspired, bursting with ideas, mercurial, revered at home, acclaimed abroad, perhaps like Wajda. Another image is that of a workmanlike professional, uncharismatic, methodically making movie after movie, some better some worse, but with name recognition and well paid. Both types are supposed to be sort of bohemian in lifestyle and even in dress, which is imagined as calculatedly casual. Neophytes in the industry waste no time making themselves into one or another of these stereotypes.

Not so Zanussi who avoided being cast in such molds. Broadly and deeply educated, something he never masked, he could easily be taken for a serious academic of a scientific bent. He is intellectually cool and careful, extremely precise in his phrasing, sharply articulate, alert for hidden implications in ideas and events, provoking others into adopting his analytic mode of reason and discourse. His lifestyle also presents something of a contrast: he possesses impeccable manners, wears a suit and tie, and is moderate in his habits. He is never a subject of gossip or scandal, avoids nightclubs and flamboyant occasions. No wonder that the members of the industry did a double take upon his appearance and asked themselves questions about this new member of their brotherhood. They would discover in due course that Zanussi's intellect and discipline would introduce a new style to the film world and show the way in dealing with subtleties and issues not yet broached by others.

The Structure of Crystal

He was at the start mainly his own screenwriter, working occasionally with his friend Edward Żebrowski. He is fond of saying that he had aspirations to be a writer but found that he could express himself more precisely in his movies. When he finished the screenplay for The Structure of Crystal (Struktura kryształu) [1969], he brought it to the "Tor" unit, then headed by Stanisław Różewicz who grasped the originality of the project, one that would involve a great deal of artistic risk in the execution. There was little plot and only a thin conflict. Mainly the piece would consist of dialogue held in a remote village. Who, the question posed itself, wanted to watch a movie like that? But it was a new idea and worth doing if only because it would be quite inexpensive, requiring no sets or decorations to speak of, and a small cast and crew. It was done.

The setting was a small village in the east of Poland that houses a meteorological station run by a young scientist, who records temperature, precipitation, wind, humidity, and so on. He and his wife await a visit from a college friend, a scientist making a good career for himself in Warsaw. The friend arrives and they do mundane things—walk, visit the local school, go to the movies in a nearby small town. Most of their time is spent talking about science, life, obligations, careers, success.

In the process the two characters and personalities begin to take on form and definition (like crystals forming?). The visitor is clearly a man of promise and ability, confident, precise, cool, and direct. He wonders at the career path his friend has chosen, especially since the two of them are equal in ability. Why does he remain hidden in this out-of-the-way location? Why has he given up the comforts of the city and the companionship of intellectuals, not to mention a more rewarding career? The dialogue between the two personalities and two approaches continues for a few days. The visitor's reasoning is clear, but what about the host's?

Comfort, prosperity, luxury, success, are not his values and priorities. He prefers to read, listen to music, contemplate life and self-reconciliation, develop relationships with those close to him. This smacks of pretense and posture, but that is not at all how the personality is portrayed. In fact the character is quite appealing, not at all moralistic. This is a man who makes no attempt to push his philosophy onto anyone and only diffidently accounts for his own choices. The film ends with the visitor returning to his active career. The host remains where he is, reconciled, at peace.

The film does not lead us to any pat conclusion. There is no preachy attitudinizing about moral integrity, compromise, activism, or contemplation. It does open awareness of choices that can be made, indeed choices that are inescapable. Life will formulate itself one way, or it will formulate itself another way. Structure will set in whether we will have it or not. What then will be the goal? It is best to understand the terms of one's existence. That is a theme that recurs in Zanussi's work.

The film was not warmly received, after all it lacked just about everything that audiences expected: story, drama, conflict. There were those in the industry also who had their doubts, but this was accompanied by a broad recognition that in this modest film, a new individuality had asserted itself, one which calculated a different approach to the audience. This was not a director whose point of view was insistent, nor was there any pandering to mode. This was a director that invited his audience to stop and think.

Family Life

He also needed to establish himself, and to that end he determined to make a straightforward story, one that would be accessible but at the same time artistically effective and thoughtful. The composition was classical, with a beginning, middle, and end, two climaxes, well-delineated characters, a hero, conflict, denouement, and unities of time, action, and place. Such was *Family Life* (*Życie rodzinne*) [1970], set in an old house suffused in an atmosphere of regret, bitterness, and defeat. The garden is overgrown with weeds, contributing to the gloomy tones which are suggestive of Strindberg or the early films of Bergman.

Into this scene comes a young man (Daniel Olbrychski), the scion of the family who returns from the real, functioning, living world that exists beyond the world of this house. He has been summoned from his job in an engineering firm on the pretext of his father's poor health. It is clear that he is returning with some reluctance and against his better judgment, bringing a friend with him as a buffer against the shock of a traumatic homecoming. His father (Jerzy Kreczmar) is jaundiced, cantankerous, psychologically skewed; his aunt (Halina Mikołajska) is old and exhausted; and his sister (Maja Komorowska) is utterly unhinged. As the action develops, further responses to these characters are evoked and they seem more to be pitied than disliked. The father is a lonely and frustrated alcoholic who has lost everything. For the sister, madness is an escape from reality. They are all, in this household, poor and lonely, badly treated by their lives, by the times, and also by this son who had more or less abandoned them. He makes an effort to be reconciled with them, but his heart is not in it. He leaves again, but clearly he cannot leave everything behind. As he blends in with the people in the world outside of the house, a close-up of his face reveals the same tic that hardened into a grimace on the father's face years ago. The ending explicates the message (perhaps too obtrusively): there is no escaping from the effects of one's family, either emotionally or genetically. Such liberation is delusion.

At this early stage in his career, Zanussi had already entered into a regular association with television production, which was an active sponsor of short, low-budget films by young directors. There was a mood of encouragement for quality pieces of serious cultural import, pieces unconnected with propaganda, and space was made for ambitious television drama. He made the documentary *Krzysztof Penderecki* [1968] and some features: *Face to Face (Twarz w twarz)* [1968]; *The Examination (Zaliczenie)* [1969]; *Mountains at Twilight (Góry o zmierzchu)* [1970]; *The Role (Rola)* [1971]; and *The Hypothesis (Hipoteza)* [1972].

Two of these deserve annotation. *Face to Face* presents a moment in the life of an ordinary person. While shaving one morning he notices a man running along a roof pursued by the police. The hunted man's beseeching eyes meet the indifferent stare of the shaver, who takes care to close his window. The man falls off into empty space. *The Hypothesis* deals with a similar theme in that a young scientist witnesses the drowning of a woman, failing to offer any help. Some time later, tried and convicted by his conscience, he dies at exactly the same spot. Both stressed the theme of responsibility for the fate of the others and underscored the guilt of those who deny such responsibility. This is an important subject for Zanussi.

Next Door

It was explored intensively in a sixty-minute television film (later given theater release), *Next Door (Za ścianą)* [1971]. The setting was banal, a huge apartment house in Warsaw, one of those grey, drab, impersonal buildings in which thousands live out anonymous existences. These were people who preferred to remain strangers to each other, preoccupied with their quotidian problems, alone in their anxieties, perplexities, and thoughts. In the same wing of just such a building live the film's two principals, several floors apart. She (Maja Komorowska) is a young scientist, unattractive, lonely, nervous, bitter. He (Zbigniew Zapasiewicz) is older than she is and a professor at the very same institute. By way of contrast he is successful, self-confident, and competent. Although they live in the same building and work together, so to speak, they barely know each other. Sometimes they nod politely on the elevator.

At a critical moment, the girl decides to seek out help from the older man. He is polite, possibly even sympathetic, but he is not moved to help her because of his reserve, his habitual distance, his irritation that this neurotic girl should have obtruded upon him with her bothersome failures. The following day he happens upon a rescue squad entering her apartment and learns that she has attempted suicide.

This is a film in which not very much happens, to be sure, but it is startling nevertheless. In the girl's restless and choked dialogue, in the polite reserve of the professor, in the atmosphere of loneliness, disengagement, and alienation, the audience recognizes something familiar, the irritating idea that no one is at fault in the sense of being bad or good, of being malevolent or deserving of benevolence. There is no passion, no resolution. What the film develops slowly and painfully is the climate of alienation, separateness, selfish isolation. *Next Door* has stifled despair as its subject and matches that with a form that suggests muffled pathos.

One wonders how such a film could have so profoundly affected the sensibilities of millions; for it did, in spite of the fact that it was aloof, abstractly moralistic, suggestively existentialist, directed so as to be low-key, short on dramatic effect, gray as the reality it depicts. One reason for its artistic success was the riveting delineation of character by two extraordinary performers, Komorowska and Zapasiewicz. They charged the film with a kind of sick, psychological fever; they showed the depth that existed beneath the prosaic story. Since *Next Door*, Komorowska has played in practically every one of Zanussi's films. He employed over and over her uncanny ability to convey the ineffable with a gesture, or with an expression in her slightly asymmetrical eyes, or with her suggestive emotional voltage that ranges from painful confusion to the verge of hysteria. Zanussi fully realized that her gifts were instrumental to bringing vibrant life, necessary life to his intellectual, exploratory, analytical themes.

Illumination

Such themes were central to *Illumination* (*Iluminacja*) [1973], a film that reflected Zanussi's continuing interest in the sciences and in intellectual search, a work that is central to his canon and extremely important in the history of Polish cinema. At its epicenter it questions the ability of the natural sciences to explain in any satisfactory way the phenomenon of human existence or define the human condition. Tactically the problem was how to express in narrative cinema such intellectual investigation.

Zanussi chose the form of a filmic *bildungsroman*, a description of one young man and what happens to him from secondary school through the university to starting a family and discovering independence. The director charts an erratic path with its turns, crossings, and backtracking, with destination unknown. The action is placed in the recent, equally erratic, history of the country, as the events of the 1960s and 1970s create social anxieties as well as personal hopes and disappointments. There was doubt in advance that such an approach could succeed on the screen, that it could make itself appealing to an audience. Zanussi had adamant faith, received approval, and made *Illumination*.

A young man from a small town applies to study physics at a university, where he tells the admissions committee that he intends to search for something more in science than a diploma and a career. Charmed by his naive honesty, they admit him to the world of studies. He enters another world as well when he is introduced to love by an older woman from a more exotic milieu. As events unfold he also comes to know death, although not the death of anyone close to him. This nonetheless leaves its mark. He experiences another love affair, this time a very serious one with a girl made in a similar mold: motivated, uncompromising, high-principled, even a bit grim. Then come pregnancy, marriage, military service, and many new demands.

While the protagonist never falters in his continuing intellectual quest, he does begin to doubt the power of science to provide efficacious answers to the great dilemmas of existence. In any case his search passes into another phase because, under the pressure of financial need, he abandons his studies to earn money, first in a factory, then as an orderly in a mental hospital where physiological experiments are conducted upon the human brain. This brings him into contact with the most acute kind of human suffering and with the relative impotence of science and medicine in alleviating it and also with the dangers involved in imperfect knowledge. He is visited by a spiritual crisis which moves him to abandon everything, job, wife, child, in order to take to the road, almost as if his blockaded psychological journey must now manifest itself physically. At one point he stops at a monastery much like the one depicted earlier by Zanussi in *Death of a Provincial*, when he probed many of the same questions. He decides to return to his family and his studies. Again the more deeply he studies the more he is convinced that science contains no answers to the questions that torment him. When finally he approaches the verge of a kind of resigned independence and a settled future, he learns that he has a seriously damaged heart. As the film ends, he stands ruefully watching his child bathing in a river.

Clearly the story lacked unity of action, the narrative switches back and forth among various environments and characters, some of them barely adumbrated, the plot movement halts from time to time to explain some physical, medical or social phenomenon. The asides themselves add up to a cycle of mini-documentaries, a sort of film within a film which charts the course of the protagonist's thoughts and his comprehension. The biography is not at all conventionally laid out. Delineation is often sketchy, elliptical—as when we see the hero exchanging glances with a girl and in the next moment making love. We go from eye contact to intimacy to him in the army and the girl among the visitors to his camp. Ellipsis is here the basis of the narrative style. Continuity is maintained by following discrete sequences, first the hopeful episode when the protagonist begins his studies, then the first love affair, then death in the mountains, then a glimpse of the girl with whom in another sequence he is to be joined. Within the sequences patterns emerge and the theme is articulated.

Ellipses, insinuations, and documentary insertions thus give the film a rhythm of hesitation rarely encountered in film, a mood of disjointed search and existential anxiety into which a sensitive audience is drawn in no small part because of the performance of Stanisław Latallo, not a professional actor but an assistant to the director, chosen because of his brooding eyes and because he could so well project the personality of a young man struggling to overcome his own shyness. Words come awkwardly to him, as if his mouth is dry; his body motions convey uncertainty; but his eyes behind thick glasses flash a strident intellectual curiosity and a lively gift of observation. By a tragic quirk of fate and coincidence, Latallo died a few years later on a mountain-climbing expedition in the Himalayas in the course of his own quest for meaning in life.

There is no verbal nugget that can summarize *Illumination*. It is worth recalling that from the outset Zanussi referred to it as a "drama of cognition," presumably one in which the protagonist struggles mind and soul to penetrate existence for whatever is worth knowing. Science, as we have pointed out, frustrates and blocks him, which was inevitable. In the film there is a conversation, an authentic conversation, with an eminent Polish scientist (not an actor) who stresses that we must not expect too much. Science takes what it has, frames hypotheses and approximations, and beyond a certain point becomes game-like. Nor does religion offer the answer, allowing another deep disappointment. What is left? Only certain rules that guide our lives, first and foremost moral rules, but they explain nothing in and of themselves. It is an error to make knowledge a goal. It is a pathway not a destination. We need it to bring necessary minimum order to our lives, to allow us approximate choices in fundamental things as well as mundane things. Other questions arise: Can we control our lives, and to what extent? What are the limits of free will? What are the chances of philosophical or intellectual rebellion? What answers can we frame?

In the context of *Illumination* it is significant that at critical junctures in the life of the hero he comes into contact with death: a mountain-climbing accident and cancer of the brain. Moreover, just as he is about to become resigned to his future he is faced with his own mortally damaged heart. Death is clearly the ultimate condition, the ineluctable goal, the entity toward which all things tend. In that this is so, it makes no sense to regard life in any other way than from the perspective of death and our own evanescence. Goals that individuals set are fragile and illusory. Does this mean that life is absurd?

That is not Zanussi's conclusion. The meaning comes not from the illusive goal and its attainment, but rather from incessant and patient striving, from ascending, to use the imagery of mountain-climbing. This thinking obviously participates in the philosophy of existentialism, and one is inclined to think of Camus's *Myth of Sisyphus*. Sisyphus's struggle was the key to finding meaning in existence. The futile struggle is itself the heroism of existence. In spite of the hero's apparent defeat, *Illumination* rejects resignation and nihilism. The child in the river is life as it is, fragile but precious. We must learn much in order to learn that, perhaps by a stroke of illumination.

The film was received enthusiastically by Polish critics and went over well with the public, especially the younger audience. Its unconventional structure, elliptical story, documentary insertions, and so on, were not an obstacle. The seriousness of the subject matter was not a detriment. It may simply be that Zanussi treated with things that lie always just below the surfaces of life, things that are seldom treated in an accessible way. Cinema is certainly the most accessible of our means of communication and dramatization. Zanussi made progress in film history by translating philosophy into cinema. Not surprisingly *Illumination* created a minor sensation in a number of countries that have a history of film sophistication. At the 1975 Locarno festival Zanussi was awarded the Golden Leopard, the jury's highest award.

The door opened for Zanussi to make films abroad, which he did from this point on with some regularity. His first venture with producer Manfred Durniok was done for the West German television company Zweites Deutsches Fernsehen. It was *Catamount Killing* [1974], a film based on the novel *I Would Rather Stay Poor* by James Hadley Chase. The German actor Horst Buchholz played the lead in the story of a bank teller in a small town in Vermont who fakes a robbery with the help of a poor widow, and then ends up involved in murder. Confession follows when they are convinced that only through punishment can they come to terms with themselves. It is a detective story with a strong moral streak. Conscience emerges as more effective than law. It was made hastily in difficult circumstances and met with poor reviews. To our knowledge it has never been seen outside of its showing on West German television.

Balance-Sheet

At home Zanussi enjoyed a portion of fame as a result of *Illumination*. He did realize that the form and intellectual heft of that movie somewhat restricted its audience and decided on a new project that would combine his style and ideas with a simple, down-to-earth story of the romance of an ordinary woman, a simple bookkeeper. For *Balance-Sheet* (*Bilans kwartalny*) [1974] he once again cast Maja Komorowska in the leading role.

She is a woman parceling out her time nine-to-fiving, marketing, practicing domesticity and motherhood, a doormat to the world, on a treadmill but glad to be of use, human and kind. From a legion of human hollow-people, she is set apart by her altruism and goodness. For example, she goes to considerable trouble to intercede for a neglected boy at his school, she helps a neighbor move furniture, she stands up for a fellow worker unjustly accused. So far this is her life because her husband (Piotr Fronczewski) is the ultimate washout, a bank clerk, dull and stodgy, the apotheosis of routine. Does she love him or he her? It is almost too much to ask. It is a question that is almost unseemly. Their apartment is a little cage and they are placid animals.

She meets another man (Marek Piwowski) who may or may not—it is never clear—be an old acquaintance. He is different—a playboy, a sport, casual, independent, more or less employed as a truck driver. He brings into her life a dimension of wit, warmth, and action. Something happens between them. Love? Again, it is impossible to say. Perhaps it is only a diversion, a necessary contrast. Perhaps it is a breath of freedom from dullness, from obligations, from the expected and the approved. Morality, goodness, and responsibility may have taken their toll on her.

She leaves her husband without crisis, fanfare, or drama. But the world does not let her off so easily. It turns out that a rendezvous with her new man does not occur, and she is impelled to return home, ruefully and with resignation to her previous loyalties and responsibilities. She was not permitted to rebel against the moral order she was a part of. It is almost as if Zanussi took up here the theme of *Family Life*. In that film, the hero walks out and his facial twitch, a family trait, seems to signal that there is no basic escape from who and what we are. In this film, the heroine must make the best of her life without kicking down the walls of conscience. While there can be some manipulation, ultimately the moral accounts must be balanced.

This is a plain story told simply and sparingly. There is no sentimentality, little drama, no explosions of passion. Narrative, mise-en-scène, and direction are straightforward, yet the movie has considerable emotional power. Much of the credit for this belongs to the performance of Komorowska, whose magic eyes, movements, and gestures convey a kaleidoscopic sense of disquiet, bewilderment, tenderness. In any given scene there is more at stake than the scene; there is always the unfolding of her personality and the making of its texture.

The response to *Balance-Sheet* by the Polish critics was shallow. They failed, on the whole, to detect any of the film's deeper values. Having been extravagant in their praise of *Illumination* and impressed with its intellectuality, they now saw, unaccountably, only a potboiler, a trite story of an unfaithful wife. The public, on the other hand, was enthusiastic. The film ran for months to full houses. It was likewise popular outside Poland, and was the only Zanussi film to get a fairly wide screening in the United States.

Nachtdienst [1975] was quite a different portrait of a woman than any that Zanussi had done so far. This was a sixty-minute film made for West German television. The script, co-written with Edward Żebrowski, is structured along the lines of a stage play. In it there is a protagonist, a rich elderly recluse (Elizabeth Bergner), looking for someone that she can bully. To that end, she engages a nurse. In spite of everything she can do, the nurse does not respond as the old lady would have liked. Balked, the millionairess has her nurse arrested for the sole purpose of securing her release, extorting her gratitude, and then starting the game over again. Psychologically convoluted to the point of perversity, the movie was well assembled with appropriately somber climate, rising drama, surprise, and superb performances by Bergner and Jadwiga Cieslak-Jankowski as the nurse.

Camouflage

In 1976, one could already detect in Poland the ozone whiff of flux, change, historical confrontation. Indeed, there were confrontations that year in Radom and Kielce, but these were only portents of the events of 1980. The cinema, as ever, was both reporter and clarion of the Polish political tides. Two films that year were especially notable and extremely influential: Wajda's *Man of Marble* and Zanussi's *Camouflage*. Their immense popular success indicated that what they had to say, morally and socially especially, was on target as far as Polish audiences were concerned.

The point of departure for *Camouflage* was not something political, but something quite philosophically general, that is, the presentation of a naturalistic view of life as contrasted with a humanistic view. To put it another way, it was an argument between what is as opposed to what ought to be.

The setting is a summer camp where university students and their teachers gather to discuss academic things in a more relaxed kind of atmosphere. Its focus is an encounter between an idealistic young assistant (Piotr Garlicki) and a seasoned professor (Zbigniew Zapasiewicz), smooth, sardonic, worldly wise, an opponent of idealism in any form. In the background are the usual activities: lectures, debates, manipulation, young revolts. But it is the dramatic dialectic between the assistant and the professor that holds centerstage from first to last, and it presents the argument and substance of the movie.

The assistant is inexperienced, naive, convinced that private life and social life are governed by certain moral principles that must be observed even at the risk of personal defeat. He believes that by living morally one can change the world, give it a more human dimension. The professor, by contrast, is a veteran of life's battles, a man with a shrewd intelligence who knows the mechanisms of this world inside out. What his younger colleague regards as enduring values—justice, veracity, loyalty—the professor considers to be naiveté, even stupidity. According to him the only rules that apply are the laws of the game, a cold, brutal game for survival and success. The assistant believes that the goal of life is to improve the world; the professor believes it is to survive. In order to survive one must learn from nature, from the animal world. A man should be able to adjust to his environment, to change his coloring, to put on camouflage as so many other species do to protect themselves. This is a conflict between nature in general and idealism, which is peculiarly human. One can call it a conflict between nature and culture.

Certainly, Zanussi does not develop these points solely in the form of verbal debate. In the dramatic situation, a student is seen as being unjustly treated and there is a student protest in favor of a colleague. There is also an instance of scientific fraud, academic double-dealing. Still, the essential conflict is between the two protagonists (or protagonist and antagonist) and the cut and thrust of their argument and conduct. The professor is determined to convert the assistant, to strip him of his illusions about the morality and nobility of human nature, to educate him in the remorseless laws of survival. In one respect the film is a study of the faustian process of temptation, an acute intelligence and a sort of diabolical charm are intent on coaxing a guileless young man onto a certain course of life.

Where does Zanussi stand? It would be difficult not to see that his sympathies are with the young idealist, but it is equally clear that he intends no two-dimensional morality tale. Rather, as in *Structure of Crystal, Family Life*, and *Balance-Sheet*, the characters face critical choices, test those choices against their own attitudes and psyches, and commit themselves to something that is not necessarily beneficial. In the closing scene of *Camouflage* the assistant, enraged at seeing cynicism and duplicity successful, physically attacks the professor, and the two of them fight to a standoff. The standoff itself is part of the message.

While the synopsis would make it seem that *Camouflage* was a general moral allegory in which naturalism faces off against humanism, the Polish audience saw through the protective coloring of the movie and read therein a scathing indictment of political and social life. The attitude of the professor, cynical acceptance of survivalism and self-interest as a philosophy of life, carried uncomfortable weight and plausibility to those caught up in the mood of Polish life of the seventies. It was a time marked by careerism and corruption. Idealism seemed unbelievably innocent and moral rebellion still seemed fruitless. Conformism, protective coloring, was the resort of the pragmatically minded. It was not surprising that the moral aspects of the film that related to Darwinist survivalism versus humanism were largely lost sight of in favor of the moral aspects that had direct application to current issues. *Camouflage* emerged as a mainstay and inspiration for a series of committed films that were to be categorized as "the cinema of moral concern."

It was an instant success upon its release in 1977, even though there were attempts behind the scenes to diminish it. For some time the censors spiked all favorable reviews, and since there were no bad notices the result was awkward silence. Actually, the aura of forbidden fruit this lent the movie only added to its word-of-mouth reputation and enhanced its appeal. Subsequently the official approach was reversed in an attempt to use *Camouflage* as an instrument in undermining the success of Wajda's *Man of Marble*.

The tactic originally adopted against *Camouflage* was silence, but *Man of Marble* was met by all out assault. The administration was concerned that Wajda's film would carry the honors at the annual Gdansk festival, and it was deemed necessary to manipulate things. To give the main award to a film of manifestly lesser importance would have made the rigging too patent and that would have ended up embarrassing the officials. Since *Camouflage* was not only known to be an important film but likewise one that was not particularly popular with the regime, it was judged that the award could be diverted from Wajda to Zanussi without inciting extreme displeasure. Zanussi's integrity would not permit this and he turned the manipulation against itself when he pointedly declined to accept the grand prize.

Zanussi's next project was done in German for Saarland television, *Frauenhaus* (*Dom kobiet*) [1977], an adaptation of a play by the Polish writer Zofia Nałkowska (1884–1954). This is a psychological piece, well structured, about a household of women, each of whom has in some way been victimized by a man. Even a young widow who idealizes the memory of her late husband learns that he has been unfaithful to her. The conclusion is a trick of theatrical irony of superb execution: the youngest of the women leaves the house with her latest lover although she knows full well that her affair will end in disaster. Some see the film as feminist male-bashing. In any case, it is a competent and respectable film, albeit not an important episode in Zanussi's career. It is distinguished mainly by the actresses: Brigitte Horney, Maria Carstens, Eva-Maria Heinecke, and Karin Baal.

Spiral

Spiral (*Spirale*) [1978] is a motion picture that is altogether distinguished. It started in a simple fashion, that is, the director heard an interesting yarn. It was about a middle-aged leukemia sufferer who decided to commit suicide and wanted to do it in a fitting way. A mountain climber, he set out in bad conditions intending to die either from the hazards of the climb or from the weather. What he failed to plan for was that his absence would be noticed. It was, and a rescue squad found him. This is exactly the right kind of plot frame for a Zanussi film. At its core is the director's central theme, death as an ironic illuminator of life. To this add the motif of the mountain-climbing, the act of ascent through struggle, of confronting nature and one's self.

The narrative is developed in a straightforward way. We do not know immediately what the protagonist is up to. He (Jan Nowicki) leaves his new car on the side of a mountain road then goes to the railing of a bridge over a deep and rocky gorge. He stares into the abyss and drops his car keys spiraling, disappearing into the canyon. In such a way he signals cutting off his connection to the modern world he was clearly such a successful part of. At the ski lodge, through a number of short scenes, we come to know of his anger, even despair, and begin to guess at the nature of his emotional crisis. During a cold night he makes a human contact with a woman (Maja Komorowska) who apparently can see through his rudeness something of the torture in his soul. Early in the morning he sets out for the mountains but does not sign out, as is the custom, or leave notice of his planned route. His disappearance is noted in the context of a bad weather situation developing, and an expedition is launched that returns him to the shelter, alive but frozen and unconscious. There are long scenes in a grim hospital and visits to him from the woman he met in the mountains. For this man, the end is coming too slowly. When he can, he drags himself to a window either to look out or jump. He either falls or jumps and in a dream shot a man walks away over wide waters.

Spiral is a film that can be regarded as a frontal confrontation with imminent death. In the first instance the movie focuses on the reactions of a man doomed, that is, his reactions to the thing that he now italicizes as *life* and the reactions he has to those that will go on living. It is as much an examination of those who must respond to his death, to their knowledge of his doom, and to their knowledge of his knowledge.

Zanussi is brutal in maintaining focus even when we would rather turn our heads away, when we would rather that things were blurred a bit, when we would rather not pay such close attention. This is the forcefulness of a relentless thinker and an insistent artist. This is an insistence that demands that we consider the fundamental questions and stay with them through some kind of resolution or until we are defeated. As usual, it is not completely certain which of those two things happens.

The critics received *Spiral* with nothing less than reverence, but it was not a success with the public. Probably it was too rigorously existentialist, too searching, and too frightening to appeal to a large audience. The mood of the viewers was also changing just at the time when *Spiral* was released. This was the winter of 1978–79 and the call was for expression of social concern.

Before things came to a head in 1980 engendering the movement called Solidarity, Zanussi made another film in Germany which has no official English title, but whose title in translation is *Roads through the Night*. Its formal German title is *Wege in der Nacht*, and in Polish is *Drogi pośród nocy* [1979]. This German venture was almost completely filmed in Poland and carries a Polish theme albeit made for a German audience.

Action takes place on a country estate in Poland in 1943. The landlords live in an outbuilding because the manor is occupied by a German military unit. A German officer (Mathieu Carriere), a man of manners and breeding, falls in love with the daughter of the Polish owner (Maja Komorowska), setting up an impossible love affair played out against the background of the reality of the war with its Nazi repressions, Jew hunting, battles with the underground, and general mutual hatred. Obviously such an affair must be doomed because the clash between the two nations fractures the emotions of the lovers. Individuals are helpless in the larger currents. As in all of Zanussi's films, there is an overarching general theme. Here we confront the fact that war erases the rules of civilization and culture. War is like biological struggle, and personal morality cannot be reconciled with it.

Zanussi was usually able to bring his generalities down to dramatic specificity in an individualistic and craftsmanlike way, as in *Illumination, The Balance-Sheet*, and *Camouflage*. This time a good artistic solution to the problem eluded him. From the start we have a stereotypical situation representing brutal Nazis and noble Poles not relieved by good character development in the roles of the two principals. The officer's humaneness and intellectuality ring hollow and manifest themselves almost exclusively through abstract dialogues with the girl and with his friends. The character of the girl is even thinner, rescued only somewhat by the acting of Komorowska. Even so, the character does not reach out beyond the stereotype of a proud Polish patriotic aristocrat. The story sinks in moralistic dialogues meant to explicate the themes.

In spite of its weakness, *Roads through the Night* gained a measure of success among the critics and with festival audiences at San Remo, Edinburgh, and Melbourne in 1979, and London and Cannes in 1980. It has never been shown publicly in Poland.

At the beginning of 1980 it was apparent that social and political crisis was imminent. This was reflected in (and perhaps even partly inspired by) a number of feature films made with intentions of social criticism, films portraying spreading corruption in the Polish economy and the expanding privileges of the elite. This was criticism directed against the elite broadly conceived, not simply the party hierarchy but all who had influence in Poland's administrative and economic system—what in the west we would call "the establishment."

Anxious about the production circumstances that might prevail during and after the impending events whose form had not yet begun to take shape, Zanussi decided to make two films at once, *Contract* (*Kontract*) [1980] and *The Constant Factor* (*Constans*) [1980]. *Contract* was underwritten by television although intended for theaters; *The Constant Factor* was made by the film unit "Tor." A single crew was organized to make both films, sometimes shooting scenes from the two films on alternate days. Zanussi simply wanted to finish both before trouble broke.

Contract

Contract, like *Spiral*, was based on an account of an event said to have actually happened, in this case in Zanussi's own family. A wedding elaborately prepared aborted when the bride, standing at the altar, answered the priest's questions with a definitive "no" and escaped. Naturally, the director invested a great deal more content and meaning than this in his movie. He placed the action in present-day (1979) Poland and his characters were types of the period, making this a biting and bitter metaphorical piece.

The intended groom is the spoiled son of a rich and enterprising physician; the girl who rejects him is the daughter of a provincial economic manager. At first impression, the doctor appears to represent the old Polish intelligentsia, while the business manager is a product of the new economic system. During the course of the wedding reception, farcically held even though the wedding was canceled, we come to know these characters more deeply and others as well. The doctor (Tadeusz Łomnicki) is prominent and rich, but his wealth is not pristine, its sources somewhat questionable. He is the director of a large state hospital and is not above receiving discrete gifts from patients. When he has a patient who is a high official, he manipulates him in order to gain advantages for himself and his family. The father of the nonbride (Janusz Gajos) is the embodiment of a local official, primitive, rude, uneducated, but shrewd, pushy, and puffed-up with his success, a recognizable type to Poles. He likewise is not reluctant to use the many privileges his post can obtain for him. There is a relative of the doctor (Leslie Caron), an aging dancer come from abroad to bring some sophistication. She turns out to be a kleptomaniac who brings embarrassment. There is a high official only very vaguely identified who seems to be involved in some fraud scandals. The groom's friends are upscale cynics who come to the wedding for whatever cynical advantages such an occasion can offer. The rest of the guests are in one way or another such as would be comfortable in that crass environment. They seem not very much put off by the fact that the marriage did not take place since they had not come chiefly to celebrate it but to make contacts, do business, and make their way among the privileged.

Only the bride did not fit the pattern here. Even so, her rebellion had shockingly small effect. True, her intended husband got drunk, lost control, and set fire to the house, whereupon he was taken to the hospital for the insane. But he might have done that anyway, and besides we know that his father will get him released the next day. She, after all this, takes a walk in the woods with her mother to try to understand everything. She suddenly notices the figure of a majestic deer with splendid horns. Admiring him she perhaps understands that there are other and finer values, and a better harmony with life. That is some consolation in light of the fact that we do seem to be tied to our fates and situations. The bride's rebellion was no enormous event, it seems. In fact, it was somewhat ridiculous and ineffective. We are left with the image of a sleazy and corrupt world and the anxiety that all of this must inevitably collapse. So let it collapse, Zanussi seems to be saying.

The Constant Factor

Before martial law was invoked in December 1981, Zanussi made and released one more film, *The Constant Factor*. It closed a sort of cycle of pieces that began with *Illumination*. It is the story of a young man, Marek (Tadeusz Bradecki), who is released from the military. His mother is the only person close to him, his father having died in a mountain climbing accident. He takes work in a company that organizes exhibits and fairs, which allows him to travel abroad, including to India. His life takes some turns for the worse when his mother contracts cancer and slowly dies. His work becomes difficult because his colleagues, who are enhancing their lives by corruption, are determined to involve him. It would be dangerous for them not to, because one honest person is a danger to a conspiracy. He is provoked, framed, and fired. Then he gets a job working on the walls of a building from a high scaffold.

So much for the outline of external circumstances. Inwardly, this is a person of great complication. He is much more than a rigorous moralist. He is a learner, a searcher, trying to find underlying sense in life and the world. The hidden rules and laws obsess him and he investigates the mechanisms of games, lotteries, dice, roulette, and studies mathematics in order to penetrate the mysteries of probability. He does learn that there are certain immutable values, constant factors, which remain the same irrespective of the changes of other elements. These are only hints at the deeper games that he is trying to fathom. Indeed he is trying to learn the terms of his own life. Did his father have to step on the particular stone that caused his death in the mountains? In what way did his mother have to get cancer? How can one's own life be rationalized? Can life itself be rationalized or is it simply an inexplicable absurdity? What is socially, biologically, or psychologically determined, and what remains undetermined, unclear, mysterious?

A response, not an answer but a reluctant response, is adumbrated in the last scene of *The Constant Factor*. The protagonist, who is ironically working from a high scaffold instead of climbing in the high Himalayas as he intended to do before he was fired for his honesty, inadvertently dislodges a big block of stone just as a child innocently runs after a ball toward the very spot where the stone will hit. We are not permitted to see if the stone and the child are in fact in the same spot at exactly the same time. The mood seems to suggest that the child will meet his young destiny just there. The point is that whether he does or not, nothing is absolutely calculable, predictable, certain. There is always variation and the unpredictable. A scientist by training and an intellectual by temperament, Zanussi yields to the mystery of things. The artist in him shows us that if there is a constant factor other than God, or collateral with God, it is death.

Because the film was shown in Poland in 1980, its interpretation was inevitably skewed by the political and social climate of the period. The philosophical dimensions of the piece were quite lost and the movie was judged largely by its social content. That is, it was seen as the description of the life of an honest man who cannot find a place for himself in a rotten world, a man victimized by a cynical and corrupt system. His co-workers were seen also as somewhat victimized. They were only playing according to the rules that they knew, the terms of the system as it exists. As far as it goes this is a valid reading, but as we have pointed out it misses the whole philosophical plane.

It is uncertain which aspect of the film accounted for its international success, but successful it was. At the 1980 Cannes festival it was awarded the best director prize and received also the award given by the international critics. In this formal way, Zanussi was acclaimed a mature, profound, world-class *auteur* of modern cinema.

Man from a Far Country

Not surprisingly, then, more and more foreign contacts were made and proposals came in. 1981 proved as busy as 1980. Of particular interest was the coming together of a project for a television film of the life of Pope John Paul II, something under discussion for some time by Italian television (R.A.I.) and by a British producer (ITC, Lew Grade). The key question from the outset was who the director would be. Supposedly and reportedly, Zanussi's name was suggested by the pope himself who was familiar with Zanussi's work and admired his moralistic and philosophical approach. In any case, it must have seemed sensible to use a Polish filmmaker to help insure capturing the special atmosphere of the pope's life. Zanussi was chosen to make *Man from a Far Country* (*Z dalekiego kraju, Da Un Paese Lontano*) [1981].

The director was very much aware of the difficulties inherent in his task, to make a film about a great and pious man without indulging in hagiography and without trivializing him. The starting point for the movie and the title was a sentence from the first words that John Paul II spoke to the crowd gathered in St. Peter's square: *"Vengo da un paese lontano"* (I come from a distant land). So the portrait of the former Karol Wojtyła, now Pope John Paul II, was to be done with the perspective of that far country in mind. What was envisioned was a series of episodes from the modern history of Poland, the history from which the personality of Karol Wojtyła emerged. That idea was accepted.

For the screenplay, Zanussi worked with two prominent Catholic writers, Jan Józef Szczepanski, chairman of the Writer's Union, and novelist-critic Andrzej Kijowski. The plan was to take account of Wojtyła as a high-school student, a university student, a manual laborer, member of the underground resistance, actor, priest, bishop, and cardinal. The film would be peculiar in not showing incidents of his life directly but portraying the reflection of his life in the lives of people who were with him at important times, for example, an actress who performed in an underground theater during the occupation, her husband, a priest from Auschwitz who built the famous church at Nowa Huta, and the like. These episodes were done dramatically with actors. The film ends in a documentary mode as white smoke rises up over the Vatican and we see Karol Wojtyła, John Paul II, on the balcony overlooking the square.

This was a very odd work for Zanussi to tackle. He had heretofore made films that were intimate, introspective, intellectual. The subject of the pope was a subject of great dimensions requiring a large cast of characters. The story itself necessarily lacked completeness and unity and could only be treated episodically. The problems were large and the results were somewhat disappointing. The film was not convincing. Intended as it was for a diverse international television audience, the historical backdrop had to be oversimplified, diminishing the films historical strength. The characters who were to reflect Wojtyła's presence in their lives never reached any dramatic fullness of their own, diminishing the film's dramatic strength. The curious idea of making a film about a man without his being represented in it did not work either. When in the final documentary section we see the real pope, we get the feeling that everything we have seen so far had nothing to do with him. The indirect approach was the film's chief weakness.

It was shown widely in Europe and the United States (in the United States it was shown as previously scheduled, which was coincidentally the night martial law was declared in Poland, ending the Solidarity era, which owed so much of its inspiration to Wojtyła). The reviews were mixed, with those in Italy and Germany tending to be more positive than those in other countries. The audience received it indifferently as simply another docudrama.

Zanussi returned to his introspective mode for his next piece, *Temptation* (*Versuchung*) [1981], made for German television (W.D.R.) from his own screenplay. It concerns a Swiss businessman (Helmuth Griem) who marries a Polish girl (Maja Komorowska). Conflicts unfold because the world of the Swiss bourgeoisie is far from anything she had known in life, and the situation is complicated by the fact that her husband is dominated by his sister. The girl very much wants to join this very orderly world and participate in it fully, but the harder she tries and the farther she goes the stronger her conflicts become. She discovers limitations, inward and outward, which seem to her to be traps. The psychological distance between her and her husband grows, so she decides to escape it all. She simply disappears. *Temptation* is the story of a restless woman, a woman whose psychological center is a trifle off balance, who cannot seem to find a focus to her life, and who seems to lose the distinction between responsibility and irresponsibility.

Zanussi was abroad when martial law was declared in Poland, working on an old project to which he had become quite devoted. It was a film called *Imperative* [1982], a quasi-religious meditation, even an argumentation, on spiritual and psychological guilt. It was a German-French coproduction under Tony Moliere, the distributor in France of Wajda's and Zanussi's films. It was made in English with an international cast, including Robert Powell, Leslie Caron, Brigitte Fossey, and Mathias Habich.

Imperative is a straightforward story about a young scientist and mathematician named Augustine (Robert Powell), working in a German university. He undergoes a series of spiritual crises which are, at the same time, intellectual crises. He has doubts about the idea of order in the universe and the sense of his own existence. He is tormented by problems of freedom of the will. When his girlfriend walks out on him he is essentially isolated from the world, except for a theologian with whom he maintains a continuing involvement. He falls in with a group of immigrants gathered around the Orthodox church, although he is philosophically a nonbeliever who is dismayed by many religious things, but by nothing more than relics and icons. Driven perhaps by a need to disprove God's existence in some tangible way, he sacrilegiously steals a holy icon. In the course of events he is committed to a mental hospital, completely overwhelmed by guilt. Augustine inflicts a cruel mutilation upon himself, which somehow helps him out of his madness.

It is an intricate and ambiguous story about madness, faith, weakness, necessity, and free-will which never quite succeeds in becoming believable, multidimensional. The questions posed seem too academic and in the form of dialogue seem to lose their dramatic autonomy. *Imperative* is an illustration rather than a drama.

That same year, 1982, Zanussi made a ninety-minute film for German television (D.D.F.) called *Unapproachable* (*Unerreichbare*). The script was done in cooperation with Edward Żebrowski very much in the form of a well structured theatrical play, and expressly written for Leslie Caron, an actress with whom Zanussi had worked before.

It is set within the walls of a rather magnificent residence belonging to a former film star millionairess (Leslie Caron). She lives quite alone, isolated and unapproachable. A brash journalistic photographer simulates an accident in order to get into the house to take some pictures for a popular magazine. His trick works. He is smart, strong, and attractive, and before long something more than a photographic interest develops between him and the star. As this happens, hidden anxieties, hopes, and inhibitions surface for both of them. When it turns out that she is ready to accept him personally, he suffers a reversal by realizing that this relationship would make him dependent. He decides to leave.

The psychological interactions are presented precisely and credibly. The attractions and alienations, all the permutations of this strange psychological relationship are developed well, yet held esthetically in check by the tight organization of the story. Leslie Caron authentically recreates the several psychological transformations within the main character. Script, direction, and acting are one. Nonetheless, taken as a whole its quality does not rise above the level of perfectly adequate television drama. In the canon of Zanussi it is significant for its play upon his theme of freedom and responsibility. In other films, for example in the *Balance-Sheet*, freedom seems illusory, and circumstances dominate. In *Unapproachable*, freedom wins out but not without evoking ambiguous moral questions.

Zanussi's *Bluebeard* (*Blaubart*) [1982] followed *Unapproachable*. It too was a television production, made for German and Swiss producers, from a novel by the Swiss writer Max Frisch and adapted by Zanussi. It is done as a court trial with, of course, Bluebeard (Vadim Glovna) as the defendant. The psychological ordeals of the wives are reconstructed in performances by Margharetta van Trotta, Vera Tchechova, and Maja Komorowska.

The Year of the Quiet Sun

From 1981 until 1984, Zanussi worked exclusively abroad. He visited Poland often, indeed continued to live there, but he made no films in the country. He was still head of the film unit "Tor," managed in his absence by Krzysztof Kieślowski, which was ready and waiting to do his next film, one to be done in cooperation with a Berlin company (Regina Ziegler) and a New

York company (Teleculture). It was reckoned as two-thirds a Polish production and one-third American and German. The title is *The Year of the Quiet Sun* (Rok spokojnego słońca) [1984].

As in the cases of *Spiral* and *Contract* the starting point for the project was a story that Zanussi had heard somewhere. In this case it concerned an impossible love affair between a Polish woman and an American soldier that takes place right after World War II on territory regained from Germany. In the film, Emilia (Maja Komorowska) is a forty-year-old woman who has lost everything during the war, husband, house, and money. She is located in the regained western territories, having been resettled there from eastern Poland, a section annexed by the Soviet Union. Her mother is aged and infirm and the two of them live a lonely, isolated, and precarious existence. Norman (Scott Wilson) is an American soldier attached to a military mission looking into German war crimes against POWs. He too is past his youth, a seasoned soldier, a veteran of some of life's most bitter experiences, including those in a German prison camp where he suffered humiliations that left him permanently scarred.

Sympathy and emotion develop between these two wounded people and later something much deeper. Their affair is played out against the background of a ruined city and a somewhat anarchical society just beginning to get itself together in these first few postwar months. This is a city of violence, of prostitutes, black marketeers, the poor and the old, a foreboding police presence.

The bleak mood of the place serves to emphasize the melancholy difficulty of such a love affair. First of all, the lovers must fight through a language barrier and deep cultural differences. Ultimately, they face the fact that he will return to America and she will remain in Poland. She is not permitted to emigrate, moreover she would never leave her ailing mother. When Norman is able to arrange for her to be smuggled into safe territory, the mother commits suicide to free her daughter from the burden of caring for her. Still Emilia does not leave, will not leave, and relinquishes the passage to a neighbor, a prostitute. She throws her life away.

There is a large hiatus in time before we see her again as an old woman in a shelter for the aged run by nuns. A message is conveyed to her of the death of Norman and the fact that he has left her a considerable amount of money to make it possible once again for her to leave. This time her body cannot obey her will. She is physically devastated. It is too late. As she dies the screen takes on brighter lighting and tones.

These are in contrast to the heavy colors and dim tones that mark the rest of *The Year of the Quiet Sun*. It is significant that the screen brightens during this epilogue of the film when Emilia learns of Norman's death and of his last gesture. Although it is too late for Emilia to be able to leave for the West, it is not too late for Norman's gesture to bring her to a kind of fulfillment. Not able to join him in life, she joins him by dying. But why did she not join him before, at the time of her mother's sacrificial suicide?

Had she done that, she would have been accepting her mother's life as a price for her own happiness. Given her personality and her religion, this was impossible. One is inclined to speculate also on Zanussi's own Catholic background and the profound influence it has had on his work. It is reflected in Emilia's and the author's implied assertion that Christian sacrifice is ours to make not ours to collect. So when Norman died and sent his fortune to her she was redeemed in a way that was good and acceptable. She could not have her happiness as a result of her mother's suicide, but she could accept Norman's valid and gracious bequest, and although she could not use it materially, it freed her emotionally and spiritually. She could die in fulfillment, suggested by the lighter tones and brighter lighting, in the same way that there is a moment of dreamlike fulfillment at the end of *Spiral* when, after the death of the protagonist, we see an illusion of a man walking on wide waters. Life may be tragic, indeed is tragic, but there is nonetheless a hope of some kind of redemption. This is, of course, a deeply religious hope.

The Year of the Quiet Sun did not meet with a very warm reception in Poland. In official circles the reception was downright frigid because, allegedly, Zanussi presented an overly gloomy and quite false picture of the historical situation. "Two lonely women isolated from the main trend of life, an American soldier, a prostitute, a priest, a secret agent, a smuggler, three thieves, and a lost German constitute a set of people which can hardly be said to be representative of the community being born at that time in the western part of Poland," wrote an establishment critic (Kuszewski, Stanisław, *Kino*, April 1985). Other opinions were mixed and included some which were enthusiastic. Audience response was likewise not enthusiastic.

On the other hand, outside Poland the film was accorded recognition and a very sympathetic audience. Reviews were generally positive. When presented at the Venice Film Festival in 1984, *The Year of the Quiet Sun* took the highest award, the Golden Lion. It played well in the United States and was nominated for a Golden Globe.

Given the depth and breadth of his accomplishment, it is hard to believe that decades of work are still before Zanussi. We can only speculate on the new psychological, philosophical, and lyrical depths he will achieve, and that itself produces a sensation of awe. It is certain that he will never be flamboyantly famous, for his films are the quintessence of intellectual cinema and will have appeal to the most sophisticated audiences. But if he is an artist of the mind, he is an artist of the heart as well. The human condition cannot be captured and understood by reason alone. In fact, it cannot be captured at all; it must be illuminated. That is as good as we can do. Zanussi crafts the doubts, fears, hopes, affirmations, frustrations, defeats, and partial victories in such a way that we can brood and think about them, and when we are at the limits of thought, his art helps us find intuition.

EPILOGUE

There was understandable anxiety among all those interested in Polish cinema that the "state of war" declared in December 1981 ("state of war" was the official term for the period of martial law) would be fatal to the more interesting aspects of filmmaking and perhaps might even be permanently debilitating to the industry as a whole. It was feared that the best filmmakers would be finally silenced or muted and that the movies that awakened the strongest emotions among the public would end up irretrievably on the shelf. To add to the anxiety, some notable young directors elected to emigrate: Agnieszka Holland and Piotr Andrejew to Western Europe, Zbigniew Kamiński and Witold Orzechowski to the United States, Ryszard Bugajski to Canada.

The darkest forebodings did not become reality. The production unit system, the organizational base of the industry which gave strength to artistic independence, was essentially maintained with two exceptions. Wajda's unit "X" and Ernest Bryll's "Silesia" were dissolved by the autorities. Personnel from these two companies drifted into other units, mostly into Janusz Morgenstern's "Perspectives" and a new unit, "Eye" (*Oko*) headed by Tadeusz Chmielewski.

The Polish Filmmakers Association, which had played a key role over the years, was suspended for a time but allowed to return to activity in December 1983. At the convention called to resume activity, Andrzej Wajda, the organization's chairman, submitted his resignation to the members and was succeeded by Janusz Majewski. It seems that Wajda's resignation was required by the authorities in return for the reactivation of the association. In return they showed sufficient restraint to refrain from hindering the free choice of Majewski who was democratically elected by his colleagues. The association is almost unique among professional groups in being allowed to function as it had before the martial law period.

Leading directors continued working, at first outside of Poland. While it is indicative of conditions that work was undertaken outside the country rather than in it, it is also interesting to note that passports were released and exit visas given, usually only with minor bureaucratic harassment, signaling that the regime had no intention at the time of imitating the harsher repressions of other Communist states. Wajda did *Danton* and *Love in Germany* abroad, and directed several theater productions in Poland. In 1986 he released his splendid new film based on a book by Konwicki, a film made in

Poland, namely *Chronicles of Love* (*Kronika wypadków miłosnych*). Zanussi, after a number of minor projects done abroad, came back to the country to do *The Year of the Quiet Sun*.

The younger lights, who contributed so significantly to the flowering of cinema in the seventies, made new attempts to continue their probing and analysis. Feliks Falk made *Idol* (*Idola*) [1985] and then a sequel to *Top Dog* titled *Hero of the Year* (*Bohater roku*) [1986], which finds his corrupt protagonist functioning under the new, post-crackdown conditions. Krzysztof Kieślowski made *No End* (*Bez końca*) [1985], a moral settling of accounts concerning attitudes during martial law. Tomasz Zygadło came out with *Scenes of Childhood* (*Sceny dziecięce z życia prowincji*) [1986], about youth and old ideologies.

As such, these works did not amount to an extension of the cinema of moral concern movement, lacking the heat and bluntness of those movies. Nonetheless, these new works are in themselves significant, thoughtful pieces that measure the mood of society following the turmoil of 1980–1982, and they do not avoid the sensitive areas of contemporary consciousness.

New directors appeared. As might be expected their offerings are uneven and their tendencies are as yet undefined, but there is certainly promise among them of an evolving cinema for Poland. One should note the following: Wiezław Saniewski, *Surveillance* (*Nadzór*) [1986]; Radosław Piwowarski, *Yesterday* [1985], and *My Mother's Lovers* (*Kochankowie mojej mamy*) [1986]; Julian Machulski, *Vabank* [1983], *Vabank II* [1985], and *Sex Mission* (*Seksmisja*) [1984]; and Andrezj Barański, *Lady from the Provinces* (*Kobieta z prowincji*) [1986]. There are of course others not mentioned here whose names will become familiar as years pass.

What form Polish cinema will take and what strength it will show over the years is not clear. More than in most countries the motion picture is a distinctive part of Polish society, politics, and culture. This art form has mirrored history in Poland, and it has even helped make history as a causal factor in events. If there is one aspect of its record that helps predict a bright future for cinema in Poland, it is this: the story begun in 1945 is marked by a series of deep artistic and political crises, after each of which the industry has emerged stronger, more independent, and more influential than before. There will be ashes, but there will always be diamonds.

BIBLIOGRAPHICAL NOTE

There is very little available in English on the subject of Polish cinema. The one general treatment along chronological lines is Fuksiewicz, Jacek, *Polish Cinema* (Warsaw: Interpress, 1973), a 100 page introductory survey. *Contemporary Polish Cinema*, ed. Jerzy Chocitowski (Warsaw: Polonia Pub., 1962) is obsolete. Film Polski publishes the series of yearly catalogues, *Polish Feature Films*, which is useful for current information but devoid of any historical or critical significance. There are chapters on Polish film in Liehm, Mira and Antonin, *The Most Important Art* (Berkeley: University of California Press, 1977), an excellent broad survey of cinema in Central and Eastern Europe. Paul, David, ed., *Politics, Art and Commitment* (London: MacMillan, 1983) contains some stimulating essays which are theme oriented. With respect to individual directors there is really only Michałek, Boleslaw, *The Cinema of Andrzej Wajda* (London: Tantivy, 1973), which is in the process of being updated for publication.

One general treatment in French exists: Haudiquet, Philippe, *Nouveau Cineastes Polonais* (Lyon: Premier Plan, 1963). Obviously it is outdated. There are also some rather out of date monographs: Trinon, Hadelin, *Andrzej Wajda* (Paris: Editions Seghers, 1964); by various authors, *Jerzy Kawalerowicz* (Paris: Etudes Cinematographiques, 1967); by various authors, *Andrzej Munk* (Paris: Etudes Cinematographiques, 1965).

In Polish the cornerstone of film study is *Historia Filmu Polskiego*, especially of relevance to this book are vol. III, ed. Toeplitz, Jerzy, 1974; vol. IV, ed. Toeplitz, Jerzy, 1980; and vol. V, ed. Marszałek, Rafał (Warsaw: Wydawnictwo Artystyczne i Filmowe). Other useful books are: Janicki, Stanislaw, *Film polski od A do Zet* (Warsaw, 1972); and by the same author *Polscy Twórcy filmowi o sobie* (Warsaw, 1966), both published by Wydawnictwo Artystyczne i Filmowe.

Among the monographs that should be mentioned are: Mkruklik, Barbara, *Andrzej Wajda* (Warsaw, 1967); Fuksiewicz, Jacek, *Tadeusz Konwicki* (Warsaw, 1976); Eberhardt, Konrad, *Zbigniew Cybulski* (Warsaw, 1976); Nurczynska-Fidelska, Ewelina, *Andrzej Munk* (Crakow, 1985).

Among the compilations of film articles, we recommend: Jackiewicz, Aleksander, *Niebezpieczne związki literatury i filmu* (Warsaw, 1971); Marszałek, Rafał, *Powtórka z życia* (Cracow, 1970); Metrak, Krzysztof,

Autografy na ekranie (Warsaw, 1974); Michałek, Bolesław, *Szkice o filmie polkskim* (Warsaw, 1960).

The relevant periodicals are: *Film*, weekly (Warsaw, 1946 to date); *Kino*, monthly (Warsaw, 1965 to date); *Kwartalnik Filmowy*, quarterly (1955–65); *Nowa Kultura*, weekly (Warsaw, 1950–62); *Kultura*, monthly (1962–81).

INDEX